brothers
(& me)

brothers
(& me)

A MEMOIR
OF LOVING AND GIVING

DONNA BRITT

LITTLE, BROWN AND COMPANY
New York Boston London

Little, Brown and Company
Hachette Book Group
237 Park Avenue, New York, NY 10017
www.hachettebookgroup.com

First Edition: December 2011

Little, Brown and Company is a division of Hachette Book Group, Inc.
The Little, Brown name and logo are trademarks of
Hachette Book Group, Inc.

All photographs are from the author's personal collection.

The publisher is not responsible for websites (or their content) that are not
owned by the publisher.

The Hachette Speakers Bureau provides a wide range of
authors for speaking events. To find out more, go to
www.hachettespeakersbureau.com or call (866) 376-6591.

Portions of the chapter "Ghosts" have appeared in the
Washington Post in slightly different form.

Library of Congress Cataloging-in-Publication Data

Britt, Donna.
  Brothers (and me) : a memoir of loving and giving / by Donna Britt.—1st ed.
    p. cm.
  ISBN 978-0-316-02184-5
  1. Man-woman relationships—United States. 2. Sex—United States.
3. African American women—United States. 4. Families—United
States. 5. United States—Race relations. I. Title.
  HQ801.B75 2011
  306.70973—dc23   2011022309

10 9 8 7 6 5 4 3 2 1

RRD-C

Printed in the United States of America

This book is dedicated to my brother Darrell,
for making me laugh, loving me unconditionally, and
making me want to be a better person.

Contents

brothers
(& me)

Introduction

The moment I saw him, I wanted him.

Lithe, black, and muscular, he was the handsomest fellow in the room. We hadn't been introduced, but he walked right up to me and looked me in the eye—so boldly you would have thought he was alone rather than accompanied by a clearly enthralled companion. He wanted me, too.

Then his companion nudged him. Turning, he strolled away, not bothering to look back. His cockiness reminded me of a saying: "All men are dogs."

If this one hadn't been an actual cocker spaniel, I might have been crushed.

It started a few weeks earlier, when it became painfully obvious that our fourteen-year-old American Eskimo was dying. Particularly stricken was my youngest son, Skye, ten. Recalling the loss of my own childhood pet—a squat cocker beagle named Taffy—I contacted a local cocker spaniel rescue and learned that adoptable dogs were being shown that weekend at a nearby pet store.

Entering the shop, Skye and I instantly spotted Woofer,

whose black fur shone like just-poured tar and who made a tail-wagging beeline for us. But an elderly man had him firmly leashed; clearly he meant to adopt him. So Skye and I checked out several females, among them Millie, a blond nine-year-old as blasé as an aging movie star, and Penny, a jet-colored cocker, who, like many black females, stood to lose a few pounds. But our eyes kept returning to Woofer. If the adoption doesn't work out, I told staffers, let us know.

Woofer's unavailability, I decided, was a sign: I didn't need another black male—even a four-legged one—in my life. Finally, fate had said, "Enough."

I'd grown up as the only daughter of a father whose specialties were bricklaying and simmering silences; I'd spent years commiserating and exchanging barbs with my three brothers. At eighteen, I left for college, where lunchtime at my historically black university found me the lone female at a table full of secret-sharing guys who reveled in the encouragement, neck rubs, and advice I was only too accustomed to offering. After years of dating, I went on to marry—twice—and looked to motherhood to redress my lifelong gender imbalance. Destined for daughters, I gave birth to three sons. If that weren't enough, my second husband and I for years opened our home to the troubled male friend of one of our boys.

Even our soon-to-be euthanized dog was an alpha male.

For decades, I'd been surrounded by men. Unable to recall a time when I wasn't outnumbered, outgunned, and certainly outmanned, I craved female energy, if only from a pet. I needed a bitch.

Guess what I got.

Woofer's would-be master took the pooch home, where his pet cat hissed and spat its disapproval. Another unjustly persecuted black male, Woofer became ours, the latest penis-bearer in a house overrun with them.

Hilarious.

Know what's really funny? I should have been as wary of Woofer—another male demanding my time and energy—as that snooty cat had been. Yet I adored him, just like all the others.

Why wouldn't I? The Divine Prankster who plopped me down at birth in Blackmanland had invested me with a compulsive desire to help anyone in need within a ten-foot radius, and an unquestioned, though hardly unquestioning, love of brothers: Brothers in the familial sense, as in my siblings. Brothers in the cultural sense, as in my African-American male friends, kin, lovers, and guys I've never met. Brothers as in a lifetime's worth of men and boys whose desires and demands often eclipsed whatever I wanted.

I'm hardly unusual in offering the men in my life whatever they need. Women are the world's most reliable, and underappreciated, givers. Anne Morrow Lindbergh, wife of aviator Charles Lindbergh and a mother of five, wrote achingly about the tendency more than a half century ago in her brilliant 1955 classic, *Gift from the Sea*: "All her instinct as a woman—the eternal nourisher of children, of men, of society—demands that she give. Her time, her energy, her creativeness drain out into these channels if there is any chance, any leak. Traditionally we are taught, and instinctively we long, to give where it is needed—and immediately."

Yes, some men are geniuses at generosity. Just as surely, some women are stingy and unaccommodating. But women are much more likely to deplete themselves by noticing—and then offering—what's needed by those whom they love. Long ago, I decided that the desire—make that the *need*—to nurture is as much a part of women's essential makeup as our DNA, as the uterus, ovaries, and other uniquely female organs that allow us, not men, to give birth.

Why wouldn't a brilliant God provide us with this survival insurance? Though men, too, give hugely to their children, sad statistics prove how much more often they turn away from giving.

No wonder my black male cocker became a metaphor for black *men* to whom I'd given. Instantly drawn to Woofer, I wasn't supposed to have him—yet he can daily be found begging for belly rubs and demanding a portion of whatever I'm eating.

The inevitable way Woofer came to me—and that I didn't run screaming when I learned he was available—symbolizes the countless times I've longed to flee black men but never could.

Over the years, I've fantasized about escaping: from black men's chilling complexity, from the gripping grace that ever pulls me in. Frustrated by brothers' troubled relationship with a world enamored of and repelled by them, I've responded by fiercely defending them, while occasionally agreeing with society's harshest judgments. Over and over, some black man's behavior—public or private, that of an intimate or an imperfect stranger—has made me want to scream. Hide. Conjure some way to make him, no, every freaking one of them, disappear long enough for me to catch my breath.

And still they can saunter right up to me, corral my heart.

White women—and brown and yellow and red ones, too—also give abundantly to men who may not appreciate it or even notice. Nobody makes us bestow so much upon the men in our lives, but we do it—even as we kick ourselves for it, even as we kick *them* for it, responding to a need greater than we or the men whom we both nurture and push away can articulate.

In one way, it's worse for black women. In a nation in which black men die younger and more often than any other group of men, black women fear for the brothers in their lives, and for themselves at the prospect of losing them. Our fear is often as unthinking as our love. But certain terrors are earned the hard way.

In 1977, when grad school was my life and being a wife and a mother were faraway dreams, my beloved brother Darrell was killed. He was twenty-six. Did I fear for black men before I lost him? Was I anywhere near as driven to give to them? I wish I could be sure.

But I do know this: Too many black women have loved and lost—to violence or drugs or prison or any of a dozen other horrors that especially haunt blackfolk—someone like Darrell. Someone who taught them that loving black men is particularly risky in a world in which love itself seems perilous. Yet still we offer our hearts to brothers—as if we had no other choice, as if a black woman today didn't have a Crayola-box array of men from which to choose.

Over and over, we choose them: The good ones, the bad ones, the conflicted ones, the ones who are clearly up to no good. Even the ones who are, well, dogs.

It's a woman thing, really. Over and over, whether we're black or white or brown or yellow, whether we're Friedan-fed feminists or Betty Crocker conservatives, women forgive, support, and prop up the men in their lives. Over and over, we choose them. Even—unless my experience is unique, and I know damn well it isn't—over ourselves.

Missing in Action

Skye jokingly shushing his mom, 2003.

From my seat in the fundraiser audience, I couldn't help admiring the woman before me. With her serene smile and hands carefully folded in her lap, this stylish woman, whom I was told is a lawyer, looked oddly familiar as she stared adoringly at her candidate husband during his stump speech. It occurred to me that this liberal Democrat was gazing as beatifically at her man as Nancy Reagan ever did at hers. So I was stunned after the speech when—upon learning I was writing a book about how women's giving often goes unnoticed by men—the lawyer's pleasant features morphed into an infuriated mask. "Will you explain why men like him"—she nodded bitterly toward the man she'd just beamed at—"can't see how much we do for them and our kids?" As I wondered, How can one calm-looking woman feel so much love mixed with resentment?, I realized why she looked familiar. I'd seen her everywhere.

Especially in the mirror.

It's a typical late summer Monday morning, so I'm a breathless blur as I dash around in the room where I so often find myself: the kitchen. Rinsing grapes and arranging sliced turkey on wheat for Skye's chess camp lunch, I flit about as the boy himself chews a scrambled egg while contemplating the relative benefits of different superpowers.

"Mom," he says, his ten-year-old voice heartbreaking in its boyish-but-how-long-can-it-last sweetness. "Which superpower would *you* want?"

Smiling, I duck my head in the fridge for juice.

"Would you like to be able to eat anything you want without gaining weight?" he asks. With vats of vanilla Häagen-Dazs dancing in my head, I think, Buddy, you can stop right there. But Skye isn't finished.

"*Or,* would you like to be able to do things at lightning speed?" Pouring his orange juice, I envision how efficient it would be—frying his egg, fixing coffee, walking Woofer, starting a load of laundry, getting dressed, and yelling "Hurry up!" to Skye eight times—in two minutes, not twenty-five.

"Sounds cool," I admit, shoving grapes into his lunchbox and thinking, No wonder this kid's doing so well at chess camp.

"Or," Skye says, winding up for his big finish, "would you like to travel through time?"

When I stop moving, he knows he's got me.

"You could save your brother!" he adds triumphantly. And though there are a dozen other things to do before I take him to camp, I'm glued to the dingy kitchen floor. Silently wondering why the words "Sure, I'd go back and change every bad thing that happened" won't come.

It's a *fantasy,* I scold myself. Just tell him you'd travel back in time and save Darrell, and by extension, yourself.

But I can't. As agonizing as my brother's death was, it contributed so hugely to who I am that the thought of obliterating it is literally paralyzing.

If a button existed that could undo Darrell's death, I'd instantaneously mash it. But Skye's supposition is a game. Games involve risk. So I'm allowed to risk wondering:

Was there an invisible reason for Darrell's leaving that I'd be wrong to undo?

No life is just one life. Each is an amalgam, a wildly textured bolt of cloth woven unconsciously by a weaver whose creation minute by minute intertwines with, seeps into, or is ripped apart by other lives.

But mine is a woman's life, a perpetual-motion cartoon

with countless hours passed in kitchens like the one where Skye has immobilized me. If a woman stopped moving long enough, she might notice her life is like a challenging recipe. Each day, she's frustrated: by her limited preparation time, the unpredictability of her equipment, her ingredients' maddening inconsistency. At times, her creation looks and smells wonderful, hints at perfection. Until without warning, it dissolves into disaster.

Somehow she salvages the mess. Again she works it; again she dares to think it might turn out nicely. Again it's a mess.

At some point, the cook realizes: She has dedicated herself to the one dish that never "turns out." Her unstable ingredients, the preparation's highs and lows, the recipe's uncertain outcome, aren't problems. They're the point. What matters is that she's tasting everything, discovering new ingredients in her cupboard, incorporating whatever tumbles unexpectedly into the mix.

By dying, Darrell overturned the bowl. It took years, but I cleaned up the mess, scraped up what could be salvaged, found exciting new elements to add. Most days, the resulting dish looks impressive — at least on the surface.

What would it look like if Darrell had never left?

Standing motionless in the kitchen, I got a glimpse. A life constructed without Darrell's death would look more like *me* — a truer, more authentic me. Who, I wondered, would that be? My brother, I realized, wasn't the only one who'd vanished. I was missing in action in my own life.

The questions sparked by Skye's game had actually begun weeks earlier. Days after my fiftieth birthday, I realized that virtually every time I see, hear of, or suspect a need in one of the men in my life, a thought so hushed and fleeting as to barely register flits through me. For decades, I had no awareness of it — until the morning its message became clear during a routine meditation: You must do whatever's needed for the men in your life. *You must.*

Someone could die if you don't. And you'll regret it forever.

I'm reasonably self-aware. I understood Darrell had died at a juncture at which we'd drifted apart in ways that siblings in their twenties inevitably do. Yet it took thirty years for me to realize part of me still believed that if I'd stayed closer to him, had been more supportive with my time and attention, he'd still be alive.

The thought makes no rational sense. But the evidence that I believed it was played out every day.

I had given and given and given. To my sons, my husbands, my brothers, to the notion of black men as bruised, threatened, and worth sacrificing for—not always as a demonstration of my love for them, but for love of a man long lost to me, and out of terror of what could yet be snatched away. No wonder I'd dreamed of escaping from black men. Facing what my giving had cost me—not just in opportunities but in resentment and regret—was tough, but no tougher than my next questions:

How could I stop giving, an act as natural and unpremeditated to me as a sneeze? *Should* I rein in a behavior that was helpful, felt good, and was an essential spiritual imperative? Had it taken decades for me to notice my over-giving because so many other women with backgrounds quite different from mine behaved similarly?

Historically, martyrs have been appreciated in war zones and medieval villages. In daily twenty-first century life, self-sacrificers are a bore; my revelations could emit an ugly whiff of self-pity. That didn't change certain facts: I was naturally generous; it was a trait of which I was proud. Yet there was nothing admirable about the lengths to which I—like millions of other women—sometimes took my must-give impulse.

Darrell's death was tragic enough. I'd multiplied its awfulness by letting it coax me to offer out of fear rather than love. It gave me unconscious permission to stay boxed inside my terror: of risking failure, of letting "my" men and boys be fully responsible for themselves.

Over the years, I'd puzzled myself by clinging to failed relationships and a spectacularly bad marriage, by being reluctant to speak up for my needs when challenged by insistent brothers, by rejecting lucrative job opportunities because I "knew" the men in my life needed me more. That such behavior could partly be traced to a whispered voice born of a decades-ago death seemed absurd.

If only that had kept it from being true.

Giving too much isn't limited to black women. My automatic behavior wasn't that different from women's of every color, nationality, education level, and income. Women *want* to give their time, their passion, their bodies, their wide-open hearts, to men. (We give to other women, too, but they're more likely to give back in kind.) We enjoy bestowing our stuff on the guys in our lives.

The problem is when our offerings aren't appreciated, rewarded, or even noticed. When we discover few men harbor the same impulse. When we don't get back nearly what we put out. When it pisses us off.

White, Latina, and Asian women, *being* women, also have issues with over-giving. Yet there's a special dynamic among black females. My friend Wendi Kovar, a Washington-based life coach, told me that several of her female clients' experiences suggest that women with serious weight problems have a hidden need to protect themselves. Her favorite example: A client whose son, fourteen, died tragically. Virtually overnight, this slim woman became obese. For a decade, she fought to lose weight, even visiting a spa whose Spartan cuisine *guaranteed* it. Her scale didn't budge. She finally told Kovar her extra pounds were "protective armor" that she'd never lose before making peace with her son's death.

Kovar's client was white. But the notion of excess weight as a form of protection seems particularly relevant to black women, the nation's heaviest group. African-American women grapple with the terrifying knowledge that their fathers, brothers, sons, lovers, husbands, and friends tend to die earlier than other men, and are more likely to be lost to incarceration, addiction, and alienation. Yet the popular image of African-American women is one of toughness, independence, and rage toward black men.

So why is it that among all American women, sisters are the least likely to seek lovers outside their race? Why wouldn't it devastate us to hear black men's rap-video and real-life bluster about black "bitches" and "hos" when we know almost every brother has had a mother, lover, and/or grandmother who gave her all for him? Why *wouldn't* we look for comfort in food—or in anything that looks or smells the least bit like love?

Now, in the kitchen, I'm equally clueless. Cemented to the floor, I feel Skye's curious eyes on me. Finally I say, "I think I *would* choose to travel through time, but I'm not sure what I would change."

Nodding, Skye says, "I knew it." He's satisfied.

I'm anything but.

I know I should explore the questions raised by Skye's game and my revelation about my brother. I'm just as certain I have little desire to probe tender, bruised places I've hidden for good reason. I'm wary of examining how the woman I've become intersects with her past, her men, her forgotten selves. But how else can I learn why I give so much and am so confused by the giving?

Traveling through time — *Skye, you do know your mommy* — I could examine when the girl whose life was all about her books, her brothers, and herself became so much about everyone else. *Was* my transformation the result of Darrell's death? Or were other factors — including growing up *as* a woman, my blackness and the vulnerability it bequeathed — as important?

Prying open doors sealed shut a quarter of a century ago would be excruciating. But I had to try.

Even without superpowers.

Darrell, Disappeared

Clockwise from the top: Steve, Darrell, Bruce,
and Donna Britt, 1962.

*O*ver and over after he left, I asked myself: *Are the dead really dead? Could those who've "passed on" move so freely, speak so clearly, occupy so much pulsing space within us if they were indeed gone? Magnified to its subatomic essence, the pebble I unthinkingly kick away becomes a seething universe. Maybe all of life is a matter of level—the level on which any being or object vibrates. If a stone can whisper its truth, what might the dead be saying to us? What does my life, as rote as the kick that sends the pebble flying, tell the lingering departed?*

If he's dead, why am I still trying so hard to save him?

Nothing in the world is more elusive than memory.

As someone who misremembers details of conversations I had yesterday, I harbored few illusions about precisely recalling the distant past about anything. Why trust memory when I'm unsure why certain events linger and others drop away until a phrase or a snatch of song rivets me in a moment long lost to me?

To this day, I have no idea why I lost my stalagmites.

I was about four when I noticed that whenever I closed my eyes for more than a few seconds, God gave me a gift: a mesmerizing and uplifting light show.

On my *eyelids.*

Sliding into bed, I'd shut my eyes and there they'd be: massive, free-floating forms in shades of smoke, tar, and midnight. Like jagged mountaintops that had broken free from some new-formed earth, they were humongous, yet floated weightlessly in slow motion across my mind. Night after night, I felt comforted by the constellations' presence, dazzled by their gleaming, prismed surfaces.

Sometimes I wondered: *Do other people see such things?* Suspecting they didn't, I told no one—not even Darrell— about my private panorama. If no one else had such visions, if watching these nightly sojourns made me weird, I didn't want to know. It was too wonderful, feeling like a small satellite to their immenseness, being the spaciousness through which they drifted.

It wasn't until third grade that I read about stalagmites and stalactites. Formations that occur in limestone caves, they're created when acidic water dissolves the limestone, dripping tiny fragments toward the cave's floor. When the water evaporates, the limestone solidifies, forming an icicle-like stalactite. Continued dripping creates a second structure—a stalagmite— beneath the original. As decades pass, the floor-bound and the suspended sections draw closer together. Decade after decade, each half reaches for the other—until finally, they meet, forming a column.

Something about the pale green shapes in my textbook felt instantly familiar. Their spikiness, slow growth, and presence in sheltering havens were like my nightly visitors'. The color was off and they were much too thin, yet I knew: my free-floating formations were stalagmites and stalactites, searching for their other halves.

Of course, I'd already found mine. The one who was separate, but part of me. Who always reached for me, to whom I unfailingly reached back.

When someone you love shifts from the firmness of flesh to the squishiness of memory, even powerful remembrances may be lost to you. Yet some stuff you never lose—like the memory of staring at a newspaper headline viewed a dozen times before, and feeling like you're seeing it for the first time:

Gary Man Shot by Police.

I was twenty-three. Sitting at the table in my mother's kitchen, I'd been called home to Gary, Indiana, from grad school by an event that could not have happened. The headline in the *Gary Post-Tribune* was supposed to make it real, so I read it over and over, repeating the words in my mind. *Gary Man Shot by Police.* I'd read them too often in my hometown newspaper not to know what they signified: a no-thought headline announcing the shooting of an anonymous thug. Such a headline couldn't possibly refer to my brother Darrell. Important people's violent passing warranted outrage, regret, astonishment—and nobody in the world was more important than the brother who loved me. *Gary Man Shot by Police?* It hit me: To most of the world, my life's most shattering event was no big deal. Because Darrell had been mistaken for ordinary.

Not the average Joe—ordinary that nearly every white guy is assumed to be. Even in Gary, the former murder capital of the United States, the shooting of the most undistinguished white man usually warranted more than a newsprint shrug. But Darrell was *black* ordinary, which meant his life didn't matter much: Not to the police who shot him. Not to the reporter who wrote the terse, six-paragraph report of yet another brother getting himself killed. Certainly not to the copy editor who took all of three seconds to compose "Gary Man Shot by Police."

Ordinary.

Well, in some ways he was. Darrell wasn't short and he wasn't tall; he was neither linebacker-thick nor tap-dancer wiry. His eyes were warm and dark and kind—but no more so than millions of other young men's eyes. At five ten he was exactly the average height for an American male. He was quietly good-looking, as tender, volatile, and doomed young men often are.

He was just Darrell. And all that he was not—striking, brilliant, wildly successful—hardly mattered to those who couldn't imagine life without him. A regular man, he was, like regular men everywhere, loved by his little sister with unremarkable completeness. My parents produced four smart, lively children—but only Darrell seemed likely to lead a typical and uneventful life, productive in the usual, unexciting ways: a stable marriage, a couple of kids, a decent job with a modest pension.

Is it surprising that he died what increasingly has become a typical black-guy's death?

Growing up, I hadn't the slightest sense that black males—my brothers, my schoolmates, my father—were more vulnerable than other boys or men. Daddy had been too formidable to be afraid for; the most dangerous thing I envisioned my brothers facing was a schoolyard beat-down.

Staring at the headline in Mom's kitchen, I examined the "facts"—Mom's torrential tears, the ashen corpse at a local funeral parlor, a familiar phone number now belonging to no one—of what surely had to be fiction. Darrell was *dead*. Like the headline, two Gary cops had mistaken him for something he'd never been. They'd received a call that a black man was trying to steal a truck in his lakeside neighborhood. Investigating, they'd found Darrell crouched in a ditch. They claimed he'd attacked them. That they had to shoot him. *Darrell?* Whom I'd never known to steal anything? Who was among the kindest people I knew?

If such an absurd mistake could be made about him, it could be made about any black man. The policemen's claims and my brother's dead body proved that the value and the safety of the people I loved most were in question. I wasn't sure I could live with that.

Perhaps it was then, as I sat dumbfounded at Mom's

dinette, staring blankly at her kitchen's cheery yellow walls, that I began pushing Darrell into my mind's dimmest corner. I did it so well that today it's easier to remember what my favorite brother wasn't than what he was. He wasn't, like my sibling Steven, older than me by five years, so taken with his own giftedness that he couldn't see my drawing, hear my singing, ponder my opinions as if they mattered. He wasn't four years younger like Bruce, whose age deficit meant I could take his admiration for granted. Sandwiched with me between them, Darrell didn't stroke or scream at people like Steve did to get his way, or seem malleable while doing exactly as he pleased like Bruce. He was something else entirely.

Remembering what he was means stepping into a bleak, little-used room inside me. Flipping the light switch, I squint and discover that my eyes don't quite focus. Feeling my way around, I bump into unresolved emotions, slip on scattered memories, prick myself on sharp-edged regrets.

I don't go in there often. As the years have passed, the light inside has grown dimmer and dimmer.

Most of my memories of Darrell take place in my childhood home, a streamlined redbrick ranch built in 1963 by my mason father. A Michelangelo when it came to laying stone and brick, Daddy designed our house's curved driveway and the balcony that hovered over my brothers' favorite hangout: the cement patio and basketball court.

The Gary, Indiana, in which we lived was strikingly different from the impoverished city whose disintegrating buildings and weed-covered vacant lots recently caused my visiting husband to marvel, "This is the bleakest city I've ever seen." When I was a kid, Gary—founded on Lake Michigan in 1906 as the site of a massive new steel production facility—was a vibrant city of 135,000 souls so connected to Big Steel that the question "Where does your dad work?" almost always elicited the same answer: "The mill."

Daddy's work was seasonal and mill-related, so the family income ebbed and flowed with the mills' fortunes. Yet we kids never felt hungry or lacking. Our parents griped about money, but if they were deeply worried, we never saw it. Daddy and Mommy, an insurance saleswoman, worked hard. Yet every once in a while, they got dolled up to go out with friends: millworkers, carpenters, and teachers transformed into glamorous sophisticates in tailored suits and peplumed dresses.

Such dazzle was on display the first time I noticed—and felt betrayed by—my giving. I was six the Saturday that my mother enlisted us kids into dusting and vacuuming for a party she and Daddy were hosting. Transforming our messy living room into the swank site of a grown-up gathering was thrilling, even before Mommy made up her face and poured herself into a slim sheath she called a "cot-tail" dress. Her metamorphosis from mom to sexpot matched Daddy's, whose sharkskin jacket made her bricklayer husband look like a guy who'd left the Rat Pack because Sinatra was insufficiently cool to hang with him. Who knew my parents were so beautiful? Proud of them and our magically transformed home, I could barely breathe.

Banished to the back of the house, Steve, Darrell, Bruce, and I put on our pajamas, whispering so we could hear clinking glasses and Dinah Washington warbling from the room where we often fought with plastic swords and watched *Candid Camera*. By the party's end, I'd figured out how I could be helpful to my parents while inserting myself into the hipster action: bringing guests their coats. The plan worked; I reveled in guests' hugs and effusive thank-yous as I retrieved their wraps. Then I made the mistake of handing a fedora to an uncle who, unbeknownst to me, had recently made a big deal out of swearing off hats. When the grown-ups cracked up, I felt exposed: a silly kid in pj's who had no business at a classy cot-tail party. Retreating into a closet, I pressed my face into a coat as my throat caught fire.

Darrell found me. Soothed me. Told me I'd done nothing wrong. "Go to bed," he said. "We'll play Life in the morning." I went to bed. Grateful he was always there, making things better.

My awareness that I liked doing things for others evolved around the time I became aware of something else that brought both pleasure and pain: I was a "Negro." It was the early 1960s. Gary, I realized, was unashamedly segregated, and all my friends, my family's friends, and most of our community's doctors, teachers, and service providers were "colored." Some might think our lack of white neighbors, colleagues, and pals lessened our lives. In fact, life couldn't have felt fuller.

My parents' generation of working- and middle-class blackfolk was determined to live the exemplary lives of which white people thought them incapable. Having done all they could to escape the oppression that had tormented their ancestors, few looked back. None of the families in our orbit suffered in any obvious way from the ills assumed inevitable in black America: harsh poverty, criminality, imprisonment, drug abuse, unmarried parenthood (folks hid it or got married). Before the civil rights movement, I rarely heard adults bristle at their lot. Life was too bursting-at-the-seams full for folks to stop living it long enough to complain—at least around us kids.

So my early years don't qualify me to write one of those anguished black narratives whose narrators had sex as preteens, were raped by family members, or were forced to join gangs. I wasn't beaten by my boyfriends or encouraged to use or sell drugs. The only liquor I ingested was the rare cupful of Boone's Farm apple wine–spiked punch at a blue-lights-in-the-basement party.

For years, I didn't even resent the white people whose lives somehow mattered more than ours. I knew none to resent. I had exactly one white teacher; my family's encounters with white people consisted of exchanges with downtown sales-clerks and workers fixing appliances or delivering milk. As for housing, Negroes in Gary respected the invisible boundaries that determined where whites lived and blacks knew better than to look.

Yet my family "knew" hundreds of white people, thanks to TV, books, and other media. White folks' habits, culture, and slang; their *lives*—or the lives they presented for public consumption—were familiar to us. Certainly, they were more familiar than our lives were to them. Our parents and grand-parents had been intimate with whites in up-close-and-personal ways; many had worked in white people's homes, seen them unguarded. We kids breathed in white lives long-distance.

Sometimes, we got closer. On special Saturdays, my par-ents, brothers, and I piled into Daddy's coral and cream Plym-outh, drove to a nearby suburb like Miller or Merrillville, and gawked at sprawling homes with precision-clipped grounds. We rarely saw white *people*. These homeowners eschewed the strolling, porch sitting, and car washing typical in our neigh-borhood. As Daddy drove slowly enough for us to see each manse, the kid who first noted a particularly cool house screamed, *"I got that one!"* adding the home to his or her imaginary portfolio. Spectacular homes inspired fierce squab-bles over who'd hollered first.

Fighting over these houses gave us some purchase on their mysterious owners. What were they up to behind their drawn curtains? Were their homes so gorgeous inside they felt no need to venture out? Who *were* these unseen, distant-though-close strangers?

The best way to learn was through TV, which we loved despite no one on it looking like us. Our lone twelve-inch black and white had the power to gather entire families for annual events: *Mr. Magoo's Christmas Carol, The Wizard of Oz,* Mary Martin "flying" via visible cables as Peter Pan, Lesley Ann Warren's saucer-eyed Cinderella. Black folks were so rarely on the magic box that neighbors threw open their doors and rushed onto their porches to shout the news when "colored" stars appeared. "Hey, Sammy Davis Jr.'s on *Ed Sullivan!*" The streets emptied.

By 1965, Darrell, fourteen—the official family clown, with Bruce running a close second—was quietly toying with the notion of a show business career. That September, NBC debuted an adventure-comedy show named *I Spy,* starring an urbane, handsome, clever, and—this part we barely believed—*black* comic. His name: Bill Cosby.

Cosby, swear to God, looked like a grown-up Darrell.

Cosby the spy was debonair and smart. Cosby the comic convulsed us with his tales of how complex life was for kids. The man was perfect. That the hippest black entertainer alive resembled my sidesplitting brother was a portent of Darrell's amazing future. We idolized Cosby, never imagining that decades later, the entertainer's only son, Ennis—mistaken by a racist ne'er-do-well as just another expendable brother—would be shot dead for no good reason.

Just like Darrell.

Once upon a time, such an occurrence was unthinkable. Darrell's presence was as warm and assured as the sun's. My family's love and constancy provided a sense of safety so deep and unthinking, I seldom questioned it. Darrell was like Mommy and Daddy and Steve and Bruce and my dolls and my friends and my welcoming bed, whose sheets were always cool and whose offer of a safe slumber was certain. At seven, you *know* these necessities will always be there. You know.

I don't remember when my stalagmites disappeared. As I grew older, images of life outside my eyelids—friends, boys, TV and movie stars—crowded the spaciousness they'd floated through.

By the time I lost Darrell, they were gone, too.

Girlstuff

Donna (left) and Shawn giggling at a house party in Gary, 1972.

Few would question a working-class black girl always having her face in a book. But these books? Printed in the 1930s with detailed illustrations, my favorite was written by a nineteenth-century New England spinster and handed down to me by my mother. By the time I was eight, Louisa May Alcott's Little Women *was my bible, and its Civil War–era heroines cherished kin: stubborn Jo, selfless Meg, calculating Amy, and saintly Beth, whose death from a fever-weakened heart devastated me each time I read it. A few years later, my undisputed favorite was* Gone With the Wind, *that love poem to the Confederacy whose servile black characters—Prissy, Big Sam, Mammy—mortified me. My earliest literary influences ignored me, were contemptuous of me, or had no clue that black girls like me even existed. And still I gave myself over completely to them.*

In some ways, girlhood for me was a long, slow period of falling out of love with myself. Three things helped mightily in the process: beauty, buddies, and my blackness.

Beauty first. At age seven, I felt good about the girl in the mirror. I liked my looks, found school exciting, and was a talented-enough artist for kids to fight over my drawings. Life was so agreeable, I thought anything I worked at—my appearance, my studies, my artwork—would pay off. Wedded to perfection, I was ripe for a lesson in the impossibility of maintaining it. My teacher: Easter shoes.

Easter was a big deal at Saint Timothy's Community Church, the creamy brick edifice where Mom, my brothers, and I were fixtures. A block from our house, Saint Timothy's was the domain of the Reverend Robert Lowery, a lion of a pastor whose pomaded mane glistened as he prowled the pulpit, roaring his sermon. Easter at Saint Tim's was exciting—the lilies! the eggs! the hats!—yet the holiday confused me. I'd seen *King of Kings* so I knew Jesus had piercing blue eyes and had died on the cross for my sins. But my Sunday school teacher insisted Christ's huge sacrifice did nothing to cancel out my everyday sinfulness in yelling at my brothers and coveting my friends' record players. More frustrating was my teacher's response to a nagging question: Where did this hard-to-please God come from? "He didn't come from anywhere," she offered, sounding somehow unconvinced. "God was always there."

"But everyone comes from someone!" I countered, stunned that she couldn't see the obviousness of it. "I came from my Mom, Jesus came from Mary." The more my teacher explained God's omnipresence—insisting that "God existed before time began"—the crazier she sounded. When I added her ravings to my nightly prayer's hair-raising suggestion that I could "die before I wake," religion became a very tough nut. Maybe only grown-ups got it.

So Easter was all about the outfit. It was the one time a year I was guaranteed a whole new ensemble, and in 1961 mine was perfect: a daisy-colored dress, matching jacket and hat, and—this part snatched my breath away—yellow patent leather Mary Janes. The shoes' beauty made them like jewels or a rare painting. Reverently, I removed them from the box to marvel at them. But they were works of art for my *feet*—feet that jumped rope, ran from boys, and walked on sidewalks bent on scuffing unwary footwear.

So on Easter, I slid on my new shoes last. Walking normally would invite creases, so I lumbered flat-footed toward church. When Mom asked, "Why are you walking like that?" I said, "I don't want my shoes to bend!" Uselessly, Mom said, "All shoes get creases!" Not mine. A canary-colored mummy, I walked locked-legged to church, where I modeled my glass-smooth shoes for friends.

Back home, I was horrified to find my treasures marred by several inexplicable scuffs. After a few more black marks, I downgraded my magical shoes to mere footwear. Yet I never forgot how futilely I contorted myself to preserve their perfection.

I'd had a master role model. From the moment my mother, Philadelphia-area native Geraldine King, said "I do" to Thomas Elwood Britt, a lanky sailor turned bricklayer whom she barely knew, she'd toiled to keep agonizing childhood memories from marring her shiny, new life. The new Mrs. Britt moved briefly with her husband to Berkeley, California, where Daddy, a former high school basketball star, played semipro hoops for the Oakland Bittners. A year later, she gave birth to a honey-skinned baby boy, Steven Elwood. Returning with her husband to Gary, my mother bore a second son, Darrell, and three years later, a girl: me. I was four when Mom gave birth again. My much-anticipated younger sibling turned out to be the last thing I needed: another boy.

It took me all of two seconds to fall in love with my baby brother, Bruce. Besides, in one way, his gender hardly mattered because it soon became clear that no two Britt kids were remotely alike. I was the brainy people-pleaser, which repulsed the rebellious Steve, who responded by teasing me nonstop and telling me grisly tales of "The Green Man," a local ghoul that snatched little girls off the street. Once Steve was jokingly waving a kitchen knife at me when he inadvertently jabbed my knuckle. The resultant gush of blood brought such horror to Steve's face that I forgot my pain in my astonishment that he might actually care about me.

Calm, funny Darrell and I were each other's instant favorites. I loved being privy to his secret joys and fears; his trust contributed hugely to my healthy self-regard. I gave him a respite from Steve's mischief and egotism; he offered me a break from keeping a close maternal eye on Bruce. While pregnant with my youngest brother, Mom had hoped to avoid sibling rivalry by telling me, "This baby will belong to you."

I believed her. But my adorable baby brother belonged to no one. At fourteen months he was a diapered freedom fighter, running back and forth across the length of his wooden playpen, banging his head in painful protest at being caged. I'll never forget accompanying Bruce and Mom to the doctor's office so he could be immunized before kindergarten. Instructed to drop his drawers, Bruce obliged—until he saw a spectral figure in white holding a long, sharp needle moving silently toward his rear.

Howling, Bruce leapt free of his pants and dashed bare-assed into the waiting room, jumping over tables, weaving his screaming way through glaring moms and panic-stricken kids. By the time the nurse caught him, his shrieks could be heard in Chicago.

Two things bound the four very different Britt siblings together: drawing and music. My brothers and I were enthusiastic artists, consuming so much expensive drawing paper for our cowboys and ballerinas that Mom finally demoted us to paper towels. We were equally passionate about pop and R & B on the radio. Memorizing every lyric, we treated hot new singles like the elegant houses we fancied in white neighborhoods, claiming them as our own as we screamed, *"That's mine!"* In 1963, Darrell grabbed an oddly catchy number before the rest of us could decide if we liked it. The British artists' corny name, the Beatles, didn't prevent "I Want to Hold Your Hand" from catapulting to number one—or Darrell from lording it over us for hesitating.

Except for Steve's needling, life was peachy; its ongoing

pleasantness was the closest thing I could conjure to the always-there God my Sunday school teacher described.

So you'd think I would recall the moment everything changed. When I realized that one immutable part of my existence—my innocuous, nut-colored skin—was irrevocably wrong. When the dissonance between my full-bodied existence and the limited one society had prescribed for me crystallized, revealing a stunning truth: my pulsing reality and everyone in it was invisible to the white people who ran the world.

Negroes—black people embraced the term's hard-won capitalization—barely existed in the pop culture I adored. Take movies. The heroes and heroines of the biblical epics, Westerns, and Rodgers and Hammerstein musicals we absorbed were all white. Yet it was years before I worried that Shirley Jones's *Carousel* ingénue and Ann-Margret's *Viva Las Vegas* hottie looked nothing like me. They *felt* like me, and that was enough. Black kids were nonexistent on TV, so I identified with Patty Duke playing mischievous twins, and the blond globe-trotter Jonny Quest. My life seemed as limitless as theirs.

The nightly news shook me out of my reverie: Brutal images of Negro men in pressed slacks and women with hushed hairdos being cursed, sprayed with hoses, and attacked by fang-baring German shepherds. Their harassers' rage turned their faces into snarling masks. *Those poor people,* I thought, until it hit me: if I were in Birmingham, Mobile, or Selma, those monsters would direct their water blasts, hurl their dogs, blow up a Sunday school around *me.* I imagined reasoning with them: "You don't understand. I'm nice! I get good grades and try hard to be well behaved so I can go to heaven." But I'd still be Negro, still have my telltale nose and skin. And they'd hate me.

It was so unfair, there had to be a way around it. I thought and thought. I'd seen ads in *Ebony* for skin lighteners. But even if my almond coloring faded, no amount of Royal Crown hair ointment would make my hair lie flat enough to fool anybody.

I was a permanent Negro.

Heart pounding, I understood for the first time that I didn't have to do anything wrong to *be* wrong. It was like realizing that one day I would die.

I was petrified. But there was no way out.

Growing up with so many guys gave me a terrific excuse for developing a penchant for giving to men. Yet I can't remember when I *wasn't* drawn to boys, often in very unsisterly ways. Local ten-year-old hunk Marty Jackson, the son of Mom's best friend, was my first crush. Unless you count second-grade dreamboat Hobert Goode, about whom I told Mom, "I've *got* my man." Or thick-lashed third grader Dale Johnson. Or...

From day one, I loved boys: their smiles, voices, and sturdiness, their different-from-me *boy*ness; I couldn't get enough of them. Yet my girlfriends were precious, too. Validating the femininity for which there was little echo at home, each in her way made up for what I bitterly lacked: a sister. I yearned for the everyday presence of someone like me. Mom was a busy adult who found my insistence on wearing her clothes and begging her to buy mother-daughter outfits from the Sears catalog baffling. I craved a close-at-hand female, someone for whom sharing feelings, magazines, clothes, and insecurities felt as necessary as it did to me. I shared what I could with Darrell. But he was a boy.

So I studied girls. I marveled at how my friend Arlene's feet twirled when she walked, how tomboyish Carolyn threw rocks as far as any boy. After I'd had a searching phone chat with my friend Mitzi, Mom found me staring moist-eyed from our picture window. "I'm sad because one day Mitzi and I won't be friends," I explained. Unlike boys, of whom I had plenty, girls seemed scarce. Sometimes I worried that my female buddies were more important to me than I was to them.

An incident a few years later seemed to prove it. My family had moved across town into the spacious brick ranch home Daddy had built with his friends. Overnight, I went from being the fourth grade's best-liked girl to being nobody. My first day at Ernie Pyle Elementary School, I stood nervously by the desk of my teacher, Mr. McCloud, who stared long and hard at my admission slip.

Mr. McCloud pointed at the page. Someone had written the "r" and "i" in my last name in such a way that the worried-looking teacher whispered, "Is your name . . . *Butt?*" "It's Britt," I hissed. Relieved, Mr. McCloud assigned me a seat.

I felt accepted by my Pyle classmates—until I entered fifth grade. My teacher, Mrs. Lewis, was a gem, but her class had an established clique of smart girls, a few of whom seemed wary of their new classmate. Typically, I offered myself to them by having them over, sharing my artwork, whispering my secrets. Just when I thought I was one of them, several decided to remind me who was boss.

The plan: Be Dirty to Donna Day.

On BDTDD, girls I'd thought were friends decreed that no one was to acknowledge me. The page bearing my name in a "slam" book circulating around the class was scrawled with details of my flaws, including "Round toes," thanks to the babyish shoes Mom had insisted on buying, and "Wore the same outfit two times in a week!" When an embarrassed non-participant explained what was up, I retreated to the bathroom in tears.

Then Claudia (or was it Claudette?) of the quick-fisted

twins whom nobody at Pyle messed with announced that she liked me and was going to kick the natural asses of whoever made me cry. When more sobbing ten-year-olds fled to the restroom, Mrs. Lewis brought all the girls together. Be Dirty to Donna's creators confessed, insisting they'd planned to dedicate similar days to other girls. Mrs. Lewis told them cruelty is always wrong. The girls apologized. The crisis was over.

Except that it wasn't. Hurt and astonished that my female friends—my ersatz sisters—had turned on me, I absorbed an unshakable sense that girls—unlike boys, whose behavior was familiar—could be dangerous. Some smirked in your face while snatching out your soul. The easy confidence with which I'd walked among my own sex vanished.

Making me more comfortable with, and more dependent on, guys.

By junior high, I had enough trusted girlfriends to focus on the people whose affection really mattered: boys. A vague sense that had begun in early grade school now felt concrete and undeniable: Beauty was the most important thing a girl could offer. It was a gift—not just for the girl who was born with it, but for everyone blessed to lay eyes on it. An unerring attention magnet, prettiness gave a girl the opportunity to share her deeper qualities, like her personality and humor. Beauty is tricky for every girl, but *black* girls' complex relationship with their bodies can make it downright calamitous.

In seventh grade, I was bused to Emerson, the mostly white high school to which scores of black Ernie Pyle graduates had been transferred for "racial balance." Each morning as we boarded the bus, I watched girls whose best features seemed luckier than mine: Shawn had satiny gold skin. Willowy Gayle flaunted a fashion model's grace. Sharon's hair was a wavy waterfall.

I had a big butt.

An ass is an asset too primitive for sonnets and too sexual to sentimentalize, especially if you're thirteen and sex is the scariest thing in the world. Even the hunched-over girls whose slumping couldn't hide newly prominent boobs were better off. It's easier to respond when whooping boys are in front of you than when they're behind.

Or so the yellow dress—whose swingy skirt barely hid the obstreperous rear beneath it—taught me. That day, I'd put on the dress, topped my ponytail with a bow, and felt as fresh and charming as a princess in a Disney movie. Grinning in the mirror, I imagined some dashing boy toppling into love with me.

Walking to school, I saw an appropriately aged boy approaching. I smiled as he walked past. He smiled back.

Then he patted my behind.

I froze. By the time I gathered myself enough to turn around, the boy was far away. But his message was clear: my "beauty" was a booty, a coarse attention-grabber that brought out the beast in boys and seemed to offer what I had no intention of giving.

"Donna Butt" indeed.

It would be decades before pop culture—via Sir Mix-A-Lot's seminal rap "Baby Got Back" and such proudly bootylicious babes as Beyoncé and Jennifer Lopez—acknowledged what boys' reactions showed me every day: my big behind had at least as much impact on boys as other girls' more lauded eyes and hair and breasts. But this was the 1960s; top-heavy sirens—Sophia Loren, Raquel Welch, the recently departed Marilyn Monroe—reigned. Flattering, body-focused adjectives—stacked, buxom, voluptuous—were usually bust-related. My most noted feature never rated public mention; having a great ass by black standards seemed shameful.

But even in middle school, I saw an irony: of the half-dozen Caucasian features Negroes had been brainwashed into worshipping, small booties weren't among them. I knew dozens of black boys who admired "redbone" black girls whose tiny noses, long locks, and golden skin were reminiscent of white girls'.

I didn't know one who preferred a tiny white-girl butt.

Was a well-rounded rear the one African feature so profound in its effect that even racism's scalpel couldn't excise it? Or was booty-love like real estate: location, location, location? Unlike her hair and skin, a woman's behind is irrevocably tied to sex. Black women's generous lower-body upholstery gives them a nature-provided cushion for life's most powerful act. Even when I was in junior high, boys and men responded with everything from whispered suggestions to shouts from across the street.

A romantic who longed to offer boys the quiet beauty of my face and heart, I was stuck with a butt whose swaying— behind my back, literally—shouted all manner of luridness. What's annoying for a woman is terrifying for an inexperienced girl, especially one already grappling with the enormity of black folks' hair issues.

In all of human history, only a handful of women of any color have actually loved their hair. But for kinky-haired black girls in the 1960s, the time and energy required for fighting, taming, and despising their hair was a full-time occupation.

I realized this at Emerson, where my white classmates' carefree attitude about their hair floored me. After gym class, I marveled at the fearlessness with which white girls swam and showered. Some even proceeded wet-haired to class! With the exception of wavy-haired fortunates like Sharon and Gayle (who dodged the jealous fists of girls eager to make them pay for their luck), black girls routinely wore *two* swim caps into the pool and showered with head coverings impenetrable enough to pass federal hazmat requirements. We'd seen photos of "Afros," proud, nappy halos worn by women in major cities. But seeing a smattering of sisters embrace their kinks was like being a 1903 buggy driver hearing that the Wright brothers were flying "airplanes": it made little sense and had less impact on your life.

In the real world, hair meant trouble. Most black girls had two painful options: a press-and-curl or a perm. Though many got their hair done in neighbors' kitchens, Mom took me to a "beauty parlor," a smoky establishment presided over by "beauticians" who had ultimate power over their clients: life or death—or cute or ugly, which was the same thing.

For a press-and-curl, my beautician swathed me in a plastic drape, washed and dried my hair, and set a heavy brass comb, or "pressing iron," over an open flame. When the comb started to smoke, the beautician grabbed a section of hair, greased it, and—as I sat as stiff as a mannequin—pulled the comb through to straighten it. When my whole head was straightened, she fired up a clattering curling iron and created rows of tight curls she combed into a style that lasted as long as I avoided rain, humidity, or sweating. Fidgeting during the process resulted in a forehead burn and a week of inventing hairdos to hide it.

Perms held other risks. The beautician applied gobs of harsh chemicals—amusingly called "relaxer"—to my hair, combed it through, and watched me sit, grimacing, as she calculated how long she had before the increasingly hot glop on my head ignited (or just felt like it). Dashing me to the sink, she'd wash the stinging goop down the drain—hopefully without clumps of my hair clinging to it.

Six weeks later—or two weeks with a press-and-curl—I endured it all again. When I griped, Mom shushed me with her favorite black-hair maxim: "Beauty knows no pain."

Except for the psychic kind. Life shrinks when water is your sworn enemy. The briefest rain shower could flatten your perm, leaving you to resemble the sodden ghoul that emerged from Naomi Watts's TV in *The Ring*. Minutes of humidity morphed the sleekest of press-and-curls into a pickaninny's mop. No wonder huge numbers of black women never learned to swim.

Worst of all was knowing that making and keeping your hair pretty (or even acceptable) required so much work that your "gift" of beautiful hair felt inauthentic, not to mention a burden. Still, black-girl hair had one advantage: versatility. We lorded it over white classmates when it came to hair *styles*, to our hair's knack for being twisted, curled, and braided in countless ways.

My hair was one more thing that gave me the sense, deep in my bones, that something was wrong with the beauty I offered the world. Like my broad nose and rounded butt, my crowning glory was deficient. My hair wasn't all that got pressed. Day after day, doubts were squeezed into my consciousness about whether I could truly *be* beautiful.

There was one more place where my blackness worked on my self-esteem: the classroom. Placed in honors courses with high-performing white students, I for the first time competed with white kids—*smart* white kids—academically. For years, I'd been told Negroes were inferior. Would I embarrass the race?

I was shocked when I, along with other Pyle kids, competed ably with our new classmates. More stunning was the warmth with which I was embraced by classmates whose Greek and Polish names reflected their exotic heritages: Toula Mantakounis; the adorable Mercuri Papakaladoukas. These kids marveled at my book knowledge, giggled at my quips, admired my wardrobe.

Why wouldn't they? I'd made it my mission to be the most engaging seventh grader alive. What better way to disprove what I assumed white kids felt: that black students couldn't measure up, or be as amazing as the kids they saw in the mirror? Of course, some black transfer students glared at their white classmates, shoved them if they moved too slowly to class. Still others simply ignored them, certain that white folks had nothing on them.

My reaction, of course, was to offer myself to them, through jokes, compliments, academic assistance, patient explanations of black hairdos and fashions. My perfect black-girl act was meant to prove my worthiness to white people, make them admire me.

It worked. So what if I wasn't so crazy about myself?

Looking back, what strikes me most about my adolescence isn't my self-esteem's inevitable slide from a kid's self-love to a grown-up's self-doubt. It's the long mornings and afternoons I spent thinking about...nothing much.

My girlhood's languid contemplations couldn't have been more different from my adult mind's bustle. Minute by minute, it whirs and sags with a thousand deliberations: about household chores; family duties; the relentless minutiae of my sons' schedules, activities, diets, health, and educations; our household budget; Mom's needs (did I call her yesterday?); my writing; appointments; the alarming state of the world; my husband and *his* career, fitness, obligations.

Yet once upon a time—the memory is as improbable as a

fairy tale—my thoughts were unapologetically me-centered: *my* friends, *my* books, *my* crushes. Me-me-me! Me flopped on my belly on a carpet of grass, eye level with a spiky dandelion, studying it. Me flipping onto my back to observe a passing assemblage of clouds, deciding what each was shaped like. Me unworried that such time wasn't well spent, or that it robbed anyone who might need me.

What woman with a mate, offspring, and/or obligations doesn't miss long mornings in bed, feeling no compunction to rise and *do* something? Little girls love "playing Mommy," pretending their dolls and the duties performed for them are real.

Can't moms occasionally pretend they're the unencumbered little girls they once were?

Can't we awaken and lie motionless as we decipher the code tapped out by rooftop raindrops? Rise slowly enough to feel the sun's drift through the curtain, hear its splash on the floor? Can't we spend a morning contemplating a day filled with games, friends, daydreams—with nothing much? We can. We don't.

But, God, do I miss nothing much.

Opposites Detract

Mom-Mommy, Mom, and Daddy at a Chicago nightclub, 1946.

She's in the basement laundry room with her back to me, hunched over the washer. Assuming she's unobserved, the small woman allows her shoulders to shudder. Tentatively, I move toward this stranger who looks like Mommy but who—it can't be true—is crying. Mothers can cry? The people who know everything, fix everything, run everything, do that, too? It's like stumbling upon God weeping. She won't say what hurt her, but I'm betting it's a man, and I know which man. At age ten, I've yet to learn about my mom's smorgasbord of past hurts. So I'm certain: no one but a daddy could make a mommy cry.

On a lushly gorgeous April day, one of the most giving people I know—my mother—sat silently in my car's backseat as I drove her home. After a long, gray winter, I found the afternoon's radiance breathtaking. Mom's uncharacteristic stillness suggested that she, too, was moved by the bright blossoms erupting around homes streaming past. Finally, Mom spoke:

"You can buy the nicest house in the most expensive neighborhood," she said. "And you have no guarantee that Hispanics won't move in next door, install a concrete driveway, and park five cars in it."

I wanted to scream, but found myself laughing instead. The words were so harsh. So uncalled for. So Mom. Over the years, I'd heard her insult every ethnicity imaginable, and her commentary seldom stopped there. I recalled riding with her though the vast New Mexico desert, dumbstruck by mountains tottering like pebbles on the horizon. "So beautiful." Mom sighed. "And so full of radiation from those experiments in the 1950s!" And there was the time after I turned forty-five, when I proudly told her a bartender had asked me for ID. Asked Mom: "Was he *blind?*"

Mom is every bit as free with a compliment. Yet I steel myself in her presence because I'm never sure whether her bluntness will leave me feeling praised or punished. She and my very different, but equally powerful, father influenced nearly every action in my life. So no exploration of my giving would be worthwhile unless I confronted two questions every searching woman asks. The first: *How much am I like my mother?*

Everyone who knows Geraldine Britt will tell you she's smart, hip, and so youthful even her doctors doubt she's in her eighties. I deeply admire her. Yet her unerring gift of ferreting ugliness from beauty and then commenting on it couldn't be more different from my tendency to uncover whatever seems wonderful about a person or a situation and to point that out.

Could I be unthinkingly trying to make up for Mom, who was born without the editing mechanism most people use to negotiate life? Though there are few ethnic groups she hasn't denigrated, Mom's favorite victims have always been black. Over the years, she has castigated blackfolk for their speech (too ignorant), lawn care (too inconsistent), fashion sense (too flamboyant), hair (too nappy), and more. Like millions raised in an era in which black people's intelligence, beauty, and worth were constantly questioned, she absorbed white culture's aggregate contempt while still managing to cherish black individuals.

Mom is just as likely to point out her own flaws, saying, "I'm too stupid to do math," or (God help the uninitiated listener) "I'm burned; I don't have a nipple on one breast." In fact, she's certain that her imagined flaws are what made her life so disappointing.

That's why my first memory of her (I was three) is so surprising. She's pregnant with my baby brother and smiling a soft, buttercream smile as she irons satiny strips of apple green ribbon. What's surprising is that Mom—whose raucous laugh can often be heard blocks away—is so silent. So happy. So *tall.*

From my toddler's vantage point beneath the board, my mother is enormous. Yet Mom is only four eleven—or four ten, or four nine, depending on when you ask. Though she insists she's shrinking, what never diminishes is her belief that her petiteness, which many people find charming, blighted her life. She is, she says simply, "too short": To be powerful. To be beautiful. To be everything she is.

Ironically, my clearest early memory of my six-foot one-inch father is quite different. Daddy seems much smaller, or at least less forbidding, than in other memories. I'm seven, clutching his hand in a kids' clothing store. Mom is nowhere in sight. I'm so excited, I can hardly breathe because my usually distant Daddy has taken me into my favorite shop.

As we approach a circular rack of dresses, a candy pink number catches my eye. "I like this one," I tell him. Seersucker with white buttons, the bell-shaped "tent" dress cost $2.99, which today sounds laughable.

But when Daddy replies, "I'll get it for you," you'd think God had dropped a diamond into my palm. My first powerful memory of Daddy is of one of the few times in my life that I recall him directly giving me something. Which raises the second vital question: *How did my relationship with my father shape my view of men?*

Another memory whispers an answer. I'm standing warily beside Daddy's chair at the kitchen table, watching his dour gaze sweep over the meal I've fixed while Mom works late. At age ten, I see "cooking" as boiling boxed mac-and-cheese or slipping frozen potpies in the oven—meals that feel special because they're fixed for my daddy (for my brothers, too, but they'll eat anything). Tonight's offering: Kraft noodles, string beans boiled to a whimper, and a square of gristle euphemistically called "Salisbury steak."

Daddy gazes. Pauses. Says, "You managed to get everything I don't like on this plate."

Which is saying something because you could fill a good-sized barn with stuff Daddy doesn't like: Intimate chats. Kids who don't leap happily from bed to tackle chores with the grim gusto he brings to every task. Wasting money on vacation spots unreachable by an all-night drive in a kid-, luggage-, pillow-stuffed car.

Sometimes I wasn't sure he liked *me*. Yet no matter how much Daddy's coolness frustrated me, Mom—whose childhood had honed her need for warmth to needlelike sharpness—felt worse. My parents' mutual irritation was at times so palpable, I was stunned the one time I saw them steal a kiss. I wasn't sure what had prompted such warmth, but it froze me in my tracks. In my thirteen years, I'd seen couples in movies exchange every kind of kiss without having seen my parents share one. The peck was so flabbergasting, it again raised a question I'd long pondered: *Why are these two people together?*

At least one explanation for my parents' connection, I felt certain, was Mom's height obsession.

Daddy was tall.

Moreover, he had no problem with her petiteness. Why would he, when Mom was cuter, more sophisticated, and more stylish than almost everyone else's wife? Why would anyone, when her stature was the only small thing about her?

I was the only girl I knew whose mom looked, well, *hot* in hot pants—and textured hose and lace-up boots. Boys my age would roll up behind her at the skating rink—she skated into her sixties—and snake flirtatious arms around her waist. Whispering, "Hey, baby," they'd lean in, gaze in her eyes— and nearly fall on their faces.

"Oh, excuse me, ma'am," they'd mutter as Mom whirled away, grinning.

This is the woman who as a high school senior won an oratorical contest judged by a young NAACP attorney named Thurgood Marshall. Mom's 1942 speech questioned why her black male classmates were heading directly from graduation to World War II, risking death for a nation that discriminated against them. I knew nothing about the speech until 2006, when I overheard Mom mention it to local high schoolers interviewing senior citizens. Forgetting the eloquence that won her the contest, Mom had praise only for the man who'd become the first black Supreme Court justice: "He was *handsome*."

Part of Mom remains cemented in childhood, waiting for things to be made right. Believing that if she had been taller— or prettier or more lovable—everything might have been different.

She might not have been stashed for years at a boardinghouse with an abusive guardian, or set afire by the backyard blaze that scorched her chest and face, leaving scars of which my mother is exquisitely aware and which I, the daughter who views her through love's prism, never notice. If she'd been different, she feels, her unwed mother might have loved her from the start.

Perhaps I would be different, too. Because if my grandmother had been able to give my mother the love she needed as a child, I wouldn't have spent decades making up for the lack.

By the time I met Theodosia Dote Houston King—"Mom-Mommy" King to her adoring grandchildren—she was in her early fifties, though no one would have suspected it. Glamorous and bitingly funny, she christened herself "Mom-Mommy" after Steve's birth to avoid the unthinkable: being called "Grandma."

Everything I knew about Mom-Mommy was cool. As a teen, she'd been offered singing lessons with Philadelphia diva Marian Anderson (she regretted being unable to afford them). During a school trip to Washington, D.C., Mom-Mommy informed a white bus driver she was *not* getting off the bus just because they'd entered a segregated city. Many of her white classmates supported her.

Confident, smart, spiritual, and as warm as toast, she was the perfect grandmother, and everything I wanted to be, including devastatingly attractive to men. Even (I didn't realize for years) the wrong men.

A Media, Pennsylvania, high school track star, Mom-Mommy was a striking nineteen-year-old when she became pregnant with Mom in 1923. Unwed pregnancy was intolerable for churchgoing Negro girls; the identity of the man responsible made it worse. The one time I asked Mom-Mommy about Mom's father, she was at first speechless. In all the decades I knew her, I never saw her so sad.

Her voice low, Mom-Mommy told me that the husband of one of her relatives—a much older, respected church pillar I'd met as a child—had offered to take her berry picking. Mom-Mommy had felt uneasy, but her mother, Nana, had insisted. When the man forced her into sex, she couldn't bring herself to tell his wife, whom she loved. Mom-Mommy soon learned she was pregnant.

No man ever took responsibility for fathering my mother. In the 1920s, "family scandals that nobody wanted to own up to were buried," Mom later told me. "That's why they hid me."

Geraldine King was born in Pennsauken, New Jersey, in

the late spring of 1924. For six weeks, Mom-Mommy cared for her newborn. Then Nana—on her half day off from her $6-a-week job as a maid and cook to a rich, white family—took the baby to Philadelphia, about fifteen miles east of Media. My infant mother clasped in her arms, Nana walked South Philly's bustling streets, asking strangers if they knew of anyone who might care for her grandbaby. A tip led her to the Seventeenth Street row house where Mom would spend her first seven years, cared for by a chilly, uneducated woman in her sixties called Mom Stevens. For years, Mom was unaware of her parents' identity, or even that they existed.

By age four, my mother was sharing the upstairs floor with two younger kids named Willie and Glorie May. She vividly recalls the home's smelly outhouse, the kitchen pump that filled the tin washtub in which she was bathed, deliveries of massive sacks of bug-infested flour, and meals of slimy oatmeal and fatback. Mom Stevens regularly "whupped" the youngsters with a heavy strap, once slapping Mom's face with a slipper. For days, Mom could smell her split lip, which was too crusted with blood and pus for her to eat.

Life was far from easy. But by the time Mom Stevens enrolled little Geraldine in first grade, my mother had a thrilling secret: Unlike the other boardinghouse kids, she had a mother who cared enough to visit.

Each week for as long as she could remember, Nana had visited her, dressed in a plain starched work dress. But once a month, an attractive younger woman in stylish clothes mounted the stairs to watch her play. Once Mom overheard a snatch of conversation suggesting that despite her fashionable garb, the young woman worked "at service" like Nana, cleaning white people's homes. Her name: Dote.

At some point Mom realized: the young visitor was her mother, the older one her grandmother. Her pride in her pretty mother was exceeded only by her terror each time Mom-Mommy left that she'd never see her again.

One hot August day in 1931, my seven-year-old mother watched Mom Stevens's husband light the trash with matches in the backyard before joining the other children in a game of tag. Dashing too close to the blaze, Mom was aghast to see her cotton dress catch fire. Bolting away, she ran shrieking as hot air fanned the flames that were engulfing her. Finally strong hands threw her down, wrapped her in a blanket, carried her upstairs. For five agonizing days, Mom sobbed in her stifling bedroom as Mom Stevens smeared cottonseed oil on third-degree burns across her entire left side. No one sent for a doctor.

After an eternity of trying to keep her scalded skin from sticking to the bed, Mom finally saw Nana—who, like most working-class people, had no phone—walk in.

Screaming that Mom Stevens should have found a way to tell her about the burns, Nana wept as she swept Mom up, flew downstairs, and flagged down the first car she saw.

At Children's Hospital of Philadelphia, Mom was placed on a gurney. Three white men in snowy coats—"doctors," Nana called them—bluntly told Nana, "We can't save this child." Nana, by now hysterical, beseeched them to try. Whisking Mom away, hospital officials for weeks limited visits from her mother and grandmother to once a week.

Five months later, on Christmas Eve, she was released to them.

Over the years, Mom told me many times about her horrific, hidden childhood. Each time, it broke my heart to consider her loneliness and pain. Yet it wasn't until I became a mother that I understood how much Mom's childhood explains her. And me.

It explained why, as a four-year-old child of working-class parents, I had *five* pairs of shoes (navy, pink, white, red, and black patent). And why at Christmas, the toys under our tree far outnumbered my friends'. It explained why Mom was more vigilant about boys, sleepovers, car trips, *everything,* than other mothers, and why her critical eyes poked my brothers and me like insistent fingers, dissecting our speech, weights, walks, hair, and everything else they prodded.

A born giver, Mom's first, most heartfelt offering to us was the protected, carefully observed early life she'd missed. We chafed under her laserlike attention, unaware that for a certain, scalded seven-year-old, love and attention would forever be indistinguishable.

For years, I assumed that my protectiveness of my kids resulted from Darrell's death. Recently, I've wondered what science has begun to ask: Could parents' traumas be absorbed by their children's DNA? I inherited Mom's round nose and gift for drawing. But what about her need to give? When I was a broke single mom, my sons had the most gorgeous (if discount-store-purchased) clothes; years later, a doctor treating Skye for a digestive problem marveled at how faithfully I prepared fiber-rich fruit for him, saying, "I wish someone cut up mangoes for me every day!"

For years, I wondered why Mom never stopped reminding me of when I was three and she swatted a housefly. I'd blurted, "I love you Mommy because you can beat up any old fly!"

In her first seven years, she felt no one cared enough even to kill an insect for her.

My father's first years were quite different, except in one key way: he, too, longed for parental attention.

Born in Manakin, Virginia, in 1920, Daddy was the only

son among a brood of four born to Thomas Sheridan Britt and Addie Snead Britt. His father, a brickmason, moved the family to Gary when Daddy was five. My serious, hardworking grandfather soon divorced my flinty grandmother. Yet he stayed close to his family, even building them a new brick home *after* his marriage broke up. Maybe he was as scared of my grandma as I was.

Imagining my father as a boy was never easy, and not just because I had few childhood photos and fewer discussions with him about those years. By the time I knew him, whatever boyishness or playfulness Daddy might have had was gone. He was a *man*, a strong, silent one with whom it was hard to talk about anything. Daddy's reticence and clipped responses to every question — "Yep," "Not really," "Um-hmm" — thwarted most inquiries. Mom loved questions, sometimes revealing too much. Dad revealed nothing. At some point, I stopped asking. I decided that men, unlike boys, were mysteries.

I did ascertain that my quiet, athletic father was close to all three of his sisters as a child. They adored him. His imposing mother was equally smitten, so my father had four females catering to, encouraging, and supporting him. His father, however, seemed less enamored of him. Long ago, Daddy told Mom one of his earliest memories: Being assigned at age five to read road signs on an overnight family car trip. Little Elwood took the responsibility seriously, fighting to stay awake so as not to miss anything important. "He was so proud of having done a good job for the father who seemed so hard to please," Mom recalled. "It was something special, pleasing his dad."

Mom, who'd never stopped seeking her absent mother's love, could relate. So could the daughter who'd expectantly awaited her Daddy's thumbs-down verdict at the dinner table.

*   *   *

When Mom finally left Children's Hospital, Nana and Mom-Mommy told her she was "going home." But rather than returning her to Mom Stevens's, they drove her to the two-story Media home Nana shared with Mom-Mommy; her older daughter, Mae Batipps; Mae's husband, Percy; and their five children. My mother had already met Mom-Mommy's half sister. Visiting her once with Mom-Mommy at Mom Stevens's, Mae had invited Mom to brush the wavy hair that fell to her waist. My mother instantly fell in love with her.

So it seemed miraculous that the new home she awoke to on Christmas Day 1932 not only had electric lights, an indoor toilet, and running water. Aunt Mae lived there! So did Mae's children: Virginia ("Din"), Mae ("Sis"), Percy Jr. ("Pop"), Francis, and Donnie. Nana told Mom's cousins: "This is Geraldine, Dote's daughter." And that was that.

Suddenly Mom was happy in ways she couldn't have dreamed. Because Nana and Theodosia held outside jobs, she became one of Aunt Mae's boisterous brood. For the first time, someone treated her like a daughter. The house was warm, the food delicious, Uncle Perce played hymns nightly on the piano. At bedtime, Sis lined up the smaller kids like toy soldiers, marching them upstairs, counting, "One-two-three-four!" Marching in time, Mom felt she belonged.

It was at Mae's house that Mom finally felt comfortable calling the woman who'd borne her "Mother." Mom-Mommy surprised her by confessing her own trepidation each time she'd visited her at Mom Stevens's, saying, "I never knew how you'd act toward me—if you would run toward me or just look at me." Mom hadn't realized how obvious her resentment had been toward her mother, how angry she'd been that Mom-Mommy hadn't visited more, so she might have told her about the inedible food, the hitting, Mom Stevens's surliness.

Finally loved and protected, my mother allowed herself to wonder, Why didn't my mother want me? An adult would find answers in 1920s culture and conventions: society's merciless scorn of unwed mothers; Mom-Mommy's unspoken bitterness that her daughter resulted from a rape by a man who never acknowledged his culpability. But Mom was a child. A child's first, best reason for any mistreatment or lack of love is "something is wrong with me." Some children never believe anything else.

Maybe that's why it wasn't until adulthood that my mother believed she had earned her mother's approval. Ask what she feels changed Mom-Mommy toward her, and Mom doesn't hesitate: "I had children."

Today I can see how Mom's unwavering devotion to her children — dedication which Mom-Mommy had been unable to show her — gained her mother's respect. I also see how freely my grandmother gave my brothers and me that which Mom never stopped craving: her full and loving attention.

Each summer, my brothers and I gleefully joined Mom at the Amtrak station to await our grandmother's arrival. Scanning the length of the Capitol Limited, we screamed *Mom-Mommy!* when we spied the lustrous woman whom bellmen rushed to help with luggage stuffed with gifts and chilled packages of the pork scrapple Daddy loved. Wrapping me in hugs, she'd listen spellbound to my breathless stories and encourage my drawing and singing and self-regard. Always, Mom-Mommy would take me downtown or to the mall to buy me shoes and dresses, sometimes more costly than Mom could afford.

My brothers and I were the human correction fluid with which both Mom-Mommy and our mother painted over the past. Mom bestowed on us the sheltered childhood that had eluded her; Mom-Mommy lavished on us everything she hadn't been able to give her own daughter. Without knowing it, my "perfect" grandmother taught me what could happen when a less-than-perfect parent didn't give her time, love, and attention to her child: Mom could happen. A lifelong sense of unworthiness could happen.

I learned well enough to know that when I had kids, I would never let it happen.

By high school, the youth who would become my father was over six feet tall, popular with girls, and a skilled forward for Gary Roosevelt High's basketball team. Though treasured by his sisters — stunning Hortense, bubbly Marian, and baby Maurice — young Elwood knew that no one cherished him like his doting mother. His father may not have been as captivated by him, but he taught Daddy to lay bricks — an invaluable skill in an industrial town — and eased his son's entry into the bricklayers' union.

Daddy was studying architecture on a basketball scholarship at the historically black Florida A&M University when the United States entered World War II. Joining the navy, he spent much of his stint playing basketball for the military on the blustery Aleutian Islands. He was twenty-five when he returned home and began assisting his dad on bricklaying jobs.

On a warm March day in 1946, Elwood was intrigued to see a cute stranger in a stylish Eisenhower jacket walking toward him with a friend. The petite woman was so impressed by *him*, she surreptitiously dumped the ice cream cone she'd been slurping into the gutter before smiling at him. She didn't want to look babyish.

Temple University graduate Geraldine "Gerri" King had just been hired as a dental hygienist at Elwood's high school alma mater. After three years with Aunt Mae, Mom had moved in with Mom-Mommy. She finally left Media when Mom-Mommy's new husband showed no interest in having a step-daughter underfoot. Gary, so close to exciting Chicago, seemed a promising place to start over.

After six whirlwind weeks, Gerri and Elwood decided to marry. Having just fled the mother whose love she still questioned, Mom did what people fleeing the past often do: attached herself to someone certain to re-create the anguish she longed to escape.

But any woman might have been drawn to Daddy. As a child, I used to stare at his black-and-white wedding day portrait. With his custom-made suit and knowing smile, he was as handsome as a movie star, radiating a suavity that spoke of cocktails and jazz, not bricklaying and bills. Yet his coolness wasn't just in his gaze and the drape of his clothes. Daddy's chilly emotional temperature—the natural detachment that magnetized and exacerbated her lifelong sense of inadequacy—also fascinated Mom.

But what inspired my popular father to marry a vivacious near stranger? Studying his old portrait, I've looked for answers—and found more questions. Nothing about the five-by-seven photo suggested the domesticity she was seeking. Did the small portrait seem bigger than Daddy because hope still filled out its subject? Because glamour was even more becoming to him than the responsibility he clearly embraced?

Did it explain why family life so rarely pleased him?

As a four-year-old, I'd jumped into his arms each night when he arrived home from work, dusty from brick mortar and cinder blocks. But by the time I was ten, my brothers and I feared him. On Saturdays, we dreaded waking to the sight of his rangy form looming over us, yanking open the drapes and booming, "Want to help with the lawn?'"

Do you think any of us replied, "Not really"?

For years, the person who'd mattered most to Daddy—his father—had demanded one thing from him: physical labor. Is it surprising that work was all he seemed to want from us?

That was difficult for my brothers; it felt punishing to me. I was an affectionate girl, and my father just wasn't demonstrative. His mother and sisters had freely given him warmth and attention; he never learned to reciprocate.

The older I got, the more I avoided him. Bounding into Daddy's arms turned to backing away from a man who couldn't offer himself—not his protection or directives but him*self*— to me. By yesterday's standards, Daddy was a good father. He came home straight from work and relinquished his paycheck. He was *there,* even if we seldom found him generous or engaging. Being there, I know now, may have been the most he could give.

In May 1946, two young people took their vows before a Baptist preacher in my grandmother's living room: a quiet groom smitten with a girl whose upbringing ensured that she'd work as hard to please him as had every other woman, and a quick-to-laugh bride as enamored of her groom's height and handsomeness as of his emotional reserve. They both sensed the other would provide what they'd been raised to expect. In retrospect, the answer to my childhood question— *why were these two together?*—was obvious:

In all the wrong ways, they were perfect for each other.

Decades later, it makes sense that a woman hidden as a child and whose husband made silence an art form would blurt attention-grabbing truths. Concealed and tamped down for years, Mom now makes sure that everyone acknowledges her.

I was an adult before I saw how famished she was for

validation, and how responsible I felt for filling the holes aban-donment had gouged in her. Yet I recoiled from her neediness, even as I absorbed what childhood had taught her: love should be stated, repeated, and then underlined, by both the giver and the receiver. For all my fretting about giving to men, she was the first person to whom I couldn't give enough. The holes were too deep.

But my mother's emotional voraciousness made sense. What was my excuse? I'd had a warm home and a mother who loved me — everything she lacked.

I had a daddy, too. The first man whom I ransacked my imagination to please was also the first whose muted responses left me starving. When I found Mom crying in the laundry room, I knew he was the cause — though she could just as eas-ily have been weeping about her frustrating mother. But I adored Mom-Mommy. My connection to Daddy was already slipping.

In 1999, my father died after his car was struck by a train that had briefly stopped at an East Chicago railway crossing during a snowstorm. According to my aunt, two cars had crossed the tracks when the train started moving; Daddy's didn't make it. A decade later, I was searching for some papers in my office when I came across a box of unfamiliar memora-bilia. Looking through it, I realized, *This was Daddy's!* Mom must have given me the box after his death; in my grief and shock, I'd stuffed it in a corner and forgotten about it.

The box was full of Donna stuff: Announcements of my induction into my college honor society and of my sons' births; holiday and birthday cards I'd sent to him as a college freshman and a grad student; columns my father had snipped from the *Gary Post-Tribune* during my syndication. There were photos of me as a bride, a young wife, the doting mother of toddlers Hamani and Darrell and of baby Skye. Daddy, I suddenly understood, had treasured every valentine, announcement, note containing news from college ("Guess what? There's a new local paper here and I am the art editor!"), correspondences in which I'd asked for money ("Sorry, Daddy, but I need a LOT this time...$45"), and milestones in his grandsons' lives. A letter from my first year of grad school informed him I'd gotten an A on my first paper and thanked him for his "cash donation to the Starving Daughters of America fund." I told him of the dates of Michigan football games he might want to attend, and in 1976 I reminded him of the importance of sending my $10 weekly allowance so I could purchase copies of my résumé, adding, "I'm glad we got to spend more time together this vacation. I feel that I know you now better than I ever did when I was living in the same house with you (isn't *that* ironic?)." In another letter, I wrote, "I hope you enjoyed the articles I sent you....I really am trying to make you proud of me."

Studying the letters and snapshots so many years later, I felt inexplicably sad. Why wasn't I thrilled to discover that I'd had a more profound connection to my father than I recalled—and that I had never stopped trying to deepen it? I'd meant enough to my "distant" Daddy for him to save every card, photo, and note I sent him. And my missives to him indicated that he'd written me back more often than I'd given him credit for. Why had I forgotten? I wondered if Mom had inadvertently shaped my memories of him. I'd been her sounding board, the child most acutely attuned to her hurts and needs. Had absorbing her disillusionment exacerbated my own? Or had my lifelong impatience with Daddy's silences blinded me to the depth of his love? The box's contents suggested I'd been a more caring daughter than I'd realized—and that my father had been more interested in and proud of me than I had allowed myself to remember.

I was unaware of that on the afternoon in ninth grade when I spent an hour in front of the mirror, practicing a disdainful sneer to employ when he demanded a beneath-me chore. The first time I used it, Daddy hissed in a Clint Eastwood whisper, "Wipe that look off your face or I'll wipe it for you."

I wiped. From then on I stared at the floor when Daddy irked me. Looking away, I felt sure of one thing:

I would never, ever marry a guy like him.

Sex, Drugs, and Rock and Roll(ing Papers)

Left to right: Darrell, Mom-Mommy, Bruce, Steve, and Donna, Christmas 1971.

*It's 1965 and we're at the dinner table, our interplay as cho-
reographed as a waltz: Steve blusters, Daddy simmers, Mom
critiques, Bruce and Darrell joke. When Darrell asks, "Why did
the elephant paint his toenails red?" the answer —"To hide in the
strawberry patch!"—makes Mom crack up in a way we've never
seen, gasping, crying, tumbling from her chair. We've barely
recovered when Steve, whose hair in this era of basketball-sized
Afros is a tennis ball's fuzz, laments, "I wish my hair would
grow." Suddenly we're howling, convulsed to hear the cocky household tough admitting a flaw. I would never love Steve more than
at that moment. Or at least until a decade later, when he
screamed at us his certainty that everyone wished that he, and
not Darrell, had died in that ditch. Again, I was undone by his
vulnerability—and by the fact that I had wished exactly that.*

It was Christmas Eve 1961, and at age seven, I was too nervous to sleep. Mom had banished us kids to bed in the back of
the house while she and Daddy got ready for Santa's arrival.

Sniffing out an opportunity to tease Bruce and me, Steve,
twelve, threw Darrell a "go along with me" look. "You better
go to sleep," he said. "I know this boy who couldn't sleep on
Christmas Eve and he accidentally saw Santa put the gifts
under the Christmas tree!" Emboldened by our shock, Steve
widened his eyes dramatically. "He was lucky Santa didn't see
him," he continued, "or he would have taken his gifts and
gone right back up the chimney!" Shaken by the boy's close
call, Bruce and I retreated under the covers of our twin beds.
Darrell and Steve left for their room; Bruce instantly fell
asleep. I stared at the ceiling, still too agitated for slumber.
Sliding out of bed, I crept to the door, where I heard Darrell

whisper excitedly, *"Let's get Donna's coat!"* Steve, too, sounded thrilled: "Yeah, she's gonna love it!" Puzzled, I returned to bed.

The next morning I found a beautiful black wool girl's coat with a real fur collar under the tree. I was confused by everyone's insistence that Santa—who I still wanted to believe was real—had brought it. But something else bewildered me more: the joy I'd heard in Steve's voice at the thought of my happiness. Steve must love me! Pondering this staggering thought, a more shocking realization followed: I loved him, too! But how could that be? Cataloging his many sins, I knew I couldn't stand him. So it had to be one of life's tricks: you loved your brothers, no matter what.

God knows I did. Nobody influenced me more, especially when it came to giving to men. For years, I had no one but guys to give *to*. Like a baby duck imprinted by the first creature it saw, I extended my early, unthinking love for my brothers to men in general. Be Dirty to Donna Day had made me permanently wary of girls, but no amount of teasing from boys could make me enduringly wary of them. Bruce, Darrell, and Steve—very dissimilar boys—ensured that my first gift to very different men would be the benefit of the doubt.

But as natural as it felt putting aside the biggest burger for Darrell or surprising Bruce with a pack of Green Hornet bubble gum cards, it was tougher to give to Steve. I just didn't know what to make of him.

I remember an afternoon when I was twelve, stretched out on my bed blissfully rereading *Gone With the Wind*. So engrossed was I in Scarlett and Rhett's chaste lust that I barely heard Steve murmuring across the hall.

Until he purred, "Yeah, baby, we're gonna fuck all night."

I gasped aloud. Praying Steve hadn't heard me—that I hadn't really heard him—I pressed my face in the pillow. And heard more: "It's gonna be so good," Steve cooed, his voice low but not low enough. "We're gonna keep fucking and fucking..."

Stunned tears wet my pillow. Even Steve had to know sex was special, an act shared by husbands and wives. He was only seventeen; he and his girlfriend weren't even engaged! I'd met her several times and thought she was great; any high school girl thoughtful enough to ask about my books, Darrell's albums, and Bruce's comics was too classy to listen to my clearly-gone-mad brother's ranting.

Yet there was no indication that she was vomiting on the other line.

My mind was spinning. If Steve was bold enough to say "fuck" to such a sweet girl, maybe he could actually do it. Maybe she could do it! Or was another girl on the line, some skank Steve was sneaking around with? Would he break his girlfriend's heart?

Could a boy one day similarly mesmerize *me*?

My afternoon was ruined. Gone with the wind.

Steve wasn't just trying to corrupt an innocent and violate the men-must-earn-sex rule prescribed by Doris Day movies. He was betraying the race. We lived in a black neighborhood, but white people took up plenty of real estate in our minds. Mom was determined that her kids would be nice Negroes who showed whites that they had nothing to fear from us while setting an example for less-dignified colored folk.

Like millions of black kids in the mid-1960s, we Britt kids knew what was expected of us: Neatly straightened or naturally curly hair—no crazy styles or excess grease. Quiet, grammatical sentences. Decorous movements in public—no running or strutting. No evidence of bodily functions: oily skin, sweating, noisy nose blowing.

"Baby, we're gonna fuck all night" warranted instant ejection from Negrodom. No wonder Steve sneeringly called me "the princess."

I was the dutiful good girl, Steve the born rebel. I flaunted my straight As; Steve skipped class, forging "adult-sounding" excuses like the one Mom found—signed with her name—in his pocket:

"Please excuse Steven Britt from class Thursday because an uncanny situation occurred."

By his teens, Steve was a talented-enough artist to paint a perfect replica of the family car's license plate when our father temporarily lacked the cash to replace the real one. The cardboard fake looked so authentic, Daddy used it for weeks. But mostly, Steve used his powers for evil: stealing from Mom's purse, creeping home late smelling of Boone's Farm wine, and trying on rings at stores where he'd ask salesclerks, "Can I look at this in the light?" Taking their wares outside, he'd dash off with them. He wore coke-spoon necklaces and hid rolling papers in his drawer. He had sex.

I made Gidget look depraved.

Years later, Steve would tell me that from boyhood, he had a powerful sense that he was born to royalty. "I felt I was a king—of what or who I didn't know." Maybe that explains why he was the first person I knew whose giving was directed entirely toward himself. He *was* like a monarch. Other people's desires hardly existed for him. Asked to explain the trait, he describes the boyhood day he asked Mom if Santa Claus, not she or Dad, brought his toys. Mom said, "Santa." When he learned the truth, Steve told her God must be fake, too. "But God is real!" Mom insisted. Too late. Unafraid of Divine punishment, Steve began doing whatever he pleased, including pushing everybody's buttons, especially his family's.

Like the memorable day when Bruce, fifteen, was downstairs in Darrell's black-lit, poster-plastered bedroom listening to music with his brothers and their friends. Everyone was smoking marijuana except Bruce, who had no use for drugs.

Steve had a brilliant idea: to introduce aspiring-rocker Bruce to reefer. It was the 1970s; weed could be smelled at every party and concert. Initiating Bruce would be a rite of passage.

Tittering, Steve tried to coax Bruce into taking a hit from the joint being passed around. Bruce declined. Steve pressed him, "*Try* it." Bruce resisted, increasingly uncomfortable. When Steve said, "It ain't gonna hurt you to take a hit," Darrell, his voice icy, warned him, "Back off." Undeterred, Steve wheedled, "C'mon, just *try* it."

Bad move. Face contorted, Darrell shouted, *"Stop it, dammit!"* Steve instantly shut up. "It's bad enough we're into this shit!" Darrell hollered. "Let him *alone!*" No one spoke.

Few had seen Darrell's rage, the ferocity of which witnesses never forgot. Like the day Darrell, furious with our parents for repeatedly putting off teaching him to drive, leapt into the car, revved the engine—and slammed into the garage door. Or the time he saved up to buy the new O'Jays album and found that the record was defective. Roaring, he'd hurled it at a wall, shattering it.

This time, an uncomfortable silence filled the basement. The party broke up. Steve never offered drugs to Bruce again.

Bruce appreciated Darrell's intervention, but the devil himself—whom I sometimes suspected Steve was—couldn't have coaxed him to smoke that joint. Bruce, too, was stubborn and independent, despite having all the empathy Steve lacked. When our big brothers left for college, Bruce drew closer to Mom and me, listening to our stories, feeling our guy-related pain so acutely that years later it was impossible for him to listen to friends' seduction stories. Each conquest was someone's daughter or sister. Sometimes Daddy worried about Mom's and my influence on him. Bruce still squirms at the memory of Daddy taking him to a 4-H-type club recruitment to forge a father-son bond. Bruce couldn't conquer his fear of him.

Daddy never tried engaging in Bruce's real passions: Hot Wheels cars, Marvel comics, and unabashed silliness. One day I heard shouts from the kitchen. Rushing there, I found Bruce chastising our dog Taffy beside a pile of dog poop. I sighed; Taffy sometimes relieved herself indoors if we didn't let her out. Bruce bent over, picked up the poop—and popped it in his mouth.

Screaming, *"BRUCE!"* I grabbed my deranged brother. Grinning, he pulled a box of Space Food Sticks—chocolate Tootsie Roll–like treats—from the cabinet and arranged another on the floor so it, too, resembled dog crap.

By sixth grade, Bruce was being terrorized by Pyle's thug contingent, kids whose idea of "black power" meant peppering their shakedowns with populist jargon. Approaching a mark, they'd ask, "Got any money, my brother?" before rifling his pockets. These punks listened to black-unity songs—"We're a Winner," "Ain't No Stoppin' Us Now"—while robbing fellow blacks, making their music seem as hypocritical to Bruce as being called "brother" during a mugging. Darrell's beloved rock music was rebellious, too, but these mini-hoods knew nothing about Jimi Hendrix or Traffic. Untainted, rock became Bruce's music of choice. By the time Mom gave him a Stradolin guitar, he wanted to be a rock star.

Like Darrell, Bruce confided his private musings to me, detailing his crushes and schooling me on the secret-identity lives of Spider-Man's Peter Parker and Daredevil's Matt Murdock. With *two* brothers so open about their feelings, I started to believe sharing came naturally to boys. Any guy seeking to connect with me, I assumed, would gladly reveal his innermost stuff.

The behavior of my family members exacerbated my giving. Daddy's cool, exacting nature made him hard to please, so I worked harder to satisfy him. Mom's need for attention made me search for ways to make her feel loved. Steve I avoided at all costs, yet I praised his artwork, acted impressed by his exploits, did all I could to minimize his tormenting. Bruce was independent, but he was still mine; like a mom, I sought to protect him.

Only Darrell required nothing from me. After school, I awaited his arrival, primed to tell him tales of my friends, problems, crushes. He never seemed bored. I felt no need to change anything, fix anything, be more of this or less of that to please him.

Giving to Darrell was as effortless as loving him.

Steve's crude attempt at phone seduction did nothing to curb my curiosity about sex. By junior high, I was discussing the subject constantly with my friends, whose emerging womanliness my big brothers couldn't help noticing. My friends noticed my brothers right back. Though five years his junior, gorgeous Gayle developed a confounding crush on my outlaw brother, Steve. Boy-crazy Sharon took one look at Darrell and, using the Spanish we were studying, archly said, *"Tu hermano es muy guapo."* ("Your brother is very handsome.") When I responded, *"Mi hermano habla español,"* my light-skinned friend turned scarlet. A third-year Spanish student, Darrell had understood every poorly pronounced word.

One day, my friends and I knew, boys would expect more than the gift of just looking at us. The prospect of sex was intriguing—and horrifying.

I'd read everything I could about the subject in the remotest corners of Gary's immense new library. I'd started devouring sex manuals the day after my fourth-grade teacher banished the class's boys to inform us girls we'd soon have "monthly periods." This flow of blood between our legs meant we could have babies. The bleeding didn't hurt, she assured, though some girls might have "cramps."

What? Mute, the girls pondered their fate: spouting blood, wearing "napkins," and getting cramps to boot. Enduring childbirth wasn't bad enough. We got to bleed for the privilege.

Suddenly I was certain: God, being male, had given boys the better deal. My smuggled books suggested sex was no picnic for females, either. A woman lay naked in bed as a man's thing got big and hard. When it was really stiff, he'd stuff it inside an area so tiny I hadn't known it existed. In one of Mom's books, the author counseled male readers, "Don't begin your marriage with a rape."

As if a sane woman would *volunteer* for such craziness.

I'd been watching TV's *Bewitched* in the den when Darrell walked in after showering. Towel around his waist, he'd plopped beside me on the couch. "Look," I said, demonstrating for him how much I'd progressed in my ongoing attempt to twitch my nose like Samantha's. I grinned when he assured me, "You're getting better." Pushing himself up, Darrell had no way of knowing that his towel had hiked up in back, giving me an unwelcome rear view of his privates. He strolled away. I froze, midtwitch.

I'd recently read a puzzling fact in one of Mom's hidden sex manuals: all women suffered from "penis envy." Now, frozen on the sofa, I searched myself for a whiff of jealousy. All I found was embarrassment—and gratitude that girls' stuff was neatly tucked away. Who'd envy "privates" that dangle out for all to see?

Only a man, I realized, could have come up with that.

It was bad enough knowing that someday a man's rock-hard thing would be pushed inside me. Now I'd gotten an up-close glimpse of the offending apparatus. Then it hit me. This was *Darrell*. "Envy" was a stretch, but if he had a penis, how terrible could it be? Nothing about him could bother me for long.

It was the same with boys. Nothing they did was a permanent turnoff. That's why sex was so confusing.

The little I knew about it had been gleaned from friends' whispers, graffiti ("PUSSY IS GOOD"), chaste movies, Mom's cache of sex manuals, and hastily perused library books. Few of these sources suggested women actually *liked* sex. Even Playmates in Daddy's girlie magazines were more jazzed by walks on the beach than by intercourse. *Men* wanted sex and would seemingly do anything to get it. The whole enterprise was so unbalanced, I wondered why females who didn't want babies even participated. Sex, I decided, was a gift born of love, a sacrifice women made to men they adored.

By ninth grade, I was questioning that one-sidedness. On weekends, Sharon and I explored the subject during long walks, after which we'd repair to Sharon's room, stack favorite 45s on the record player, and melt onto her twin beds as Smokey Robinson warbled, "Here I go again, walking into love," and Eddie Kendricks swore to "try something new" to win *us*, not skinny Diana Ross, his duet partner. When we weren't limp from love to come, we conjured situations that might justify us having sex:

Sharon: How old do you think you'll be when you do it?
Donna: I don't know. Old—like twenty. You know it'll hurt.
Sharon: I know. But what if you were stranded on a desert island...with Jermaine Jackson? You wouldn't give it up?

Donna: Jermaine? And there's nobody else there but us?

Sharon: Just you and him. And he says he loves you. And he starts singing "Bridge Over Troubled Waters," just like on the *Third Album!*"

Donna: (after a long pause) How long have we been stranded?

Sharon: Six months. And nobody's coming to rescue you.

Donna: I guess I would have to...DROP MY DRAWERS!

By eleventh grade, boy-crazy Sharon had developed a Sophia Loren–esque beauty that lured guys of every type. One, a cute sophomore named Gary Sewell, was so likable, I comforted him when she inevitably moved on. But Gary kept calling; I found myself searching for him at school. I was a goner even before the night he confessed that his brother had called him a "chump" for displaying a photo of me on his dresser. "I don't care," Gary told him. "I love her."

I had stumbled upon a prince.

Does anyone forget first love's shell-shocked sweetness? I can still see myself in our darkened kitchen, perched on a stool with the wall phone's receiver pressed into my temple. I hear— no, *feel*—Gary's voice, deep inside my ear, saying, "I love you." The words filled me like helium. Only the cabinet bolted to the wall above me kept me from floating away.

I'd had crushes since kindergarten, but this was different. I'd never felt such a need to give to a boy other than my brothers. Now I picked out cool clothes for Gary on his birthday and introduced him to new music and movies— *The Great White Hope, Love Story*—whose plots and cinematography he surprised himself by discussing. Neither of us had a driver's license, so I begged Mom or Steve to pick him up from his home so we could visit. Once Gary joined me at a party hosted by my art teacher. Hanging out with "creative types," he later said, connected him to his artistic, spiritual side, making him confident the thug life that beckoned nearly every young black man wasn't for him. His openness in expressing such things, and knowing that I'd inspired him, were enchanting. Did I mention he was the world's best kisser?

As the months passed, Gary and I both craved more than kisses. Stealing into empty rooms at my house or vacant corridors after school, we pressed against each other, exploring his hardness, my softness. I felt every melting thing I'd dreamed of while lying on Sharon's twin bed. Yet desire couldn't subdue my sense that I wasn't ready for sex. More daunting was the thought of Mom's devastation if I got pregnant. Two years earlier, a girl named Cheryl, the smartest, prettiest sophomore at Emerson, had gotten pregnant. The news had exploded through the school like a nuclear blast. Leaving school briefly, she'd returned...a *mother*.

Not me. Finally, there was something I wouldn't— couldn't—give to a man I cherished. My "gift of love" would have to wait. When I finally told Gary, "I can't," we slowly, inexorably drifted apart. Dazed, I tried to understand it. True love—the fairy-tale event I'd awaited since childhood, the reason I'd worked to make myself attractive and desirable— had arrived. Now it was leaving, apparently because I refused to do what no fairy princess would even consider. As horrible as I felt, I was comforted by a thought: a boy who couldn't wait for something so precious couldn't be "the one." I'd passed an important test.

I would keep waiting.

I may have been incapable of changing my views about sex, but I'd known since ninth grade that my country was in upheaval. Without warning, "Negro" had turned to "black"—

and by 1968, black wasn't just proud, it was dangerous. April had brought a shoot-out between the Black Panthers and police, leaving Bobby Hutton—seventeen, Darrell's age!—dead. And just two days earlier, fate had finally caught up with the outspoken Atlanta preacher whose aliveness in the face of hatred had astounded me. Mom made us put on our church clothes to watch Dr. King's funeral on TV. No one complained.

The world was becoming more threatening to black men just as my favorite brother was preparing to leave our home's safety for college. But Darrell wasn't an activist, a radical, or a criminal. He was *nice*. That, I told myself, would keep him safe.

Meanwhile, I spent as much time with him as possible. One summer night, he, Bruce, and I attended a house party. I was dancing downstairs when I heard arguing outside and learned that a boy had accused Darrell of hitting a girl. Darrell had denied it, but he wasn't backing down. Dashing upstairs, I found a tense group gathered around the two; someone whispered the other guy had a knife. *But Darrell never hits people!* I thought as I heard Bruce implore Darrell, "Let's get out of here!" I don't remember what defused things, but both guys eventually backed off. What I never forgot was my terror—or Darrell's refusal to retreat.

Suddenly I remembered how in fifth grade, a "mean girl" had inexplicably followed me home after school, taunting and shoving me. I'd considered telling Darrell, who would surely have found my tormentor and terrified her. But I couldn't do it. What if *she* had a vengeful brother? I couldn't put Darrell at risk.

After the party's near fight, I thought: *What if he risks himself?*

Such idle fears didn't consume me for long. In August 1969, Darrell left for Indiana University. Bloomington was "only" three hours away, but it may as well have been in Greenland.

Yet amazingly, the emotional cataclysm I feared never came. Darrell's frequent trips home and my fascination with watching him transform his basement room into a hippie haven, complete with a water bed and a parachute suspended from the ceiling, softened the blow. Besides, Bruce quietly slipped into the brother-confidant role. Another funny, sensitive brother had my back.

I would survive.

Date Rape 101

Donna in her Hampton Institute dorm room, 1973.

*T*he doctor, whose darkness isn't just a matter of pigment, looks contemptuous as I sit before him, naked except for an office-issued gown. He thinks he knows me: another foolish, knocked-up girl home from college. His questions are brusque; his examining hands worse, squeezing my breast hard like it's a rubber dog toy and he's locating the squeaker. Scowling at my grimace, he says, "If you're old enough to have sex, you're old enough to handle that." My terrible need of him doesn't keep me from thinking, If you knew me at all, you'd know I'm not supposed to be here.

When I think back to that sunny, wish-I-could-take-it-back day, it's the white ceiling that surprises me. I couldn't have known the countless ceilings I would gaze at, occupied but disengaged, from my back. This was the first, the one whose blankness engrossed me as something unsalvageable was ripped away. You'd think its details would be seared into memory, but they aren't. That I even noticed what was above my head—with so much pain and disbelief and *no!no!no!* distracting me—was a miracle. Yet like millions of ceiling-struck women, I just observed.

Women can tell you about ceilings. How absorbing they can be when your spine is smashed under the weight of a man—a man you love, or tolerate, or don't even know, but whom you wish was anywhere but inside you. How lazily time passes as your eyes sweep their expanses, how transfixing their slenderest cracks become. Such ceilings are as intimate and as unknowable as the body pressing yours, whose panting urgency and smothering heft can't be denied—and yet are so unfelt, the whole business could be happening to another woman. A woman who wants him there.

This man, my first, had no idea who I really was—and cared as little as the ceiling that had swallowed me.

It was 1974. Two years earlier, at the height of collegiate affirmative action, I had been a black, urban, working-class National Merit semifinalist, the type of high school graduate who wasn't just welcomed at prestigious Ivy League schools but who received substantial tuition assistance.

I wasn't interested. Without exploring my options, I accepted a partial scholarship from the historically black Hampton Institute and boarded a train to a Virginia campus I'd never visited.

Was I insane?

Not entirely. I wanted to be a writer who explored the complexities of race and culture, and neither Darrell nor Steve, who was studying art at Indiana State University, seemed especially enamored of their majority-white universities. A black college could help me wrap my heart more completely around my blackness, allow me to engage in fiery debates about Malcolm X's and Martin Luther King Jr.'s legacies, and tutor kids at a school that a century earlier had taught former slaves in defiance of Jim Crow. I knew nothing about my worth on the college-freshman market, but well-regarded Hampton wanted me. That was enough.

Until I arrived. Hampton's campus seemed ancient and threadbare next to the sparkling structures and emerald lawns I'd seen at Indiana and Purdue. Freshman girls were housed at century-old Virginia-Cleveland Hall, a medieval, turreted dorm that seemed the perfect castle for imprisoning a Disney princess. My sweet Atlanta-born roommate, Debbie, was a delight, but hardly seemed the type to discuss W.E.B. DuBois's musings. *Why was I here?*

Then Debbie and I stepped outside. Scores of male students had gathered at Virginia-Cleveland to ogle the new talent. Everywhere I looked, crowding the lawn and perched two-deep along the stairway, were men: Men with sandy, inky, and loosely curled Afros. Men whose tight T-shirts snaked over broad shoulders. Men of every height, weight, and shade "fine" came in. My head spun back and forth with a speed that invited whiplash.

I'd been hasty. Hampton deserved a chance.

I never found the activists I'd envisioned. At Hampton, being late for lunch was a radical act. Or maybe I overlooked the philosophical set while stuffing myself at Hampton's all-you-can-date buffet. Still looking for helium love, I fell "in like" with three guys before Christmas. But the buffet went both ways. Most men were less interested in romance than in sampling every dish.

I wasn't alone in adjusting to changes. At Indiana State, Steve stunned everyone by marrying his winsome—and pregnant—girlfriend, Irene. Steve... *married?* Miles away, I tried to believe it.

Bruce, who had made faces and cracked jokes as he waved good-bye to me at the train station as I left for Hampton, had returned home, shut himself in his room, and cried. Weeks later, he unexpectedly broke up with his first girlfriend. It wasn't enough that I had abandoned him to Gary's dreariness. Now he was really alone—and the only kid left at home to satisfy Mom's need for connection. Taking refuge in the basement and FM radio, he listened to underground rockers like Alice Cooper ("I'm eighteen...I gotta get out of this place"), practiced his guitar tirelessly, and dreamed of a rock career.

Then there was Darrell. The aspiring actor took advanced acting and stagecraft classes at Indiana and pledged Alpha Phi Alpha, moving into the homey brick frat house's biggest $63-per-month room. In a letter to Mom, Darrell called himself "penniless," asking for $35 for burgers and pizza, as well as curtains and paint to spruce up his "pitiful" space. Social life at I.U. was pretty nice, he wrote, though he wouldn't bore us with his "feminine conquests." Apologizing for the letter's brevity, he wrote finally, "Tell Donna I'll write later when I get more time."

Soon afterward, he shocked us all by earning a spot on Indiana's junior varsity basketball team. Darrell—who at five ten had never made high school varsity—walked on during tryouts for the Big 10 squad and went instantly into "the zone," defending taller opponents, making impossible shots, outplaying even future NBA star George McGinnis. Making the squad was thrilling. But Indiana's team had just come under the direction of the soon-to-be-infamous coach Bobby Knight. Darrell hated him.

When he didn't make the varsity team the following year, Darrell quit playing hoops for Indiana. A year later, he left college altogether. The university wanted him to declare a major; Darrell just wanted to make people laugh. He was working odd jobs in Gary when a friend asked him to share the driving on a trip to California. Finally seeing his chance to pursue stardom, Darrell moved in with our aunt Hortense in Los Angeles. I could hardly believe that my beloved brother was living in a city I'd never visited, his life a complete mystery. One day soon, I told myself, we'd pick up where we'd left off—maybe after he became a star!

Back at Hampton, I finally fell in love—with my school's bottomless diversity. My fellow students included midwestern badasses, southern belles, swaggering urbanites, and flat-out nerds from across the United States. But my closest new friend was—big surprise—a man: a funny, drug-loving introvert who told me everything.

A voracious reader, fellow Mass Media major Jeff Rivers had grown up on Philadelphia's tough streets, where he'd developed fascinating theories about African-American invincibility ("After a nuclear blast, ten thousand brothers will be hanging onto one hanger in space"), black people's real purpose ("God keeps niggaz around to make Him laugh"), and death ("Rich, white people never die; they fake their deaths and move to a posh hidden island when life gets too deep"). My own ideas were so comparatively lame that my role in the friendship seemed to be dragging the reluctant Jeff to class and praising his humor and creativity so much he called me his "cheerleader."

Of course, having just one close male friend to coddle was unthinkable. I soon became the unofficial female mascot for an entire group of trash-talking young men, unthinkingly re-creating what I'd had at home—emotional intimacy with several very different guys. Insightful Philly Dog, probing Slim, cynical Marty, and goofy Dr. J became the "brothers" to whom I gave—pomading their scalps, encouraging their romances, rubbing their shoulders even after they'd engaged in such questionable behavior as a spirited cafeteria debate over which is better for a woman to have: a great ass or big boobs. Outnumbered but unbowed, Dr. J leapt on a table and shouted: "I am a TITTY man! And proud of it!"

Once again, I was surrounded by men. Yet sex remained a coming attraction. By late sophomore year, I was twenty—and increasingly aware that I still hadn't "done it." Plenty of guys would have gladly cured my "problem." An unidentified male once shouted, *"Give it up, Donna Britt!"* from a men's dorm window. But I was, as Jeff put it, a "closet square" whose tight jeans belied her clamped-together knees and who was so romantic I could sing entire Broadway scores. Lovemaking, I still felt, should wait for love.

Yet I was looking forward to sex—glorious, poetic, earth-shattering sex—as soon as I found a man worth sharing it with. After passing on intimacy with Gary, I felt that my first time had to be magic.

Among the guys who'd stop by my room to chat or offer

me a lift to McDonald's was a thickset Baltimore senior whom I'll call Ted. Because he never said or did anything to suggest his interest was more than friendly, I assumed Ted, a member of a popular fraternity, saw me as a baby sister. One bright day, he invited me for a ride. Stopping at a park, Ted gave me slices of bread to throw to ducks circling a pond. *How sweet,* I thought. But it wasn't until Ted asked to show me his apartment that I felt his interest might be romantic. I wasn't terribly attracted to him, but why not share a few kisses with a guy nice enough to take me duck-feeding?

At the apartment, Ted introduced me to his roommate, a popular senior. In his room, we sat side by side on his mattress on the floor. He kissed me. I kissed him back. By now I was an expert at corralling my desire while keeping a guy's at a safe simmer. But Ted kept probing, pushing me into the mattress, fumbling with my zipper. When I realized he was actually trying to have sex with me, I said, "No! *Stop!*" sharply, vehemently. "Really. *Stop!*" He didn't. Stunned that he was ignoring me, I shifted beneath his strength, insisting, "No! *No!*" Why didn't he stop? Finally he did; we both lay panting.

But again, Ted's lips sought mine. Grateful that my friend had come to his senses, I accepted what I thought would be a light, concluding kiss. Emboldened, Ted pressed harder. Disbelieving—*hadn't this ended?*—I struggled more. Crushed under his weight, his hands everywhere, I started to feel like we'd been tussling forever. But I didn't scream. What if his roommate told people about the hysterical sophomore who thought Ted wanted her for more than a fuck?

How could I have been so stupid, misreading Ted's intentions, putting myself in this ugly, desperate situation after years of waiting for magic? Overwhelmed by shame, weariness, hopelessness, and self-recrimination, I finally stopped struggling. When he tore inside me, I muffled my own scream.

I don't remember whether I moved or lay frozen as Ted finished. What I do remember is staring at the ceiling, feeling myself being absorbed by it. Its emptiness seemed as involving as the intensity roiling in Ted. Then it was over.

I got up, walked dazed to the bathroom. Wiping the scarlet from between my legs, I stared out of the bathroom window at a green field. Words swooped like restive birds around my mind: *I'm not a virgin anymore. Not a virgin...* Had I been standing there ten minutes? Twenty? Rousing myself with a new thought— *maybe it was dumb to have waited for...this*—I emerged. Ted, stunned that the woman he'd forced into sex had been a virgin, seemed subdued. He patted my back—a tentative, brotherly pat—as I got out of his car. Lying on my bed, I stared at the ceiling in my own room too. *Not a virgin.*

I wasn't outraged or angry. I just felt flattened. It never occurred to me to tell the police. "Date rape" had yet to penetrate the public consciousness. Besides, wasn't it my fault?

My fault that a near stranger whom I'd stupidly trusted had stolen what I'd been saving for years. My fault that I hadn't run away when I could have, and that my lame attempts to stop him were ineffective. My fault that I didn't scream out of worry about what he—a liar, a manipulator—and his roommate, whom I didn't even know, might say. My fault that I'd be the one left to weigh and relive, cry and beat myself up, about this violation for years to come.

My first impulse was to tell myself, and a few friends, that the incident was no big deal. To prove it, I had protected sex with a guy I'd dated for most of the semester. Afterward I snickered about how cool I was, having sex—yes, I'd reframed the rape that way—with two guys in a month. Back home for summer vacation, I tried to forget that duck-feeding afternoon as I waited for the monthly period whose appearance had never been a concern but that now was stubbornly absent.

Finally, I told Mom everything. When a doctor verified my fears, she asked, "What do you want to do?"

My honest response—"Go back two months and lock myself in my dorm room"—wasn't helpful. Abortion had recently been legalized in the United States, but issues of legality hardly affected my inner battle. I wanted nothing more to do with Ted, whom I'd phoned to inform of the pregnancy and who spoke vaguely about being supportive. I neither believed nor wanted him.

I was being punished—for having gone to Ted's apartment, for letting the ceiling take me. Whatever I chose, I would suffer. I didn't want a baby, especially one conceived like this. I didn't want to kill a baby, either, no matter how often I asked myself why *I* should pay—interrupt my schooling, bear the stigma of unwed motherhood—for an act I'd neither wanted nor enjoyed. I recalled how much I adored Steve's and Irene's baby; surely I would love my own. But would I resent a child who stunted my dreams and made me look like just another careless, unwed black mother? I imagined carrying and bearing an infant and giving it to strangers— a *black* child whose adoption wouldn't be assured. Back and forth I went, replaying every argument I'd heard: Abortion was murder. A fetus wasn't a real baby.

It was real enough for me to feel devastated by the thought of destroying it. If all I would be destroying was this tiny being's potential, that potential deserved my acknowledgment, my concern. There was no escaping my heart's yes-no swirl; every thought was a reproach or a prayer. Mom—ever the abandoned child picking at the scab of her unwantedness— wasn't conflicted. *It's your decision,* she said. *But if you have a baby, it will change your life forever.*

At the time, I didn't know Mom-Mommy's story. But Mom did. She knew that fifty years later, I'd unwittingly repeated her mother's—and her own—misfortune: pregnant after my first, unwanted sexual experience. The prospect of me giving birth to a baby like her must have raised the specter of her own rejection.

I asked my mother what she thought I should do. When she told me the truth, I asked her to make the appointment. The doctor was haughty and sullen, but I was grateful when he said I'd be unconscious for the procedure. Before I fell asleep, I stared at another white ceiling and begged my baby and God for their forgiveness. After the procedure, I awoke feeling relieved—unaware of the hundreds of nights I'd lie awake, certain that I'd removed myself from the circle of God's love. A decade of prayers later, I knew: God had forgiven me long before I forgave myself.

Although I doubted Ted had trouble pardoning *him*self for what had happened, I sometimes wondered how he'd processed that bright afternoon. Years later, I described my first sexual encounter to a street-smart male friend. He said it's not uncommon for certain men to physically push a woman toward sex until, overwhelmed, she stops struggling. "They're *waiting* for you to relax," he said. "It's part of the seduction." Would Ted somehow remember our encounter as something that I'd wanted? Did he have any idea that he'd taken something irreplaceable? That I saw him as a rapist?

All I know is this: Almost twenty years later, I was a mother of two and a columnist at the *Washington Post* when I opened an envelope with a Baltimore postmark. Inside was a note from Ted. *"You may not remember me,"* it began. *"If you have a free night, maybe we could have dinner..."*

I never answered.

For years, I told myself that my sex life's painful beginning had no lasting effects. Human beings are survivors. We keep walking, talking, working, laughing, and behaving as if everything's fine when we're a crumbling mess. I was too shrewd and hip, I decided, to be thrown for long by my girlhood fantasies ending on a frat boy's mattress. So what if my dreams about this once-in-my-lifetime moment had been shattered? All I could control, all that mattered, was *now*. Now I was free. Now, unburdened by naive expectations, I could be like other women my age and enjoy sex with whomever I pleased.

The truth was that I was neither shrewd nor hip. I hadn't just lost my virginity to Ted; some measure of my sexual confidence, and my trust in men's basic goodness, went with it. It was impossible to feel like the liberated woman I presented to the world when I doubted most men and my very soul's worthiness. No wonder "sex with whomever I pleased" often wasn't pleasing.

I fell into bed with a couple of men in the following year, including one I'd adored as a freshman who'd dropped me when my "sex must wait" rule proved nonnegotiable. I hardly enjoyed any of it. I wasn't sure why. After all those years of refusing to give myself completely to a man who gave equally back, Ted had happened. That experience was all about *him* — his intention, his desire, his taking. Giving had nothing to do with it.

Sex became more about what I could get, and I never got much. My desire wasn't for pricey gifts or fancy dinners but for acknowledgment and appreciation. Without them, the letting go required for satisfying lovemaking was impossible. Relaxing had resulted in the worst pain of my life; letting go was *dangerous*. For all my giving, I had trouble allowing myself the sweetest abandonment life could offer. No matter what my body was doing, part of me stayed remote, kept something vital for myself.

Sex became pretty much pointless. Which didn't keep me from having it.

The next two years were full: a summer internship at *Redbook* magazine, the return of True Love in the form of a witty and thoughtful New York University basketball player named Michael, and in 1976, graduation from Hampton, followed by admission to the University of Michigan's graduate journalism program through Booth Newspapers' minority fellowship program. My first day of classes, I fixed my hair in a topknot so businesslike that no one would guess I was cowering inside. Many of my fellow students would be white graduates of colleges more prestigious than mine. Could I compete? When the program chief asked us about ourselves, I self-consciously recited my résumé.

Weeks later, I discussed that first day with my favorite fellow master's candidates, who of course were men: Garth, a Michigan farm boy, and John, a wry Ohioan. "You were so gorgeous and intimidating," John said, sounding like he meant it. Added Garth: "You worked for *Redbook*! You made the rest of us feel like crap."

Me gorgeous? Intimidating? It hadn't occurred to me that my white classmates might see *me* as threatening. All I thought they'd see was black. I still assumed every white person must be secretly contemptuous of me—and might hurt and reject me. I remembered being six and seeing black protesters hosed and beaten.

Becoming friends with white students challenged many such assumptions. Like Hampton, Michigan taught me about diversity—*white* diversity. If all white students secretly disdained blacks, many put on an astonishingly good act. If they were innately more studious and mature than their black counterparts, I had no explanation for U of M's obvious slackers or the rivers of vomit outside "kegger" parties. White prejudice had shaped my life. Yet I hadn't realized how little time I'd spent around actual white *people*.

Now they were everywhere. And I was drawn to my fellow master's candidates, despite part of me feeling that I should know better. My quandary came down to a question: *Could* my white classmates have any inkling of how it felt to be black in America? Or of all that their whiteness had bought them?

The sensitive ones, I figured, had to have imagined what being African-American was like, perhaps even envisioned themselves enrobed in blackness. Had they been shaken by the thought of being trapped in the skin they feared in restive places hidden by their goodness? Was their kindness toward me an acknowledgment of that revulsion, of their unspoken gratitude for the haven their whiteness provided? If it was, then I was grateful for it. That might be the best a white person could do: try to rise above his or her aversion.

But imagining something is one thing. Living it is another. Racism had wounded and angered me for so long, I had plenty to rise above myself. Like feeling that for my white classmates, my blackness—a natural, unbidden fact of my existence— overwhelmed all else. Life had taught me that the skin and the culture I was born into, which I might easily have seen as a full-throated blessing, were somehow a curse. Yet the racism that had ravaged my self-regard had been a blessing for each and every one of them. Because no matter how ugly, clumsy, stupid, poor, or untalented a white person was, he or she could take a bit of comfort, feel some spark of superiority with this thought: *At least I'm not black.* Did my classmates know what a gift it was, not to feel rejected before they could utter a word?

Yet my suspicion and resentment couldn't stop me from giving: giving white students (who, as far as I knew, hadn't beaten or hosed a soul) a chance. I understood fellow black students who separated themselves, whose hurt and mistrust led them to negotiate U of M from the protection of a safe, black bubble. But I couldn't join them. I couldn't deny white classmates the opportunity to know me, an open, honest-to-God black woman, or deny myself the chance to know them as *individuals*, through discussions, debates, and one confession I'll never forget.

Our class had been passionately discussing racism when I noticed that Katie, a sharp-faced blonde, looked like a child working herself up to admitting something she'd be spanked for. "My father told me that black people don't feel romantic love," Katie began. The room went silent. "Carnal lust, yes. Real love, no."

With classmates' gazes beating like hailstones against my skin, I was flooded by images: of every man who'd sent my soul soaring, of every poem, flower, love letter, and secret a brother had entrusted me with. People like Katie's dad weren't content with denying us respect or jobs. They would deny us our humanity, our *love*. I admired Katie's courage for her admission, but I don't recall having the courage to ask, *Did you believe him?*

It didn't matter. Admitted or denied, racism was too slippery to contain or make sense of. I already suspected what later would become undeniable: the same fear of racism that had made me suspicious of *them* had also made me better. I worked to avoid being like black folks whom racism had silenced, whom it had crushed into "what's the use?" paralysis. I was a giver, so that's how I'd fought it: by giving more. *They* thought I couldn't be brilliant or insightful? I studied harder, worked longer, analyzed more deeply, to prove them wrong. In my every public moment, I'd been representing the race. An ambassador for blackness, I'd sharpened my speech, fattened my vocabulary, spoken out in every class, never giving *them* the satisfaction of my mediocrity. The responsibility felt as heavy and palpable as a boulder.

There was sweetness in the irony of knowing that something so hated had helped me to excel. Yet I would have happily traded it for the gift every white girl held, unknowingly, in both hands: the chance just to represent—to *be*—herself.

I adored my tiny studio in Ann Arbor, with its makeshift meals cooked in a tiny oven, its easy-to-stow sofa bed. With no Mom to urge it, I washed every dish, symmetrically arranged each pillow, and set a table so pretty that I rarely marred it by eating from it. What filled me was the joy of providing beauty, good food, and a warm home only to me.

But my beloved apartment cut deeply into my stipend. Learning about a job opening for a resident director at the Helen Newberry women's dorm, I envisioned living cost-free in an ivy-kissed Colonial manse housing one hundred freshman girls—a dorm full of the little sisters I'd never had. Interviewing for the position with several young residents, I adopted the offhand insouciance I'd once used with Bruce's friends ("I'm older and hipper but you're cool too") and got the job.

I was now in my second year of teaching freshman journalism, a requirement of my grad school fellowship. I was surprised by how little my students cared that a segment of their journalism class at this pricey, Big 10 university was taught by a graduate student barely older than they were. Among my most engaged students was sandy-haired Jon, who one day after class grabbed my books and walked me to my dorm.

At Newberry, Jon pretended not to notice my young charges' delight at seeing a cutie their age accompanying me. He began walking me home after every class, chatting up whichever young women were hanging outside my room. When some-one suggested Jon actually had a crush on me, I laughed. Please.

Although I'd feared losing the autonomy of my apartment, I loved being an R.D. After years of catering to men, I enjoyed assuring girls of how pretty and smart they were, providing hugs and tissues when they cried. Girls were so *grateful*. I'd never realized how entitled guys had seemed to my praise and neck rubs.

Was gratitude, like the giving that inspired it, a woman thing?

Bruce had graduated from West Side and to everyone's horror had rejected college, which — after observing Steve's and Dar-rell's checkered college experiences — he had no interest in. Working as a grinder at U.S. Steel, Bruce saved every cent and within months had paid cash for a new Chevy Nova. But he hated the mill, whose chief lesson seemed to be that hands encased in work gloves all day can stink as much as sweaty feet. Weekend after weekend, Bruce drove to Ann Arbor to bask in the admiration of Newberry girls, who convulsed at his jokes and gushed about his cuteness.

Darrell never joined him. He'd gotten an apartment in Miller, a beach community on Lake Michigan, and a job at Bethlehem Steel. I rarely talked to my still-beloved brother, not even about important things — like how, after thirty years of bitterness, Mom and Daddy had gotten a divorce, a move that was surprising only in that it had taken so long. Painfully familiar with the marriage's problems, my brothers and I felt little need to discuss it. We felt not grief but relief. I didn't talk much with Darrell about his experiences in Los Angeles, either. He seemed chastened somehow, still warm and hilarious but hardly encouraging of questions about his California adventure. Stifling my curiosity for the time being, I kept up with him largely through Mom and Bruce.

I didn't worry overmuch about the distance between us. I knew in my bones: two people who'd been as close as we had would always be there for each other.

Losing Darrell

*Mom and Darrell striking a pose
by their Gary home, 1975.*

Sometimes, he comes to me in dreams. Each time, he is as young and solid and whole as he was when he left. He's as real as the red flannel shirt that I buried my face in after he died, which obligingly clung to his scent for years. As real as the afternoons when we chatted as I watched him practice on our backyard basketball court, when he'd slide to his left, set up, shoot the ball, and retrieve it, talking to me throughout. As real as the times he searched the refrigerator for bologna to fry for sandwiches we could share. That's how alive he is. Like in the dream before I married Kevin. There he stood in a tree-dotted field. Smiling. Clasped in his hand was a bouquet of balloons, white and red and straining toward heaven. "I'll be at your wedding," he said, kissing a hurt I hadn't realized I had. "Don't worry," he said, his smile as buoyant as the balloons he held out to me. "I'll be there."

Some things you don't forget: like my first words when I learned during a late-September phone call in 1977 that Darrell might be dead.

I was in the midst of talking to my mother, updating her on my fall classes and the girls at Helen Newberry. An official-sounding male voice identifying itself as from the Lake County Coroner's Office cut into the line. When the voice asked if Mom knew Elwood Britt, Mom said, "I'm his ex-wife." The voice paused. Without thinking, I blurted: *"Where's Bruce?"*

Hours and days and years later, I replayed the two words that demonstrated how completely my younger brother had usurped Darrell's place in my consciousness. The desolation I'd felt when Darrell left for I.U. was long gone; by the time he moved to Miller, his absence rarely troubled me. Bruce's wit and openness matched Darrell's; his chumminess with my friends in Ann Arbor was the icing. He had become my most indispensable brother.

The voice asked Mom if she knew *Darrell* Britt. When she said, "Yes...is he all right?" it asked her to come to Mercy Hospital. Panicked, Mom said she'd call me back. I hung up. Waited.

But I already knew I had betrayed my brother.

A sharp, regretful pang echoes inside me each time I remember my instinctive words. "Where's Bruce?" suggested that I, too, had abandoned Darrell, who must have felt terribly alone in that ravine when the policemen fired their guns at him. Did his spirit, already freed from that dear body, hear my response? Did he feel I loved him less? Darrell had developed an independent life. His secrets were no longer my province; his thoughts, frustrations, and activities were largely unknown to me. I had a life, too, and little time to keep tabs on an increasingly distant brother.

Though I'd told myself it was okay because someday we would pick up where we'd left off, what actually happened was that I stopped looking for him. I stopped seeking him out as the one to coax confidences from, confess secrets to, comfort, and be comforted by. Suddenly our growing apart, a process inevitable among even the closest siblings, was unforgivable. Darrell had stopped looking for me, too, but that hardly mattered. He was gone. And he'd left me with a question:

How could I have stopped paying attention?

After what seemed like an eternity, Mom called back to say what I already knew: Darrell was dead. He'd been shot to death by Gary police; she had no idea how or why. I should come home immediately. Hanging up, I sat very still, tried to absorb it. *Darrell* had been shot. By the police. But Steve was the one who courted trouble, stole things, bucked authority. That afternoon, I caught a bus whose passengers must have wondered why the girl with one of the window seats wouldn't stop sobbing.

As the days passed, I learned more about Darrell's death. None of it made sense, starting with what the police had reported:

On the morning of September 27, a male homeowner in Miller (the mostly white lakefront neighborhood where Darrell was renting an apartment) called to report that a man had tried to slip his hand into the window of his truck. The truck's owner had told the police that he had confronted the stranger—Darrell—and asked what he was doing. "I've got to get home," Darrell reportedly said, trembling. "Will you take me home?"

Convinced that the interloper was on drugs, the truck's owner told Darrell to wait while he called the police so they could take him home. In fact, he told them something quite different: he was "holding" someone who was trying to steal his truck.

The two white patrolmen who responded, Officers Jerry Cyprian and Daniel Mattox, said they found Darrell in a nearby ravine, a tire clutched in one hand, a broken bottle top in the other. Without provocation, they said, he shouted, "I'm going to kill you!" and—despite their having fired two warning shots—charged at one of them with a chain, a brick, a plastic baseball, and a three-foot length of pipe. They pumped one .357 Magnum bullet into his chest and another into his left thigh. Within minutes, he was dead.

One more thing: According to the police, the man in the ravine was barefoot and wearing an aluminum cooking pot on his head. The truck owner had told them he was crouched "like a native hunter" while chanting something unintelligible before standing and saying to no one in particular, "Take me higher."

This was the official report that I'd hoped would bring clarity to Darrell's out-of-nowhere killing. Instead, it shifted an already confusing incident into the surreal. Darrell, who was working as a laborer at Bethlehem Steel, had no history of mental problems. An autopsy would find no alcohol or narcotics in his blood.

The world as I knew it slipped free of its hinges. As it floated untethered, a deepening sense of unreality permeated everything.

I remember those days, weeks, and months as if they were a movie, a confounding indie consisting of long stretches of indistinct images intercut with scenes of cut-glass clarity. Hazy footage included a large meeting at our house among family members and friends about whether to take legal action against the police, who were performing their own investigation. The room was thick with rage, fear, and despair. Steve was the most vocal among those who felt we should aggressively challenge the absurd circumstances claimed by the police. Others suggested we await autopsy results. Still others felt we should cut our losses, let the police be. They'd already demonstrated they were brutes. What if our prodding and questioning inspired them to prove it again?

As the different factions argued, I sat mute, my customary feistiness extinguished. *Darrell really must be dead,* I thought. Why else would a dozen family members be screaming at one another in our den? I had no strength to challenge the ridiculousness of my assumption that the universally apparent wrongness of Darrell's killing would be recognized. I mean, really—two men with guns against a guy with a tire and a broken bottle?

Much clearer is my picture of Darrell in his coffin at the

funeral home, his thick eyelashes meeting his cheeks, the skin and mouth that resembled his except for their pallidness. Darrell's stiff body looked vacant, like a sturdy building whose occupants had inexplicably fled. While I stood there, Darrell's friend and roommate Fred entered the room, took one look, and shook his head, saying, "Naw. *Naw!*" He tore away.

Most vivid is the memory of my mother taking photographs of that bewildering corpse; why would she want to preserve such an image? I was more empathetic a few days later in a department store dressing room as she tried on dresses for her son's funeral. "I want to look nice for him," she said.

Each family member reacted differently to Darrell's death. As always, Daddy said the least. But the pained disbelief on his face as he described watching a morgue staffer separate his son's nude body from an assortment of naked black corpses spoke volumes.

Mom had been driving down Fifth Avenue when she heard a radio announcement of a shooting in Miller of an unidentified man. *Killing, killing, I'm so sick of this killing,* she'd thought. Like me, she had countless questions and not a single satisfactory answer. Were the police lying? Why had they killed Darrell rather than wounding him? Had Darrell tried LSD or another drug that might have lingered in his system, roaring back to spur his puzzling behavior that day? She knew he'd done drugs; he once described trying something that made him feel he'd left his body. The week before he was killed, Darrell had fasted, ingesting only water and juice. Could cleansing his system have made him susceptible to some weird delayed drug reaction?

For weeks after her son's death, Mom, who worked for the state of Indiana canvassing local businesses for job openings, stopped every policeman she saw to ask if he knew anything about the incident. None said yes. My uncle John knew Officer

Mattox; he sometimes drank at the same bar as the redheaded cop, and described him to my mother. One afternoon Mom spied a short, red-haired policeman, walked up to him, and asked if he was Mattox. When he said yes, she shakily told him her name. Then, looking in the eyes of one of the men who had killed her second-born child, she asked, "Why was my son killed?" Instead of answering, Mom recalls, Mattox started asking *her* questions. "Have you got any proof we were wrong? If you do, bring it forward." Mattox told her the shooting was Darrell's fault because he'd had a length of chain with a lock on it that he'd swung around his head as if to hit them. Standing her ground, Mom told him that shooting "someone" in the leg or knee would have stopped him.

Mattox was very angry, Mom said. "I kind of felt threatened so I left it at that. But I let him know I thought it was unjust. That this was a valuable person they had killed."

Steve—who by now had changed his name to Ben Melech Yehudah to reflect his association with the Hebrew Israelite culture—realized for the first time that his closeness in age to Darrell had made him regard his brother almost as a twin. As someone who'd always been, and would always be, around for him. Steve-now-Melech had thought of Darrell as Robin to his Batman, his little *compadre*. He kept thinking about what Darrell's roommates had found on his water bed after his death: a poem Darrell had written called "Love Is All There Is." The poem said love is the only thing worth living for, that everything else was "an artificial bore."

The poem, Melech felt, was proof that Darrell had been serious about something he'd told the family a few weeks before his death: he had embraced God and intended to enter the ministry. Darrell's espousal of the religion that he'd paid little attention to since childhood surprised Melech, despite his having undergone a spiritual metamorphosis of his own.

He and Darrell had spent years being freewheeling and hedonistic—drinking, partying, experimenting with drugs. When Melech had talked with Darrell about his own conversion months earlier, about "the beauty of living in the Word," Darrell had told him that if you go too deep into the Bible, "you'll die. God just takes you." He had said, "I'm going to have fun, live my life."

So Melech couldn't have been more surprised when Darrell did a complete 360. "The last time I saw him," Melech said, Darrell was a Christian. "His face radiated a glow and a peace that couldn't be faked." It was obvious he'd experienced a sincere conversion, Melech said, that he was no longer dealing with religion as most people understood it. His brother hadn't said, "I'm interested in God and going to start going to church." Darrell was *transformed* and had an entirely new aura about him. Listening to him, Melech looked at himself—and realized that as serious as he was about his faith, religion hadn't altered his personality. Though he was more biblically knowledgeable, "I was still kind of crazy," he said. But Darrell had *changed*. Weeks later, he would be gone.

Consumed by rage and pain, Melech hurled at Mom and me his certainty that we'd wished he'd been the one to die in that ditch. Our muted denials must have sounded hollow. Yet in a way, Melech did die that day. Darrell's death gave him his first inkling of how conflicted his family members were about him. One of their number had died. Yet Melech—the Britt who'd taken risks, courted danger, loved life on the edge—was still among them. No one was prepared for even the possibility of Darrell being taken.

For Melech, Darrell's death was "an awakening." The family's most facile liar decided it was beneath him to lie, to be phony, to be veiled in any way. Darrell's death inspired Melech to tell people the truth, regardless of the consequences.

Bruce's reaction to his brother's slaying was the most puzzling: fury directed at Darrell for, as he put it, "getting himself killed." The police report suggested that his big brother hadn't done what every black man knows to do when confronted by cops: be calm, restrained, conciliatory. Knowing Darrell's rare but explosive temper, Bruce assumed he'd lost control. Bruce was even more incensed with Darrell for having abandoned him. How dare the brother he most enjoyed leave him alone to face Gary's hopelessness? As the weeks passed, Bruce became a virtual recluse, spending so much time in bed that once, when he tried to rise, his knees buckled like a newborn calf's.

I neither understood nor related to Bruce's anger. How could I, when I'd never been mad at Darrell in my life? Even when he'd disappointed me—like the time he got so high on one of his visits home from college that Bruce and I found him passed out naked on his bed—my major concern had been making sure Mom didn't find out. People you adore can and will mess up. My job was to forgive them, protect them. Darrell had never even raised his voice to me. How could I accuse him now?

My accusations were directed at me.

Maybe that's when the seed was planted. When my guilt provided fertile enough soil for what had been a tendency toward giving to blossom into a near addiction. If my relationship with Darrell had been troubled, I might have felt less remorse for having allowed us to drift apart. It didn't matter that the drifting had been natural, even necessary. His death had made it traitorous. Now I knew: inattention toward a loved one, even for an instant, was perilous.

It didn't help knowing that the last time I spoke to Darrell, he had reached out to me.

Darrell phoned me three days before he was shot. Pleasantly surprised to hear from him, I was astonished when he said he'd missed our childhood closeness. Couldn't we try to recapture it? Touched beyond speech, I sputtered something like "I want that, too." Then he told me about his decision to become a minister.

Years ago, he explained, Mom had told him that at his birth, Nana had laid hands on him and stated, "This boy is going to be a preacher." Said Darrell: "I resisted that my whole life, but it was always there." Then he said, so quietly, "When I was six or seven, I used to talk to Jesus. I heard Him, felt so close to Him...but I never told anybody because I knew people would think I was nuts."

Nuts? Never you. Not the most reflexively good person I'd ever met, not the brother who, when he and Steve played cowboys as toddlers, resisted when Steve used his big-brother status to force Darrell to be the villain. Darrell sobbed for Mom to make him stop because "bad guys always lose."

Sometimes, in fact, they do. Like the policemen whose use of deadly force was ruled "justifiable homicide" by the powers that be in Darrell's death. The day after his bullet punctured Darrell's thigh, Officer Mattox hit and kicked a handcuffed Hispanic suspect, shot up his car, and slammed the door on the man's legs; he was sentenced to three years' probation for violating the man's civil rights. At his trial, Mattox attributed his behavior to having participated in Darrell's killing, saying, "I'd never shot anyone before." Five years later, he was ousted from the force after being convicted of theft. Officer Cyprian had been arrested by Portage, Indiana, police a year *before* Darrell's killing for shooting at his estranged wife and pointing a loaded .45-caliber pistol at her head. In 1979, he too was kicked off the force after his conviction for sexually assaulting a girl of ten who had babysat for his children.

I don't remember how Darrell and I ended that last phone conversation. But I didn't insist that he come to Ann Arbor for an extended visit, or call me every night, or avoid going out by himself in his neighborhood, where somebody might mischaracterize his request for a ride home as an admission of thievery. I didn't save him.

The haze that enveloped me after the shooting followed me to Michigan, where I finished the semester in a fog. I still counseled my girls, attended classes, taught journalism. I kept breathing and moving and smiling and doing everything required of me. None of it felt real. I wasn't offended when people treated me like the walking wounded; that's what I was. Consumed by thoughts of a man who'd left me for regions I could neither imagine nor see, I began to feel as invisible as he'd become.

So as the weeks passed and Jon—the nineteen-year-old in my journalism class whom I'd insisted had no interest me—became a constant visitor, I accepted it. I let myself notice his compact wrestler's waist and acre-wide chest. I appreciated his obvious concern, the kindness and hesitancy in his green-flecked eyes, even his youth itself. His lingering simplicity was a sweet antidote to all that had become rudely complex.

There was no shelter anywhere. No one could see me, so there could be no consequences. When Jon's desire for a relationship became unmistakable and he reached for me, I reached back.

Jon's whiteness, I suspect, pulled me to him as much as his thoughtfulness. Embracing a white man after such an essential black one had been stolen by his kind kept me from hating the rest of them, helped me continue to move among them. I was clinging to my friendships with Garth and John, so I wasn't entirely surprised to find myself loving Jon when I needed to. His unique purpose, I believe now, was to preserve white men's humanity for me. Our liaison was too brief to describe as serious. But its meaning—connecting me to a group that suddenly seemed unsalvageable—was almost sacred.

As the weeks and months passed, I wondered if I would live long enough to experience an afternoon, an hour, or even five minutes free of the breathless hurt crowding my chest. Still unable to accept Darrell's death, I repeated the fact of it to myself as if that would help me digest it. Whether I was trying on a pretty dress or savoring a perfect slice of cheesecake, I'd pause to remind myself, "Darrell's dead," or "My brother died," purposely short-circuiting my pleasure.

Would Officers Cyprian and Mattox have cared that the shot that pierced my brother's chest had excised my capacity for joy? How could I be happy when Darrell was dead? When each laugh had to wind its way around a knot of guilt?

I wanted to remember my brother, to never let him go. I also wanted to stop hurting. I tried to do both, but each memory was a knife that slashed at my wound. It hurt, replaying my mind's video of Darrell taking over the basketball court at I.U., the day he made the junior varsity team. It hurt, recalling the good wishes I'd sent with him to California, and my certainty of his impending stardom. It hurt, recalling how he'd enchanted me with tales of Hollywood egos and nights sleeping under starry Arizona skies.

It was agonizing, remembering how he'd loved living in Miller, close enough to Lake Michigan to walk to the beach and gaze wonderingly at the water. How meaningful his work as a drug counselor had been to him, and his disappointment when the program's new funders fired him after decreeing that every staffer had to have a college degree. How after he'd taken the job in the mill, I assured myself such work wouldn't long satisfy a man of his curiosity and intellect. Soon he'd be back on his path.

Most torturous to recall was his humor. Like the times Darrell tied a bandanna around the smooth, black head of our dog, Taffy, whose patient expression made her resemble the homeliest of peasant women. And how he'd "sneak" into a room, purportedly slipping unnoticed behind Bruce or me to scare us. Sidling past us in a burlesque tiptoe, Darrell would move in plain sight from one inadequate hiding place to another, "concealing" his 175-pound body behind a slender vase or a fourteen-inch footrest. His impish "I'm invisible" look convulsed me, even before he leapt at me shouting, "Boo!" I'd recall Darrell and Bruce sitting astride (in fact, inches above) their "horses" Taffy and her son, Scooter, posing with their short-legged steeds as if riding into battle: plastic swords raised, nostrils flared, Napoleon and Simón Bolívar in Afros and sneakers.

Happy or sad, memories of Darrell tightened the knot that never left my throat. So without quite realizing it, I started doing what I'd unwittingly done before he died: turning away from him. Slowly, subtly, my least vivid memories slipped away. Next I unconsciously shifted his laughter, his voice, his smell, his *Darrell*-ness, from too-vivid constancy to a cranny so deep, I was barely aware of it. Cut off from consciousness, Darrell started visiting my dreams, where his presence was welcome; where it didn't hurt to linger with him.

I'd begun the decades-long task of forgetting him.

True — or Just Accurate? — Love

Donna kissing Hamani, 1983.

Was it his diminutiveness that threw me off? Six additional inches, half a foot more in height, and I might have seen the similarities between him and the man I'd left behind: The whip-thin muscularity. Curly-wavy-shiny hair. The effortless way he wore a suit. All features I'd admired in the most influential man in my life, the father whose defenses I'd never penetrated, who in his seventy-plus years couldn't express his love for me. This man was as bantam-sized as Daddy was tall. Still, I must have sensed the impossibility of making this new love—so like my first—happy. So I married him, and quickly.

In 1985, I knew little about the things people do with their eyes wide open that are entirely hidden to them. We take jobs not because the work thrills us but because it's what Mother expects. We bed inappropriate strangers and call ourselves liberated, though fecklessness born of past hurts is hardly free. We marry for love—not for love of the person we've wed but for love of someone long gone, whose memory we've tucked deep in one of our heart's unexamined pockets.

I did know this: my first marriage ended because my cocaine-addicted husband smoked his car. Or was it because I accidentally incinerated the diamond engagement ring I had paid for myself? Either way, the symbolism was clear: the disastrous union had finally gone up in smoke.

I'd met Greg in Detroit in 1980. I'd landed in the Motor City after leaving Michigan, where it had taken me three years to complete U of M's two-year master's program. What I remember most clearly about the months after Darrell's death is the tears. Everything else is murmurs and shadows.

At some point during that last year of grad school, it

occurred to me people might actually be able to look through me. The whole-body invisibility I'd felt after Darrell's death had contracted, becoming a hole in my gut so palpable, I could feel wind gusting between my ribs. Spanning the space from breastbone to navel, the emptiness was so tangible, it rendered organs and muscles irrelevant. All that was real was the void, and the mantra echoing inside it:

My brother is dead. My brother is dead. Darrell is dead.

But just as in grad school, my feet kept taking me where I had to go. I have no recollection of graduating from the master's program, though I have paperwork attesting to it. Bruce had moved to Ann Arbor and joined me in a light-filled basement apartment. He'd gotten a job selling shoes after he saw a Help Wanted sign in a window, strolled in, and told the manager, "You'll love me!" His presence was my one solace. Every time I'd thought of him in Gary, vulnerable to errant police, accusatory white people, local thugs, I'd felt a stab of panic. Now he was out of danger; my presence would protect him as I traversed streets I barely saw, took classes whose lessons didn't penetrate, and turned in papers produced by the automaton who resembled me.

Repeatedly, I was drawn to men younger than I. Not dangerously, illegally younger, but younger nonetheless. Jon was the first, then came Tony, a dashing, whip-smart black Detroiter four years my junior, a journalism major who for months was a perfectly satisfactory boyfriend — except when he acted his age, which was often. After one passionate argument, Tony stood in my doorway and announced, "At least you've known *one* good man in your life!" That this immature eighteen-year-old would pronounce himself the best man I'd known when I'd lost one far better incensed me so much that I envisioned — no *felt* — myself jabbing the pair of scissors I'd been using into his back. The impulse scared me into breaking up with him. At one point, I felt hugely attracted to a youth of seventeen whom I was mentoring. I actually let this kid kiss me before asking the woman who moved, looked, and sounded like me, "What are you doing?" I wasn't sure, even when a female friend pointedly asked, "Don't you like any *adults*?"

I couldn't see it then, but my intent seems obvious: I'd just lost my childhood's most admired and gallant youth. I wanted him—his openness, his lack of guile, his desire to take care of me—back. So I'd found several boys—or boyish men. But not him.

Careerwise, I'd had successful summer internships at the *Charlotte Observer,* a highly regarded Knight-Ridder paper in North Carolina, and at the *Ann Arbor News,* the folksy Booth paper that served U of M's home city. Editors at the *News* wanted to hire me full-time; I was thrilled because it would fulfill the terms of my Booth fellowship. In my new, risk-filled world, the prospect of remaining in Ann Arbor—and in Bruce's safe, familiar orbit—seemed ideal. Ann Arbor's rambunctious students were so full of themselves that they distracted me from my emptiness. But Booth fellowship officials insisted that I work at a smaller paper in tiny Bay City, a ten-square-mile town more than an hour and a half away. Only 2 percent of Bay City's 15,000 residents were black.

The thought of being alone with the hole in my midsection was harrowing. I appealed to Booth to be allowed to stay where I felt safe, editors wanted me, and I had a shot at meeting a mate. Booth's response: Bay City or nothing. I felt duty-bound to take the job, though I had no contractural obligation. I'd been so certain that I'd stay at the *News* that I'd sought no other offers. I felt trapped.

Weeks before graduation and unbeknownst to me, Neal Shine, a top editor at the venerable *Detroit Free Press,* looked around his large, vibrant newsroom and noted, "There are no black people here." He said nothing of his revelation when he visited Michigan to speak to our graduate program, but was intrigued by a pushy black female student's pointed questions, not realizing that people without insides have nothing to fear. I became the first Michigan journalism master's grad hired by the exalted *Freep*.

As thrilled as I was, everything in life still felt squishy and unsettled. Yet I was sure that Detroit, a hardscrabble city as racially divided as any, was the perfect place for me as a journalist to address the most solid fact of my existence: Darrell would still be alive if those policemen had known whom they were shooting. Whomever they thought they saw in that ditch—and I was sure they saw black—they had no inkling of the valuable human being they'd blown away.

Before Darrell's death, I wanted to be a great writer. After he died, I knew what I wanted to write *about:* the agonizing wrongness of such losses, not just for me, but for thousands. So what if I'd never confronted Darrell's killers, sued the police, or found the grace to forgive his murderers? I could do something for my dead brother that I'd never had to do when he was alive: make people know him, what he meant, if only to me.

Detroit was full of Darrells, men young and old whose blackness had obscured their humanity for my newspaper's wary white readers. It was full of little girls who could shrivel up inside if something horrible happened to their daddies or their brothers. My words could tell people how it felt to be twelve—everyone was twelve once—coming home to Darrell after a long day of trying to ignore girls who snickered as they cataloged my inadequacies. The balm it was, knowing one person didn't judge me for my hair, my outfit, my relative attractiveness on the sliding Negro scale. My words—powerful, Darrell-inspired words—could tell how essential it was to be adored for no good reason, to have someone see you more generously than you saw yourself, to be bathed in a golden, undeserved light.

Didn't everyone have such a person? Someone so crucial that the mere thought of him or her would make them hesitate to kill? Someone whose image would inspire them to fire into a shoulder or a knee or some other nonlethal place when confronted by a guy armed with a chain when they had guns?

It would be a decade before I could actually write about Darrell. Just thinking about him threatened to rip off the gossamer substance with which I'd papered over my heart. So I wrote about other black men, women, children, with the sensitivity and knowingness I couldn't yet use to describe him.

Detroit, thank God, was less than an hour's drive from Bruce. I found a studio in a flatiron-shaped building in a neighborhood a quick bus ride from the *Freep*'s downtown offices. Assigned to the city desk, I found myself covering a municipality whose murder rate had placed it atop the nation's "Most Homicides" list, and whose mayor, Coleman Young, was an annoyance to whites and a take-no-shit hero to many blacks.

Racially and economically, Detroit was surreal. A seven-mile drive down Jefferson Avenue zapped you from affluence to poverty to flat-out riches in fifteen head-spinning minutes. Beginning in the city's then-vibrant downtown, Jefferson morphed quickly into destitution, cut through middle-class pleasantness, and ended up amid breathtaking lakeshore mansions built by auto magnates Edsel Ford and Horace Dodge. Window shades and curtains were always pulled tight in the shabby flats occupied by poor, inner-city Detroiters. But as the neighborhoods grew richer, the more curtains you could peer into. By the time you got to wealthy Grosse Pointe, nothing was veiled; passersby got unobstructed views of folks' expensive

TVs, music equipment, and artwork. Entire families could be seen reading, eating, and otherwise living their lives. The message: *Look all you like. We are invulnerable.*

Fascinated by the city's contrasts, I enjoyed my job and appreciated earning a real salary. I even started dating actual grown-ups. Like the brilliant lawyer who seemed drawn to me but who never made a move. One brutally lonely night I phoned him and said, "Let's just be physical. No strings." After a pause, he said, "I can't. I know we would get more involved," as if that was the worst thought in the world. And there was the happily married TV reporter whom I interviewed and found myself laughing with for more than an hour. A dozen riotous calls later, I realized I felt more in sync with him than with anyone I'd met since my New York beau Michael. I'd never slept with a married man, but felt dangerously close the one time he visited my apartment. After a passionate kiss, he left. He never called again.

Bruce was more successful at romance, for a while. Patty, a coworker whose hippie skirts and up-to-something smile he'd admired, invited him roller-skating. Depositing Bruce on the sidelines, she spun off for some solo laps to James Taylor's "Up on the Roof," whirling in circles, her brown hair flying. Bruce was a goner. So was Patty—for three months. Then she cut off their sexy relationship with no explanation. Still wounded from Darrell's death, Bruce had resisted getting close to any girl, especially a white one. Now what Bruce had seen as a passionate love match looked like Patty's opportunity to explore the black-men-are-hot dynamic and bolt before getting in too deep. Bruce kept working with her until the day Bob Seger's plaintive "The Famous Final Scene" played over the sound system and he discovered his face was wet. He decided to move to Detroit.

Together we found a two-bedroom apartment with gleaming hardwood floors. In the fall of 1980, Bruce began work as a *Freep* copy aide, a support position in which his wit and serious work ethic endeared him to the newsroom. An interview with the Canadian rock group Rush led to his writing reviews and articles for the paper's music section. My rocker bro was a writer!

As the chasm inside me filled, I became more engrossed in my work. I adored my local New Age church, enjoyed exploring spirituality with my sweet pal Denise, and laughing about men with new buddies Geri, Jeanne, and Mireille. I loved my life.

So why was I drawn to a twenty-eight-year-old youth in adult clothing? I can't claim I had no forewarning of Greg's issues: he snorted cocaine the night I met him. But he was a smart, good-looking man with an exciting job. In the early 1980s, coke was still thought of as the "perfect" drug, the clean, nonaddictive source of a breezy high. Watching this boyishly attractive stranger doing the trendy, naughty-but-nice drug cemented his coolness. Besides, I was already mesmerized by his huge, thick-lashed eyes. They were like a guileless child's, an impression heightened by Greg's five seven frame.

A more observant woman might have noticed a theme.

I'd met him at a party at the home of an up-and-coming black GM car designer, where my buddy Jeanne promised we'd meet "lots of single guys from the auto industry." Walking into a pretty brick Tudor vibrating to "Rock with You," I spied Larry, an attractive businessman whom I'd dated briefly in Charlotte and who had since moved to Detroit. I introduced him to Jeanne, who in turn presented me to one of her former flames.

I was immediately smitten. Greg was a GM public relations executive who reeked worldliness, at least to a girl who'd just left a town where a tattered sport coat passed for formal wear. I can still see him studying me, his shirt a blaze of white, his head cocked as he nursed a drink. When he confided that he was about to snort some coke, I asked to watch, curious about this safe new drug. Even more fascinating was the European cut of the jacket he had draped over a chair. I said it looked too small for a well-muscled man; Greg slid it on, pivoted like a model, and asked me to Sunday brunch.

The next morning, he had smoked salmon and mimosas waiting for me at his downtown apartment, a Mies van der Rohe–designed high-rise. The floor-to-ceiling windows in Greg's living room offered a panoramic view of the Detroit skyline. After reading the *New York Times* and the *Freep* together, we rode in his silver Cutlass Supreme — my favorite car, a sign! — to the swanky Renaissance Center mall to window-shop. Mostly we walked silently. Though I lived for penetrating conversation, I was charmed by Greg's unembarrassed quietude. Our first kiss in a dim RenCen corner was slow, deep, unhurried. Later I called my ex-roommate Pam to tell her all about my new beau. "Oh, he's *sophisticated*," she sighed.

An only child, Greg had been raised in St. Louis's middle-class suburbs by adoring parents who couldn't have been prouder of him. When one of his friends told me that he had for years had almost everything done for him, I shrugged. Finally, an attractive, popular, athletic guy who wanted marriage and a family was pursuing me.

So what if he favored cool silences over searching conversation and was used to having attention lavished on him? I saw no connection between him and the quiet, distant man in my past whom he resembled. Why would I connect Daddy (a grown man if there ever was one) to a guy whose most striking feature was his boyishness? At any rate, I rarely talked to my father, and no longer yearned for acknowledgment of his love. Greg's huge, innocent eyes suggested he'd never hurt me. I believed them.

Before the month was out, I was in love.

For all that I didn't know about Greg and my own motives, I was sure about one thing: I wasn't going to mess things up by heedlessly jumping into bed with him. I'd had it with intimacy that wasn't intimate and with "liberated" sex that mostly liberated you from getting a phone call the next night. One morning, Bruce opened my bedroom door and found me on my knees, praying that this relationship would stick.

And it was delightful, letting a real gentleman court me. For weeks, Greg took me to dinner, concerts, and movies. I courted him right back with home-cooked meals, weeknight massages, probing questions about work. I did everything for him but have sex. I told Pam that unlike most women we knew, I was determined to forge a serious relationship that precluded intimacy until I knew we were headed toward permanence. This being the 1980s, Pam asked, "Can you *do* that?"

I could try. Three months into our relationship, Greg said he loved me and wanted to marry me. Two months later, I was pregnant.

I hadn't planned to get pregnant, but I hadn't tried terribly hard not to. Greg was the one. I was twenty-seven; I'd always known I wanted marriage and a family, and Darrell's death had made frittering away precious time criminal. Unsure of how Greg would receive such news five months after we'd met, I said I had good news and bad news. Which did he want first? When he said, "The good news," I said, "I'm pregnant." Greg threw up his arms in triumph. When he asked for the bad news, I said, "I'm pregnant!" laughing with the knowledge that everything was going to be okay.

My work life, too, was going swimmingly. After a stint on the city desk, I'd joined the *Freep*'s feature section, "The Way We Live," as a fashion writer. What could be more fun than making use of my accumulated knowledge of clothes? Two years after Darrell's death, I felt like I was back on course. I'd lost a brother but gained a whole new life.

Engaged and expecting a baby in six months, Greg and I told our parents the news, which was greeted happily on both sides. Mom, of course, would have preferred a taller son-in-law. But Greg's glossy curls and deferential manners enchanted her. I found a curve-hugging gown of Alençon lace with a mermaid train and made my own rose-kissed mantilla-style veil. Pam, Gayle, Sharon, Shawn, and Melech's cute daughter, Shcoma, were enlisted as my attendants; my brothers and several longtime buddies were Greg's. A jovial *Free Press* coworker named Harry performed the wedding at a gorgeous Episcopal chapel.

It was perfect—except for the trivial fact that my groom and I hardly knew each other.

Our all-white wedding was followed by a Canadian honeymoon—Toronto, Montreal, and Quebec City—that fortuitously coincided with the end of my morning sickness. I returned with my new husband to my Palmer Park apartment (Bruce had found a flat on Detroit's East Side). Although my building prohibited kids, the manager said he'd try to overlook the newborn soon to be under his roof. "How much trouble can a little baby be?" he asked.

I had everything I wanted. But on the way to nirvana,

something weird happened: Mr. and Mrs. So-in-love discovered they didn't much like each other.

My need for openness and validation had always been met by Darrell, Bruce, and numerous friends. Greg's need was for privacy and solitude; his natural secretiveness had been intensified by his being an only child. We admired each other's looks, style, and ambition, but not who we *were:* a moody charmer who kept many of his deepest feelings to himself and a talky prober bent on coaxing people to reveal what they'd stashed. The problem crystallized one afternoon during an out-of-the-blue quarrel that began as we unwrapped wedding presents. Our words were so explosive and our viewpoints so at odds, arguing was useless. Exhausted on the sofa, we looked at each other. A chilling thought filled the room: we'd made a mistake. Frozen in an awful clarity, we *knew.* The illusion of our being even a decent match evaporated.

We kept unwrapping. Greg and I were married. We loved each other. We were having a baby. We would make it work.

Boys, Big and Small

Hamani, Donna, and Darrell in their
Detroit apartment, 1985.

Every fairy-tale princess awaits the love that will liberate her—from a flame-spouting dragon, a jealous stepmother, or a long, dreamless sleep. Real-life princesses—who toil in offices, work as cashiers at Safeway, and rush to get the kids before day care charges extra—also look to love for liberation. Their princes, too, will save them: by reminding them of their beauty, slaying their insecurities, making weary places inside them burst into song. But in real life, as in storybooks, few princesses seek to learn why their rescuers love them. They don't ask themselves, Do I adore this savior for who he is, or just for showing up? Grateful for True Love's arrival, a princess may not question the wisdom of linking her life to the stranger's whose kiss has set her free. Like her prince, she never pauses to ask:

If I'm loved for the wrong reasons, can I have a happy ending?

Five months pregnant with my first child in 1981, I told Mom-Mommy I was considering telling friends and coworkers the good news. "Lord have mercy," Mom-Mommy said. "We just got you down the aisle." I laughed. Greg and I had met before Christmas, wed eight months later, and become parents the week after New Year's. My wedding photos featured a woman who strongly resembled me except for the stripper-worthy cleavage bubbling out of her white gown, courtesy of the four-month-old fetus underneath it.

For once, even Melech approved of my choices. He'd abandoned his pseudo-pimp wardrobe and manner and was now in full religious-prophet mode. Appalled by my feminism, Melech suspected that my insistence that women have the same privileges as men had doomed me to life as a childless crone. Seeing my married-and-pregnant self, he smiled beneath his turban, patted my belly, and offered the loveliest compliment he could conjure: "You're beautiful, now that you're no longer a barren tree." Whatever. Once an ultrasound revealed my child's sex, I felt certain: my little boy would grow up to be the perfect black man.

My life, I'd decided, was a do-over. Creating a flawless new family would wipe away all that had gone terribly wrong with the first. Even before he was born, my baby would be given the best I could offer him.

Yet for weeks, I had the nagging feeling Greg and I weren't married but playing house. He *looked* like the husband I'd wanted—attractive, elegant, bright. I looked and sounded like a woman who'd be right for him. But I couldn't help wondering if what we cherished most in each other was what mattered in a marriage. Greg's silences were as vital to him as my sharing, yet I resented them. And when we did talk? He listened politely as I explored emotions, spirituality, and people's subterranean feelings. I stayed focused as he discussed sports, politics, current events. Our emotional styles were like different parts of the ocean: Greg's natural habitat was the waveless tidal pool; mine the roiling, fathomless blue. Each has its beauty. Yet they seldom meet.

Before my concern could blossom into alarm, the man I'd worried might be a bit too enamored of the status quo startled me. The agent of my surprise: a forward-thinking doctor whom a less open-minded brother might have dismissed as a kook.

The perfect birth required a special doctor. Jewel Pookrum was a respected physician who'd trained at prestigious Henry Ford Hospital before rejecting Western medicine and starting an obstetrics practice as organic as Eden. On my first visit, Dr. Pookrum looked me in the eye and asked, "Do you plan to have your baby at home?" My blank stare reflected my unspoken thought: As opposed to the mall?

"Um, no," I said. "At a hospital." Whereupon Dr. Pookrum presented a half-dozen reasons why no sane woman would consider giving birth anywhere as filthy and intrusive as a hospital. Reporting back to Greg, I steeled myself for his derision. He asked to learn more. Dr. Pookrum directed us to persuasive books by holistic physicians and described the intensive nutritional and educational preparation we'd receive. Our home's location, minutes from two hospitals, she assured, would protect us in an emergency. Despite Mom, who reacted as if we'd invited a blind Zulu witch doctor to deliver her grandchild in a cave, we decided to go for it.

My son Justin Hamani was born on sheets Greg had boiled and stretched over a sterile layer of newspapers in the brass bed we had conceived him in. He had his dad's portal-to-heaven eyes. *Perfect.*

A week later, my newborn started crying nonstop. Only two things seemed to distract him from his sobs: being carried on his belly, airplane-style, and quaffing breast milk as lustily as Henry the Eighth attacked his flask.

The rest of the time, Mani cried. And cried more. Then he really started sobbing, his tiny body writhing, his purple face convulsed. "It's only colic," our pediatrician shrugged, which did nothing to calm me or the upstairs neighbor, who started banging on his floor with a frying pan during my son's hourly wail-fests.

The intrusion of imperfection into my do-over world had the unexpected benefit of drawing Greg and me closer as we tried everything with Mani that a half-dozen counselors advised: swaddling, rocking, singing to him, slipping him whiskey, massaging his belly, begging for his pity. Only feeding him quieted him for long.

Mom—wary of any infant nourishment that wasn't a canned, factory-concocted brew—helpfully offered, "Maybe something's wrong with your milk." But I knew the problem was more basic:

Something was wrong with me.

Not surprisingly, the stress, sleeplessness, and uncertainty arising from my baby's torment caused submerged feelings of inadequacy to surface. I was to blame for my baby's agony, despite having faithfully gulped Dr. Pookrum's liquefied grass drinks, meditated daily, and exercised into my eighth month. Yet unlike Darrell, whom I'd failed through my inattention, my newborn had been given every benefit I could think of. And still I had failed him. Knowing nothing about postpartum depression, I asked and re-asked myself the obvious question: *What's the matter with me?*

After four months, Mani's colic disappeared, just as the doctor had predicted. So I wasn't to blame. My real problem, I began to realize, wasn't my insufficiency but the fact that everything had moved so fast between Greg and me. With my new husband, home, and baby, I'd been too dazed, busy, and hormonal to consider: first-time motherhood is a thrill ride few women are prepared for.

With our household blissfully silent, a pleasing calm descended upon Greg and me. After surviving a quickie marriage, new parenthood, two moves, and colic, we'd found our footing as a contented couple. We were different but loved each other and our baby. We had jobs we enjoyed, supportive families, and a desire to build a life together. Mismatched couples made it with less. We'd heard that layoffs were imminent at GM, but assumed my husband's close friendship with his boss would protect him.

It didn't. Laid off, Greg looked for work but found nothing. Suddenly he was a proud man entirely supported by his wife. With too much time on his hands, my dispirited husband returned to his occasional drug use. Before long, it flared into something more sinister.

As Greg's experimentation with cocaine morphed into an addiction, I was examining dependencies of my own. Stumbling upon Marilyn French's seminal 1977 feminist novel, *The Women's Room*, I devoured the book, and took my first hard look at my unquestioning giving to men. I pondered everything—encouragement, support, cash, advice, and, always, the benefit of the doubt—I'd offered my beaus, friends, brothers, and now husband.

Why, I seriously asked for the first time, did I offer so much? Women growing up in the 1950s and most of the 1960s were socialized to give, by society, by their families, and by every book, magazine, TV show, and movie they encountered. Did that explain my inborn desire to give? It couldn't have been home training. In the Britt family, everyone had worked. Mom was a force to be reckoned with; nobody rivaled Daddy in the tireless toil department. But my father had been stingy with his soul. More and more, that was the first thing I offered all comers. Because I hated thinking about Darrell's death, I never considered that it might have anything to do with my propensity. The best reasons I could come up with embarrassed me: I *enjoyed* giving. I remembered meals cooked for Daddy, artwork drawn for Darrell, the Green Hornet trading cards I'd bought for Bruce, the coats that I'd retrieved for my parents' party guests. Giving gave me pleasure.

More unsettling was the suspicion that my ratcheted-up giving was inspired by wanting the men in my life—and the men I *wanted* in my life—to love and admire me. In some panicked place, I felt that if I didn't give generously, they might not either.

French's book shook me into seeing what the "perfect" wife I hoped to be was trying to ignore: The increasing absence of even shallow conversation between Greg and me. The frigidness of exchanges we couldn't avoid. The questions I didn't dare ask.

One evening, I arrived home from work to find that Greg was out. He'd had a job interview and mentioned he might stop for a drink at a local lounge. Leaving Mani with our teenage neighbor Nyasa, I headed to the pub. Entering, I let my eyes adjust to the dimness.

Directly before me, in a booth with friends, sat my husband. Stylish in his three-piece suit, he was engrossed in a conversation, throwing his head back with laughter. I noted how expertly he balanced his Newport in one hand, his cocktail in the other. Something about the cigarette (which he knew I despised), the gale-force gaiety, the oddly unfamiliar laughter of my husband of more than a year, made me ask: *Who is this guy?* Worn out from work and distrust, from denying that my husband was uninterested in everything I liked best about myself, I regarded this stranger. Greg looked like he had the night I met him: confident, worldly, dashing. And I wanted none of it.

The glamour before me had no relationship to our lives. Money was disappearing from our joint account at an alarming rate; Greg's explanations were increasingly unconvincing. His uncommunicativeness, I'd told myself, arose from his frustration over his joblessness. I couldn't hurt him by being too intrusive about money or his job search. Yet my patience was draining away; I could barely recall the love that dropped me to my knees when we were dating. Regarding this dapper man-about-town, my mind uttered a staggering truth: *this man is not my husband.*

This handsome stranger wasn't "bad" or unattractive. He just had no authentic connection to the real me. I left without a word.

Just like that, I knew: I'd had it with my self-imposed blindness, with giving unconditionally to an out-of-work husband whose comings and goings were increasingly murky and for whom I—ever the troopless Girl Scout—provided the perfect cover. Week after week, I could barely breathe while paying our bills; watching our limited funds evaporate with no explanation sucked the air out of me. Guardedly, I told my coworker Marty, also a wife and mother, about the feelings French's book was stirring. "That book made me so angry," Marty said. "I had to keep putting it down."

So did I. When your kid is tiny and your mate is disappearing before your eyes, when you're neither brave nor self-preserving enough to say, "Something horrible is happening and it has to stop," putting the book down seems a sensible option. I was a God-fearing black girl weaned on the Bible and *Essence* magazine. I knew the Loyal Sister Mantra by heart:

The black man is even more burdened by the white man's hatred than you are. He needs your support. Yours has lost his job; you're supporting him. Would you further emasculate him by leaving him, by separating him from the black male child he adores? He's his daddy, even if he's destroying himself.

As the sister, friend, daughter, and lover of brothers, I knew everything that deeply affects American men affects black men more harshly. Being human is wrenching for everyone. Yet the level of hostility and suspicion directed at black men is so palpable, their culturally inflicted wounds so raw, I understood how a decent brother might be drawn to anything that eased the pressure. My husband was a good man grappling with demons he wouldn't acknowledge. I had to stay. Had to help him.

Despite knowing better, despite sensing that the man I'd married would never be my true husband, I put the book down. Eyes burning with "don't bullshit me" intensity, I told Greg, "Tell me what's going on."

He was, he finally admitted, an addict. This was scary but honest, a step in the right direction. His defenses and bravado gone, he promised to get help. He meant it.

But my husband was an *addict*, a bright, likable guy in the thrall of one of the most addictive substances known to man. Despite his assurances, things went from bad to worse to god-awful. There was nothing special about the lies, evasions, and mounting financial losses I experienced as the wife of an addict. Greg, too, must have felt let down: by my impatience, by my rage, by the deliberate distance I kept from him in bed and everywhere else, by every subtle indication that I was girding myself to leave him.

Inching toward that inevitability was torturous. Four years earlier, I had spectacularly failed a good man who'd needed me. Now I was failing another whom I'd promised before God to love, honor, and cherish, in sickness and in health. I begged Greg to confess that he'd been sexually unfaithful, committed some sin that would meet God's requirement for my leaving. "I haven't," Greg insisted, knowing he had me.

I knew that the drugs he was using, not to mention the people who sold them to him, could kill him. After Darrell, could I live with that? Underlying everything, a voice whispered, *"No one has ever needed your generosity more."*

But I had nothing left. I felt my mind being made up.

Then I learned I was pregnant.

It was impossible. Pregnant by a man I barely was speaking to? Because I had no memory of the sex that must have occurred, I jokingly called my second son my "immaculate conception." But the pregnancy didn't feel like a joke. This inexplicable development had God's fingerprints all over it. I knew what it meant: I couldn't leave.

In August 1985, my son Darrell was born. As beautiful as his brother, my newborn almost never cried, which *did* seem like a miracle. For more than a month after his birth, Greg was a changed man. Gone was the snarling brooder who vanished for unexplained reasons. My husband was happy, helpful, engaged in family life and in finding work. He played with his sons. He and I talked, planned, and—unbelievably—laughed together.

Hopeful, warily, I reached out to him again, in small, just-testing ways: Fixing his favorite dishes. Offering my hand for holding. Nestling into the curve of his body as his arms wrapped around me at night. As my maternity leave lengthened, I warmed to the notion of even trusting him again. Daring to think we may have weathered the worst, I asked what had shifted. "I'm not sure," Greg said. "I'm just different."

I had scheduled a train trip to Media with Mani and Darrell to introduce Mom-Mommy to her new great-grandson. Wary of leaving when things were going so well, I confessed my concerns to Greg; he assured me he'd be fine. Still, I bundled my checkbook, ATM card, and diamond engagement ring into a paper bag and thrust it into Bruce's hands. Consumed by anxiety, and distracted by my two small kids, I feared I might lose them. And I couldn't risk leaving them with Greg.

Each day I was away, my husband phoned to reassure me all was well. Returning home, I learned two things: My bank account had been emptied, courtesy of a forgotten ATM card buried in my jewelry box, which my drug-craving husband had located. More astonishingly, Greg had smoked his Cutlass, literally trading our one source of transportation for a high. My despair was so acute that when Bruce returned my paper bag, I distractedly removed the ATM card and checkbook and tossed the bag in the garbage. It was days before I realized I'd trashed the tiny oval diamond I'd bought myself through monthly payments Greg had promised to repay. Mortified, I borrowed $800 rent money from a sweet male coworker whose eyes counseled, *Leave* him. My marriage, I told him, was over, but how could I leave? I had no money. Where would my boys and I live? What would happen to Greg?

A few days later, my work phone rang. It was Joe Urschel, a former *Free Press* coworker whose writer wife, Donna, was a close friend. The Urschels had moved to the nation's capital when Joe was named managing editor of the "Life" section at *USA Today,* the colorful new daily that was revolutionizing newspapers. "I'd like you to work for me," Joe said. "As a writer or an editor, whichever you like. When can you fly in for an interview?"

My retreat from Detroit in 1986 for Washington, D.C., was as speedy as a battle-weary woman could have wished. My coworkers threw me a lovely good-bye party, at which Greg looked so poised that Helen Fogel, a friend who knew every detail of our saga, pulled me aside in alarm. "Is Greg coming with you to Virginia?" she asked. She'd overheard him telling someone that he'd be joining us in Alexandria, where I'd found a town house. The ease with which he said it made her believe it.

Whatever. I flew with my boys to Virginia, settled in, and for the first time in months felt free—breathing my own air, responsible only for my sons and me. I waited for guilt to consume me for having left my husband at his life's toughest juncture. It never came. I recalled how, at the height of the madness, I'd confessed to Greg that my distress was so intense, I feared becoming seriously ill. "If you get sick, I'm not going to blame myself," he'd said. I could shrug, too.

In the months to come, Greg would hit rock bottom, move back to St. Louis, and kick drugs for good. I admired him; several of his friends would struggle for years to free themselves from the "nonaddictive" poison that had decimated their lives.

But my focus was entirely on my sons. Darrell was five months old; Mani had just turned four. Raising them alone was something I'd never planned. My worries were every single mother's: money, child care, discipline, my own capabilities. What if my generous nature made me give them too much? Some nights, I even lay awake wondering if grabbing the life preserver of *USA Today* had been a mistake. I'd read a dozen books about black boys' need for male role models; I'd kicked my sons' loving father to the curb.

Always, there was the subconscious lesson of my brother. For eight years, I'd pushed memories of Darrell deep enough to shush them. But forgetting as a survival tactic exacerbated my sense of having betrayed him. Darrell had shown me how dangerous the world was for black men. Now I'd let another significant brother be consumed by it. Could I teach my sons to successfully negotiate such a minefield alone?

All of this was on my mind when I phoned a local Montessori preschool as a possible choice for Hamani. Everything about the soothing female voice on the other line suggested the school was top-notch. Warm and wise, the voice felt like a much-needed balm as it rubbed the wonders of the school's curriculum and class size into my consciousness. Then I asked, "How many black students do you have? I wouldn't want Hamani to be alone."

The babbling brook of a voice sputtered, then stopped as

abruptly as a turned-off faucet. Its owner could hardly believe her mistake. She was speaking to one of *them*? Recovering, the voice smoothed itself out. "Is your son...nice?" it asked. "We've had some problems with some of our black boys." Panicked— *we're not like the bad ones!*—I was poised to assure the administrator of my son's sweetness when two questions screeched me to a halt: This school hasn't had "problems" with *white* four-year-olds? Is this what my beautiful little boy will face?

By the time we finished chatting, the voice's concerns seemed allayed. Invited to set up a time to visit the school, I never called back. But I couldn't shake what the voice's words portended. The question it raised was never far from consciousness:

Who was I to try to raise two black boys alone in a world poised to reject them?

Perfect

Donna and Kevin, 1990.

Mesmerized, I'm watching the driveway basketball court where my sons, three and six, play hoops. But today three ballers are weaving, tossing, leaping beneath the basket: my boys, their high voices screeching with excitement, and the man whose baritone encourages them. Black boys and backyard hoops I know by heart: Darrell and his friends trash-talking; Melech-once-Steve hacking his way past every opponent; me serving lemon Kool-Aid, though I'm the one drinking in the moves, the competition, the joy. Seeing this man play hoops with my kids plays havoc with my heart. Note to self: buy lemonade.

It happened one sunny afternoon in 1988, two years after I'd left Detroit. I hadn't abandoned my dream of raising perfect sons. But the demands of single motherhood were so overwhelming, the only thing I envisioned doing perfectly was qualifying for institutionalization.

But on that bright day, something so amazing happened that I forgot that I'd been expecting it my whole life: I found the perfect black man.

As challenging as my life as a single mom was, I felt a new equanimity permeate my life. I loved my babysitter Tonya, and I enjoyed working as an editor of the "Life" section at *USA Today*, whose newsroom in a gleaming high-rise overlooking the Potomac seemed totally unrelated to the grit-and-grime of daily journalism. I'd never been an editor. But when Joe offered me a choice between writing and editing, I couldn't imagine crafting nuanced prose at a paper whose every sentence seemed to beg for an exclamation point. My brilliant boss, Linda Kauss, and talented staff soon schooled me on the expertise required to write informative, engaging stories in a quarter of the space "real" papers used.

A year after I arrived at *USAT,* Joe Urschel called me into his office and asked, "Are you happy here?" Refraining from blurting that my gratitude for having escaped Detroit was such that I would have daily polished his loafers, I said, "Yes." With a crafty-cat grin, Joe asked, "If you could do anything here, what would you do?"

Wary—was this a trick?—I reiterated that I really liked my job. Undeterred, Joe asked, "But if you could design any job for yourself here—anything at all—what would it be?"

What the hell. "Okay, I miss writing," I began. "So I'd be a writer again. Features...or maybe movie reviews; I used to love that." Then I froze. "But if I was a writer, "Life" wouldn't have any black managers...so there'd be a management aspect."

Joe's feline grin widened. "So where would this job be?"

"In L.A.," I said without hesitating. Bruce had just taken a job as music writer at the *Los Angeles Daily News.* I missed him. "I'd love covering Hollywood."

Still smiling, Joe said, "Okay, thanks," turning his attention to papers on his desk. I returned to my desk, deflated after the high of fashioning my perfect job.

Two weeks later, I was back in Joe's office. The grin was back. "In three weeks, we'll have an opening for a Los Angeles bureau chief," he said. "We'd like whoever takes the job to write entertainment features and be our backup movie critic. Are you interested?"

That was the moment I learned the magic of saying what you want aloud.

I was on my way to Los Angeles.

*   *   *

A year later, I'd adjusted to the Los Angeles sledgehammer sun and taught Mani and Darrell how to stand under doorways with pillows over their heads during earthquakes (the Whittier Narrows quake hit during our first week in town). I'd had a blast interviewing such disparate celebs as Kevin Costner (flirty), Pee-wee Herman (cagey), Barry Manilow (engaging), and Don Johnson (resplendent). Feeling that I'd earned a week away, I left my sons and new home to attend the National Association of Black Journalists' meeting.

The annual conference was my brief yearly shot at confabbing with my peers and pretending to be the unfettered young thing I no longer was. On the second night, I met up with Jeanne, the Detroit friend who'd introduced me to Greg and who was now a recruiter for the *Washington Post*. She'd married Larry, the guy I'd acquainted her with at that fateful party. Now we were both mothers of two, briefly emancipated from family, and headed to a riverboat soiree.

Yes, riverboat. NABJ's 1988 meeting was in St. Louis, Greg's hometown and where he'd lived since our breakup.

After checking into the convention hotel, I dropped off Mani and Darrell at Greg's parents' suburban home and listened warily as my estranged husband suggested we try again. My satisfying work life notwithstanding, I was weary—of shouldering too much alone, of beating myself up for having separated my boys from the daddy who loved them. Greg said he had stopped using drugs, and something about his manner made me believe him. Our total incompatibility seemed less important than our children's welfare. I said I would consider it.

Not so fast, a kind God interjected. Climbing onto the bus to the riverboat, Jeanne and I sat behind two guys, one of whom turned, spoke to Jeanne, and blinded me with his dimples. Kevin Merida was a Washington, D.C.–raised political reporter for the *Dallas Morning News,* whom Jeanne hoped to lure to the *Post.* As she chatted with Kevin's seatmate, I put this new prospect through my first-meeting mental checklist. *Attractive?* Oh yes. *Interested?* Almost certainly. *Holds up his end of a clever, preparty conversa*—wait, what did he say? Damn that smile!

By the time we got to the boat, the night's blessed trajectory seemed assured. Then Jeanne inexplicably morphed into Recruiter Girl, pulling Kevin away to discuss careers at the *Post.* That left the field open to a smarmy editor I'd been avoiding. It took twenty minutes to shake him; Kevin was nowhere to be seen.

Scanning the dance floor, I spied my quarry at the bar, sitting with the guy from the bus. It was now or never.

"Excuse me," I said, tapping his shoulder. Both men turned. "When you're done here," I purred, staring deeply into Kevin's eyes, "find me."

Twirling, I slipped away. The men looked at each other. Kevin's friend said, "Man, I would find her."

He did—but too slowly for a single mom on a forty-eight-hour crazy-life furlough. Mr. Smarmy had reemerged, pulling me onto the dance floor. By the time Kevin caught my attention, my teasing mood had evaporated. Two precious hours of my dwindling freedom—and my first-ever cinema-worthy opening gambit—had been wasted. So when Kevin said, "I've been looking for you!" I sidestepped him as I would a squashed roach.

"Why did you want me to find you?" he asked.

"Because I felt like flirting and picked you to do it with," I answered truthfully. Shrugging, I added, "But I've lost the urge."

Grinning (those accursed dimples!), he said, "C'mon. You can get it back."

Another shrug. "A woman can't turn that kind of thing on and off."

"So it's my fault you were dancing with twenty other guys?"

And on it went, for weeks afterward. It didn't take me long to decide that Kevin was as close to "the perfect black man" — a real-life prince — as any beau I'd had. Intelligence, integrity, and generosity beamed from him; he reminded me more of Darrell than anyone I'd dated. Kevin was a "real brother" whose blackness was vital to him but who was equally comfortable around whites, moving seamlessly between tough urban streets and the halls of Congress. What wasn't to like?

Suddenly the boys were thriving, and I had a tailor-made job and an exciting, long-distance relationship with a guy whose position — covering the Michael Dukakis presidential campaign — required visits to Los Angeles for campaign events. Kevin cherished traits I valued in myself but that had sent other men fleeing — particularly the Kev-christened "Donna Britt dig-deeper program" of inquisitive probing. I still had financial problems as a single mom receiving a fraction (and during many months, not a penny) of assistance from my ex. Once a month, I felt the breathless discomfort of lining up my bills, staring at each, and calculating which to pay, which to put off, how much I could spare and still feed my kids. Yet life was grand.

There was just one snag: the all-consuming nature of covering a presidential campaign meant that in those pre–cell phone days, half a week might pass before I heard from Kevin. This was intolerable. He'd call, we'd have a great chat, I'd be floating... and days would pass before I heard his voice again. Kev patiently explained his "unbelievable" busyness; I less patiently countered, "Single motherhood's no joke, either." When a whole week passed without a call, I told Kevin sporadic talks didn't suit me. "Call when the campaign is over," I suggested. "That way I won't be looking to hear from you." He seemed miffed, but he'd get over it.

Something else nagged at me: I missed writing. *Writing*-writing, the kind I couldn't do at *USA Today:* long, cunningly crafted sentences that wrestled with insights requiring more than ten words to relate. *Washington Post* "Metro" editor Milton Coleman had approached me about a position on "Metro," but I had no desire to cover the kid-crushed-by-school-bus beat. So when I got a call from "Style" editor Mary Hadar about writing for the *Post*'s legendary features section, it felt like a summons from God.

God, it turned out, was a perpetually smiling brunette with dancing eyes who reminded me of the pre-devastation Judy Garland. Meeting at a journalism event in Nashville, Mary and I attended the Grand Ole Opry, where we laughed and clapped as I tried to make sense of her warmth. Was it a ruse? Just seven years had passed since the *Post* had endured journalism's worst scandal: Reporter Janet Cooke's fabricated article about an eight-year-old heroin addict. Cooke was black, my age, and an adept writer; I'd felt inordinately proud when she won the Pulitzer. Learning that she'd lied felt calamitous. Didn't black journalists have enough problems? Did white editors understand that Cooke's lies reflected only on her?

Cooke's downfall sparked a slew of articles describing the *Post* as a tense workplace where reporters competed for stories in gladiatorial contests of ego and ambition. But I yearned to write for "Style," and Mary seemed as genuine as she was smart. So I was thrilled when I was invited to the *Post*'s Fifteenth Street offices, where I was shepherded from one editor to the next before being led into the sanctum of Ben Bradlee, famed architect of the paper's Watergate coverage. He and Len Downie, Ben's deputy, engaged me in an obligatory question-

and-answer session that to a dig-deeper girl felt distressingly . . . polite. I was talking to *Ben Bradlee,* the legend for whom the scandal that had broken my heart must have been a body blow. Would he subconsciously hold Cooke's lies against me? The Cooke debacle might be the last thing Bradlee wanted to discuss, but when else would I get such a shot?

"What happened with Janet Cooke was incredibly painful for me," I began. "Do you think that on some level it might affect how you look at other black journalists?"

Bradlee, who had seemed only semi-engaged, paused. Really looking at me for the first time, he spoke. The Cooke scandal was his life's deepest disappointment, he said. He described his profound sense of betrayal and disbelief, how attractive and imposing Cooke had been—"She looked like that singer, Diane Ross"—and how tragically she'd snookered his beloved newspaper.

I knew his pain. Cooke's behavior, I responded, had been nearly as wounding to black journalists. "We took incredible pride in her triumph," I explained. "How could we not feel crushed by her shame? . . . Now we have to worry that every editor might judge us by her." At last Bradlee and I were having a conversation, one as revealing—for a job interview, anyway—as I could have asked for.

Back at my hotel, I weighed whether to phone Kevin. The presidential contest had ended three weeks earlier; I was still awaiting his call. Clearly, I'd underestimated his anger over my inability to handle off-and-on communication. Now I was in D.C., with nothing to do besides ponder my uncertain future. Calling his mother's home on the chance that he might be visiting, I heard Kevin answer. Sounding thrilled to hear from me, he invited me to dinner that night and a Redskins game the next day.

Days later, I got an offer to write for "Style." The Janet

Cooke exchange, I learned later, had sealed the deal. As excited as I was, part of me hesitated to accept. I loved Los Angeles. The town was about bullshit, but it was *fun* bullshit. Washington, D.C., bullshit got nice boys shipped overseas to die in bogus wars. Los Angeles spoke to every shallow, self-involved cell in my being. Abandoning spandex-and-sweats Hollywood for trench-coated Washington felt like leaving a tropical bird sanctuary for a nest of wrens.

But the job I'd yearned for was in Washington. So was the man. Kevin hadn't just swept into my life; he and the boys had adored each other instantly. He'd brought thrills, fun, and grown-up maleness of the best type into our home. I wanted more. A fear that had long haunted me evaporated. I'd found the ideal role model for my growing sons. Kevin savored the role, which surprised some who'd known him as a serial monogamist with a girl in every career "port" in which he'd settled. I wasn't worried. Whatever Kevin thought was going on, I knew: He was it. My perfect man.

There were just two problems, neither of them obvious. The first: What *wouldn't* a woman who'd given her all to clearly imperfect men give to one who deserved it?

The second: There is no perfect man, black or otherwise. Just perfect intentions.

I rented a cozy, tree-shrouded house in suburban Takoma Park, Maryland. During my final walk-through, its owner, Mark, pointed next door and said that his neighbors, Mary Jo and Tim, "have kids the same age as yours. You should get to know them." I thought, Yeah, right. What if these white folks (how many black Mary Jos do you know?) were less welcoming than Mark assumed? Mani and Darrell had no such doubts, becoming instant buddies with towheaded Jacob, who like Darrell was four, and his baby brother, Jonathan. Warily watching my boys pal around with them, I took my time getting friendly with Mary Jo, a social worker, and Tim, who ran group homes for developmentally disabled adults.

Every white person, Darrell and the black-and-white footage of beaten civil rights workers reminded me, was potentially dangerous.

Of course with children, there was plenty besides racism to worry about. But not so much with Hamani. If Kevin seemed to be the perfect man, Mani gave every appearance of being the perfect boy. Charming, affectionate, and academically sound, he was so affable that I sometimes wondered if he'd sobbed away every ounce of irritability during his first months. This was a seven-year-old who patted my back when I was discouraged, happily reciprocated Mom's constant hugs, won numerous school Citizen of the Month awards, and exclaimed, "You shouldn't have!" when opening gifts, sounding as if he meant it. He was so open that at age eleven he blurted, "Mom, I can't wait to kiss a girl!"

If Hamani had been my only child, I would have congratulated myself on my parenting genius, assuming that my wisdom—not blind luck—explained his awesomeness.

Darrell cured me of such notions. The opposite of colicky-turned-cheerful Mani, Darrell—who seemed bent from day one on rejecting his brother's model-kid image—was a tranquil cherub who daily grew more challenging. Never as slippery or as incorrigible as Melech, Darrell was more likely to apologize after he lied, smart-mouthed you, or otherwise mashed your buttons. He was also resourceful. Once when I was out of town, a friend inadvertently dropped Darrell, six, at school before it opened. This tiny boy walked five blocks, crossed the area's busiest commuter route during rush hour, knocked on Mary Jo's door, and calmly told her he'd like a ride with her kids. She almost fainted. Darrell inherited his namesake's convulsive sense of humor and gift for mimicry: he'd put on a wig, toss a coverlet over his shoulders, and *become* Mom-Mommy King. Driving us to distraction, he'd then make us laugh so hard, we'd forgive him. Until the next time.

My sons made life full, satisfying—and overwhelming. Lacking a spouse or housemate whose interest in our home's smooth functioning matched mine, I developed the self-defeating habit of doing everything myself. Moms without partners—and that's black women more than any other group—have no extra time. It's faster to do stuff yourself than to spend a half hour teaching, correcting, and coaxing reluctant kids to iron or fold clothes. Blind to the problems I was creating for myself, I knew only that with working, cleaning, cooking, helping with homework, ferrying kids, meeting with teachers, managing finances, and shopping for necessities, I hardly had time to breathe. My friends didn't get it. The single, childless ones hadn't a clue how it felt, never having a second to yourself. Those with husbands had someone to step up when they ran out of juice.

For weeks after my move to Maryland, Kevin would arrive after work, plop on the couch, and read the paper—while I supervised homework, did chores, and cooked, often still in high heels. Noting the absurdity of my Donna-Reed-in-blackface routine, I started asking Kevin to help out. He did. But whenever my do-it-all nature kicked in, he went along with that, too.

Perhaps he felt he already had his hands full. He'd never courted a full-time mom, let alone taken on an entire family. Dating me meant being involved in three relationships, not one. The dynamic was tricky for me, too. Months after Kevin and I became physically intimate, I was reluctant to let him stay over. Several nights a week, Kevin left late, exhausted. Finally I sat Mani down to discuss it.

"You really like Kevin, don't you?" I began. Mani nodded solemnly. "Well, Mommy likes him a lot too. How would you feel about him, um, spending the night?" Mani's eyes became huge.

"*Could* he?" he blurted. Off he rushed, yelling to Darrell one of childhood's magic words: *"Sleepover!"*

If only everything were so easy. As the months passed, Kevin drew ever closer to the boys and me. Yet three years after we'd met, I realized that he'd said nothing about making things permanent. Had I been wrong in my instant certainty about him? Kevin was in his midthirties; maybe he was one of those guys who'd never pull the trigger on marriage—or on taking on a ready-made family. Or was it that he loved my kids but was unsure about me? Discussing my concerns, Kev and I weighed whether we should date others or take a brief hiatus.

About this time, Kevin was assigned to an out-of-town story, leaving me dateless for a major political banquet. I was considering staying home when a fellow journalist—a thoughtful, attractive brother I didn't know well—offered me a lift. Unwilling to pass up the chance to trade my customary harried-mom sweats for a formal gown, I accepted. The day of the banquet, I dutifully bought a ticket at a school raffle— and won a $600 pearl necklace. My first thought: "It'll be perfect with my strapless dress!"

The night, too, held surprises—especially my increasing interest in my escort. It had been three years since I'd been drawn to a man other than Kevin, yet there was no denying our attraction. My date, too, was in a relationship that seemed stuck. Feeling I shouldn't, I invited him in when he dropped me at home. Feeling I *really* shouldn't, I let him kiss me—and kissed him back. I'd experienced this instantaneous connection only a few times—the last being when I met the man whose inability to commit was more bothersome every day. What was happening seemed as fated as winning the necklace. Was I supposed to be with this guy?

Bidding this perplexing new love interest good night, I went to bed. The following day, my new flame phoned. When I explained my plan to tell Kevin everything, he paused. "Maybe you should wait," he said. "See where things lead." His girlfriend would be visiting soon, he said. "Maybe the four of us could go out."

Go out? So he and I could play footsie under the table while Kev and his girl exchanged pleasantries? The truth was glaring: I didn't know this man, and my irritation with Kevin made me place more importance on our attraction than it deserved. I wanted a commitment from Kevin, something more concrete than the attachment he showed each time he helped with homework, took the boys to ball games, bought dinner, and invited us to his mom's for holidays. My head was still spinning when I picked up Kevin from the airport. We headed to a party we'd planned to attend.

Guess who was standing on the stoop when we arrived? Wrapping me in a friendly hug, my new fling grabbed Kevin's palm for a "brother" handshake. This was too much. The party passed in a guilt-drenched whirl. The next day, Kevin and I were heading home after buying groceries when I told him everything. Face impassive, Kev slowed the car, his foot growing so heavy on the brake that he stopped in the middle of the street. Catching himself, he pulled into my driveway. We talked for a long time.

Incensed by my date's actions—especially the ten-minute "Hey, bro, what's up?" party chat—Kevin insisted he wasn't angry with me. The incident, he admitted, had brought a welcome new clarity to his feelings. He *did* have concerns about commitment; my flirtation showed what ignoring them could mean. I, too, was grateful for the slap-in-the-face reminder of the sexy-but-untrustworthy guys I'd had enough of. And of what I already had. Just like that, it was clear: We were both in this relationship for keeps.

Ghosts

*Left to right: Steve, Mom-Mommy, Donna, and Darrell
at the Gary train station, 1959.*

*A*wed, I cradled her in my hand — not, as I had envisioned, *in my arms. My daughter. The length of my little finger, she was rosy beige, like sand at sunrise. She had emerged lifeless from me after hours of cramping escalated into a labor that couldn't be. Yet she was perfect: Round black eyes. Blips for hands and feet. The bumpy curve of a spine curled in forever sleep. Four months after her conception, she had arrived, a "she," I knew, because I'd done the math: Mom-Mommy was twenty when she'd had her only daughter; my own mother was thirty. At forty, I held mine in my palm, the baby I'd longed to conceive so that my new husband could raise a child of his own blood. My heart had expanded when he'd told me he was hoping for a girl because "we already have two sons." Our daughter. Come and gone.*

On the September Saturday before my outdoor wedding to Kevin, rain exploded from heaven like tears from a tantrum-throwing child. Rehearsing between cloudbursts at the river-front mansion where we'd scheduled our outdoor nuptials, bridal party members walked their paces in soaked-through shoes. With more torrents forecast for Sunday, we anticipated moving the nuptials inside the manse's peach-colored drawing room.

The next day dawned as hot and dry as toast. Gayle did my makeup, Kevin's sister Leisa cracked jokes, Mireille and Retha adjusted the gardenias in my hairdo, secured with enough hairpins to set off every airport alarm between Washington and Greece, our honeymoon destination. Malcah and Mary Jo buttoned and smoothed my lace dress. With its full Scarlett O'Hara skirt, it was exactly what Darrell, eight, had demanded after nixing a photo of the slim, sophisticated sheath I'd thought perfect for a second wedding. "You can't wear that," he said. "You're supposed to look like a fairy princess!"

During the ceremony Darrell and Mani, resplendent in tuxedos, joined Kevin and me on the mansion porch. After lighting four individual candles, we together lit a larger one that symbolized our new family. The gesture, the look on Kevin's face, the commitment we were celebrating—all were profoundly moving.

Most days, life itself was close to ideal. After years of being courted by the *Post*, Kevin had accepted a job covering Congress. I felt I was in heaven in "Style," writing serious features as well as profiles of celebs such as warm but wary Denzel Washington (who had turned down the interview until I sent him a searing piece I'd written about my brother Darrell) and Will Smith, twenty-two, the rapper-turned-star of the new TV show *The Fresh Prince of Bel-Air*. Mani and Darrell idolized Smith, so I arranged to bring them to the interview. The boyish star grabbed the plastic sword Darrell had with him and playfully chased assistants with it around his publicist's office.

Yet as satisfying as my work and home life were, there was always a nagging thought: *Remember, you felt safe and contented before Darrell died. You let yourself relax into happiness. Stay armed. Be ready for whatever awful thing could visit your boys, Kevin, you.* Meditating and reading spiritual books banished such Darrell-related musings, but never for long. Primed for tragedy in the midst of joy, I was haunted by the dearest of ghosts.

How could I have avoided it? Working for a newspaper made it impossible to ignore the awfulness that stalked the world, claiming both the unwitting and the prepared. But Darrell's death hadn't just devastated me; it had deepened me, sharpened my vision and my voice. Although I enjoyed writing features, I wondered: Should I be doing more? Would challenging myself somehow appease the specter that was never far from consciousness? That's when *Post* "Metro" editor Milton Coleman blew me out of my size eights by offering me my own column. Asked what I could write about, Coleman said, "Anything you want."

Anything I want? What reporter doesn't dream of hearing those words? A column would allow me to shed my objectivity, to explore whatever struck me. I'd written many first-person pieces in my career and several well-received essays at the *Post*, including the Pulitzer-nominated piece I'd used to persuade Denzel Washington that described what Darrell's death suggested about the value of black lives.

I'd arrived at the *Post* in January 1989 and found myself writing for a paper that drily reported the murders of fifty people in that one month, most of them black men killed in the drug wars that were decimating U.S. cities. Hardly anyone — at the newspaper, the grocery store, bustling down the street — seemed perturbed.

Darrell had made turning away from such carnage impossible. The men who were dying were real: flesh-and-blood fathers, sons, and brothers. How could I make them real for readers?

By making Darrell real for them. By putting flesh on my ghost, making the man I, too, would have dismissed as another nameless "Gary Man Shot by Police" real for them. I could describe his wit, his warmth, the quiet radiance that made him my hero. Excavating everything I'd buried, I reopened healed-over wounds, coaxed memories from the corners where I'd hidden them. My fourth article for the *Post*, the essay was the first substantive thing I'd written about the man slain twelve years earlier whose name I still couldn't say outside my family. Writing it rebroke my heart.

It was worth it. A deluge of calls and letters from readers suggested that I—that Darrell—had made them see the dying underneath their noses. Their responses gave me a sense of journalism's tremendous power. They also got Coleman's attention. So did my popular "Valentine for Black Men" (who else would I write one for?) on Valentine's Day 1990. Praising brothers' undervalued grace, impact, and import to the world and to me, the essay won the National Association of Black Journalists' commentary prize and inspired more than three hundred grateful phone calls, as well as roses from the president of a historically black men's college three years running. One call was from an executive who'd read it in his glass-walled office. He said his employees were pretending not to see the tears streaming down his face.

All my essays evoked powerful reader reactions. So why did Coleman's offer astonish me? Because I'd never expected *them*—the *Post*'s predominantly white power structure—to see my value, let alone reward it. The trust the offer represented humbled me.

Yet I was terrified I would fail. Like many African-Americans and more than a few women, I was more comfortable railing against the limits that racism and sexism had placed on others than acknowledging the beating my own spirit had taken from them. In America, sexism and racism are inescapable, as if nature excreted them into our water and air. No one is immune. Millions of women are secret sexists, harboring questions about women's ability to lead corporations, local municipalities, the U.S. government. Countless black folks decry white racism without acknowledging how totally they've absorbed it, how instinctively they suspect and demean their own people. Who among us rushes to admit how well we've learned to question our own worth?

And who rushes to be vilified? I knew that writing a column would inspire some readers to say nasty things, to send letters scrawled with personal beratings and racist slaps. Anonymity grants people a pseudo-courage that frees them to spew verbal assaults far more rank than anything they'd actually say. It would be "Be Dirty to Donna" all over again—multiplied by several hundred.

But even that prospect paled next to my most deep-seated fear, the real reason for hesitating: What if I just wasn't good enough?

I couldn't do it. Deciding to tell Coleman "no, thanks," I listed my reasons for Kevin. Looking at me as if I were crazy, he said, "But, Brittski, you were born to write a column!"

I accepted the offer.

Next I chose an editor, Jo-Ann Armao, feisty enough to ensure that I took Coleman at his word. Indeed, I wrote about everything: Black women's outsized booties. The dangerous meaning of the word "fine" when snapped by a fed-up female. My conviction that testosterone should be designated a controlled substance. Though I celebrated black culture, I also expressed the many ways it frustrated me. I was baffled by some sisters' tendency to defend seemingly any black man accused of a crime—think O. J. Simpson or Marion Barry—or of just being weird (Clarence Thomas's Coke can accusation by Anita Hill). It is the justice system's imperative to presume innocence until guilt is proved. But why was it so many sisters' imperative to assume that brothers—even those like Simpson, who had no interest in them—couldn't be culpable?

I wasn't surprised that my new column generated mail. What stunned me was the *type* of mail: warm, effusive, grateful. Yes, there were attacks, some blistering. But many readers appreciated my efforts to bring a new openness to the paper. In 1994, my column won several honors, including the prestigious

American Society of Newspaper Editors (ASNE) Distinguished Writing Award.

Basking in this approbation, I loved knowing it honored work that was often a tribute, a paean, a kiss blown to my brother. After that first, harrowing essay, I'd again tucked my most intimate memories of Darrell safely away. But I now had a twice-weekly opportunity to reveal to people—particularly to *white* people, some wielding power as policemen, politicians, and employers—black folks' humanity. What purpose was more sacred, since I felt certain that two such men's lack of understanding led to Darrell's death?

Fifteen years after he left me, I could still give to my brother.

In 1993, I became the reluctant owner of several pre–World War II treasures: a dainty lace cocktail glove, a pastel-tinted photo of a couple in 1930s dress, a gold watch with chains as delicate as new grass—all inherited from Mom-Mommy after her April 13 death.

I'd gotten the late-night phone call from my mother...on my birthday. Mom-Mommy, eighty-eight, had suffered a stroke. Mom had the flu, so I'd be representing us both when I made the two-and-a-half-hour drive to Media to be at my grandmother's side. A few years earlier, I'd gotten a similar call. Rushing to Media, I'd found Mom-Mommy laughing with nurses, the latest victims of her relentless charm, who tempted her with the hospital kitchen's delicacies.

This time was different. The woman who'd always seemed invincible lay still, eyes closed, her hair flat against her head. Most alarming was a pool of moisture in the corner of Mom-Mommy's mouth. If the most glamorous person I'd ever met could have spittle on her face, nothing in the world was solid.

The athletic teenager who'd hidden her forbidden pregnancy had become an award-winning saleswoman, society doyenne, and church pillar. Still sexy at sixty, Mom-Mommy in the next decade seamlessly morphed from hottie into adorable grandmother. The fact that she was personally protected by God was proved each time I got into her car. Driving with impunity in the wrong direction down Media's one-way streets, Mom-Mommy was unfazed by motorists' blaring horns. "Don't worry, darling," she'd cluck. "I always do this."

Dabbing her mouth in the hospital, I asked silent, desperate questions.

Why would you, the grandmother who'd always had special gifts for me, have a stroke on my birthday? Is my gift the privilege of reading spiritual texts to you as you doze? Sitting within whispering, hand-clasping distance as you heal? Learning that even wiping up spit can feel like a blessing? Or is it seeing what I never noticed before—how despite my penchant for giving, I've never given myself over so completely to love?

Mom-Mommy's stroke gave me a sliver of time between taking-for-granted and loss, a moment in which a love I'd thought pure was distilled into unimaginable clarity. I'd never realized how dangerous Darrell's death had made love seem to me. I hadn't stopped *feeling* love, but I had unknowingly constricted its expression, even with this beloved soul who'd never shown me anything but devotion. I feared telling any adults how much I loved them. What if it sparked revulsion, or caused my beloved to be snatched away?

Now, fearless and unashamed, I told Mom-Mommy, *"I love you so much. Come back. Let us care for you as you've cared for us. I love you. Come back."* The more I pleaded, the more she reacted, stirring, shifting, tightening her grip, until a nurse marveled, "Look at how she responds to you. I really think she's going to wake up." I prayed she would—yet at some point, my love overwhelmed my fear, filling me with a certainty that however Mom-Mommy left this sacred space, she'd be fine. Six days after the stroke, I was smoothing her hair when her breathing slowed. Feeling the tender throbbing in her neck go still, I whispered good-bye for my mother, my children, and my brothers, murmuring it was okay if she had to go. And I knew her gift to me: the honor of being with her at her parting. This time, I knew I wouldn't feel haunted.

The hardest thing would be telling the boys, who were as captivated by their great-grandmother as I had been at their age. Sitting my sons on the couch, I held their hands and said, "Guys, I have good news and bad news. The bad news is that Mom-Mommy died. The good news is she's in heaven, and that we were blessed to have had her so long." Mani just sat, blinking tears. Darrell, ever his opposite, burst into wails, screaming, "It *isn't* good, it *isn't* fair, and it *isn't* right!" I couldn't argue with him.

Besides, arguing with Darrell was useless. I'd learned that a year earlier when I put him and Mani on a plane to visit Greg and his parents. I'd looked forward to their annual St. Louis visit. My sons would be lovingly cared for; I'd get a needed break. Yet part of me hated seeing them go.

Driving to the airport, I cheerfully described the adventures and spoiling ahead of them. Darrell sat stone-faced. "I'm not leaving," he said, frightening in his calmness. At the airport, he announced his intention to strangers at the ticket counter. At the gate, he started crying; by boarding time, I had to carry him, bawling and struggling, onto the plane. Strapping in his thin body as he wriggled and sobbed, I felt my heart rip. I'd never been so needed, or so frightened by my own need.

So it's no wonder I was horrified by the approach of Mani's twelfth birthday in 1994. My son was nearly a black teenage male, a fact beside which all else—his affability, academic excellence, citizenship awards, and capacious knowledge of all things cinematic—was meaningless. Before he could open his mouth, people would condemn him. My slain brother had made it only too clear that Mani could be targeted by police, who detain, harass, assault, and "justifiably" kill black males—some culpable, many not. Any black man can tell you what mild-mannered Jeff, who's a slight five six, once said: "I've been stopped by the police at least a dozen times. And I have never committed a crime." Mani could also become a target of other kids, youngsters who pull a knife or a gun on another teen for an imagined slight, or for nothing at all.

Kids of every color feel their mothers' wary eyes on them as they hurtle toward their teens. Few black boys realize how regretfully their mothers track that trajectory. Staring at my eldest curled in sleep, I marveled, "Look at the space you take up!" while despising my terror of his lengthening form. I recalled the stranger who'd sat next to him several years earlier on his first solo plane trip. She'd phoned me at work to say, "Your son is so smart and self-possessed. I had to let you know." Awash in love, I thought, If people could know you, they could never hurt you. But women's children are hurt every day.

Like millions of black mothers haunted by their own ghosts, I made sure Mani knew the rules every African-American boy should know: Never be brash or make any fast moves with a cop. Never fight if you can walk away. Know that your manhood isn't defined by what's in your pants or on your back, but by the responsibility and self-respect in your heart.

Never do anything that could make someone take you away from me.

*   *   *

At some point, perhaps, I grew tired of worrying only about boys. Or maybe my need for an infusion of estrogen in our testosterone-soaked home got the best of me. I certainly believed that Kevin, a wonderful stepfather, deserved a child of his own, one that carried on his family's genes and traditions. Whatever my reasons, I became more and more certain my new husband and I would soon be expecting a daughter. It didn't entirely make sense: Marrying Kevin had ended the wearying mental and financial marathon of single motherhood. I could have chilled for a while, enjoyed our family.

But now that I was in a loving, supportive marriage, I wanted another child. By early 1994, I was pregnant, and certain I was carrying a girl. Exhibiting none of the exhaustion, yeasty scent, and constant nausea typical of my boy-producing pregnancies, I decided male fetuses were like occupying forces whose nine-month encampment caused upheaval in women's bodies. With this pregnancy, I felt energized. My stomach stayed settled. I smelled like *me*, as a woman carrying a female child should. I was so sure a girl was on the way that I bought a girly dress-up frock for her in shimmering navy, babylike and elegant all at once.

In my tenth week, I kissed Kevin good-bye as he drove off to play in a three-on-three hoops tournament in Richmond. Two hours later, I felt a twinge. And another. *Cramps.* An hour later I was curled on my bed in fetal position, praying, weeping, trying to meditate away my uterus's insistent clenching and my growing certainty that my daughter was arriving—and departing—too soon. "Don't leave," I pleaded, rubbing my belly. "Please, stay here with me." Two hours later she emerged, so perfect in her minuteness that I stared at her, bewitched. *Why didn't you let me be your mother?*

Driving myself to the hospital, I was examined by a kindly nurse who said there was no reason not to get pregnant again soon. She'd borne six children, she confided, yet had never forgotten one long-ago miscarriage. "No one knows why these things happen," she said, before adding, "We'd like to examine the fetus." I balked. "We want to make sure there's nothing that might cause this to happen again," she explained. Hesitantly, I handed over my daughter, whose tiny form I'd hurriedly placed in a sandwich bag. Instantly I regretted it. I should have buried her in some hallowed place. Not relinquished her to a stranger for having abandoned me.

But she was gone. Another ghost, another specter whose reason for leaving would be forever hidden from me. My daughter's first, last secret.

Women who miscarry are beset by apparitions. They're haunted by phantom moments that will never take place, cuddles forever unshared, the never-formed faces of the babies they've lost. Had I miscarried because my daughter had grave physical problems? Had I somehow repelled her? I recalled my friend Geri's comforting words after my abortion: Every baby chooses its parents, even the abusive, drug-addicted or tundra-souled mommies and daddies no child would seem to want. A flawed parent might be the perfect one to teach a soul its most needed lessons. A fetus might learn enough in three months to happily take its leave of the mother who rejects it. Was that my daughter's secret? That though my nostrils grieved at never tingling with her scent and my fingers at never braiding her hair, she'd gotten all she needed from me?

For weeks after the miscarriage, I felt demolished. Trying to forget, I did everything I'd done before in a daze—wrote columns, chased our dog, Silverado, fixed peanut butter and jelly lunches for Darrell five days a week. Puzzling over a charge on the cable bill for a movie titled *Booty on the House,* I was about to alert Comcast when, on a hunch, I showed the bill to Hamani.

"I'm so sorry, Mom!" he said, blanching. "I just wanted to see a black woman naked!"

I almost smiled. This is what you get with boys, I thought. How would my daughter have surprised me at age twelve? Giving birth to a girl would have taught me different lessons. It might have filled the emptiness I'd had since I'd yearned for a sister in childhood, and redressed a hurt as old as my betrayal in fifth grade by girls I'd thought of as friends. My daughter could have resurrected the joy I'd briefly felt at Helen Newberry, the joy of giving to *women,* whose need and validation and appreciation of me were so unlike those of the men I'd offered myself to. By now, I knew I was a caring and thoughtful mother. Hell, I was *good* at it. Was it my fate, my blessing, my curse, to always give the best I could offer...to men?

Resigned, I thought perhaps it was. Until one of the men to whom I'd given the most put everything in a whole new light.

Holes in the Heart

Darrell, Skye, and Hamani, 1997.

We all have our secrets: the hatreds we conceal, the loves we'd die before confessing, the particular way we touch ourselves for pleasure. Even minor secrets can be hard to admit: A decade passed before my son Darrell confessed to the trick he and his pal Jacob used in grade school to get out of class. Pulling blades of saw grass from clumps behind the school, each boy drew a spiny strand sharply across his palm, creating a wound much like a paper-cut: bloody enough to ensure an hour's freedom from class, but not so alarming that parents had to be alerted.

Some secrets' pleasures make their sting worthwhile. Other secrets just sting.

In 2002, I uncovered a secret whose holy-shit unbelievability was belied by the innocuous words that introduced it: *two years.*

In the months following my miscarriage in 1994, there was nothing secret about my despondency. Kevin penetrated it enough to convince me we should to put an end to equity-free home rentals and buy a house. Driving through unfamiliar neighborhoods, I felt myself come back to life as my real estate agent, Felicia, shuttled me from house to house. I'd started writing my column from home, so I was interested in a dwelling with a decent-sized office. Otherwise, we were searching for Kev's dream home: something new, low maintenance, and on a manageable piece of land.

So of course when Felicia showed me an old, high-maintenance house cresting two rolling acres, I fell in love. The fifty-year-old Cape Cod that Felicia called a "mini-estate" sat atop a leafy hill; its nooks and stonework were reminiscent of Mom-Mommy's Media home. Kevin needed convincing.

But two months later, we moved into our half-century-old "new" home in time for Kevin's birthday. Though exhausted, we celebrated well into the night.

Weeks later, I knew I was pregnant. This time, I was hideously nauseous, looked like hell, and smelled like a bakery at dawn. But I was in enough denial that when a staffer from the amniocentesis center informed me I was again having a boy, I blurted one word: "*Shit!*"

It was my first and last unwelcoming response to Skye, my youngest—and most imaginative, independent, and determined—child. After the loving pregnancy I had envisioned, Skye appeared, impressing visitors with his gorgeousness, calm, and skin so ivory he was barely distinguishable from the hospital's white infants, causing my editor Jo-Ann to blurt, "What fun is that? I see white babies all the time!" Skye's skin deepened to gold, but his calmness remained. Just one thing excited him: animals. Though it's rare for four-month-olds to sit up, the purplicious sight of Barney, PBS's dinosaur megastar, caused Skye nearly to levitate.

By age six, Skye was obsessed with everything critter-related, from plastic tyrannosaurs to the safari book he was describing to his pediatrician during a routine visit when she placed a stethoscope over his chest. "Mmmm, he has a murmur," Dr. Virgo said, almost to herself. I wasn't concerned. Heart murmurs, I'd read, aren't uncommon. People live long, healthy lives with them.

So I was stunned when the pediatric cardiologist Dr. Virgo referred us to informed us that Skye had an "atrial septal defect," a hole in the heart, requiring open-heart surgery. Symptoms could take years to develop, she said, but would progressively worsen. If you don't take care of this, another cardiologist said, the defect could eventually become life-threatening.

Excuse me? I wanted to ask. Skye couldn't have seemed

healthier. For months I put off the operation, praying, meditating, visualizing his healing. How could an invisible, symptomless "defect" threaten my lively little boy? But Kevin pressed forward, dragging me along until we found ourselves in a Johns Hopkins Medical Center waiting room, swathed in vomit green scrubs. With us was a balding cardiac surgeon whose soothing manner was at odds with the forms he presented to us describing our understanding that Skye could die during this operation. Eyes wide with disbelief, we signed.

Holding Skye on my lap, I watched him grow groggy after nurses administered his initial sedation. Gathering his son's limp body into his arms, Kevin cradled Skye for a long moment. Then he stood to surrender him to the medical team. Looking straight at the surgeon, he said, "I need you to have a great day today. The best day of your life." The doctor nodded as nurses wheeled Skye away.

Later, sitting in a waiting room surrounded by loved ones, I read Bible verses and assorted spiritual texts. Closing my eyes, I breathed, and was filled with so much pure, buoyant love that my heart, the sunlit room, the sedated child whose sternum was being cracked open down the hall, all fused into one overwhelming sense of okayness. For long stretches of Skye's four-hour operation, I wore the bemused half smile of one seriously submerged in Spirit, as calm as a mom could be under the circumstances.

In such states of perfect clarity, everything seems illuminated: The terror in your husband's hand as it grips yours. Friends' and relatives' forced cheer. The tension radiating from other tiny patients' parents. But when all you feel is love, some things are impossible even to suspect. Should I have noticed when my husband slipped away to phone a woman I'd never met? Updating her on our son's condition, on the status of their off-and-on union?

The hole in my son's heart was successfully repaired. A larger fissure would soon appear in my own.

How long is two years?

Far more, and less, than 730 days. It's the forever it took for the windswept cavern in my gut to begin filling after Darrell's death. It's the age at which my sons—once helpless, immobile baby-lumps—became talking, running individuals. A 2006 study says it's the time it takes for the body chemistries of two lovers to shift from producing hormones that spark white-hot lust to creating oxytocin, the "cuddle hormone" common in established couples. It's an interminable number of minutes, hours, and days for anyone keeping an explosive secret.

In December 2003, "two years" swept away everything I thought I knew about my husband and me. We were facing each other in a Cambridge, Massachusetts, hotel room. Kevin was propped on one elbow on the bed, his expression unreadable in the moonlight. We'd traveled to New England so I could address a gathering of journalists; afterward, we'd bantered with colleagues like we had a hundred times before.

Except this time, I knew my husband—my perfect black man—was seeing someone else.

I'd suspected something for weeks, mostly because Kevin couldn't fake an ardor he no longer felt. Though he participated in every family event, he seemed half-there where I was concerned.

Yet for months, I was clueless. Returning home from out-of-town trips, I'd find a pleasant but unengaged mate who exuded none of the sizzle that had linked us for more than a decade. Each time I asked if there was anything he wanted to tell me, he said, "No." When I added, "If there is, it would be *better* to tell me," he insisted there was nothing to reveal.

Believing an untruthful spouse means doubting yourself. It means speculating about whether the coolness that has crept between you was inevitable, whether it's natural for the passion that united you to downgrade from a boil to a simmer to a remembered glow. It's asking if *you're* crazy, feeling the ground roil beneath you when everyone swears it's solid. Countless confident women have been shaken by their mates' insistence there was something wrong with *them* for daring to suspect them. One such wife brought a camera to the hotel where her husband was trysting with his mistress. Pretending to be room service, she burst in when he cracked open the door, snapping pictures as the guilty couple leapt into their clothes. Photos were the only proof, she explained, that would prevent him from later denying what her eyes had seen.

Kevin's natural discretion and concern about the consequences had made him extremely careful not to be found out. But finally, a name was whispered to me of a woman I'd never met. I kept the name to myself, even on the day before the Cambridge trip when I sat my husband down, clasped his hand, and said please, *please* tell me: Something's going on. *Just give me that.*

"I don't know what you're talking about," he said.

In our hotel room, Kevin had kissed me and dozed off. Beside him, I sat tensed, like a runner poised to hear the pistol shot that would release her. Incapable of sleeping another night next to a body whose inhabitant's attention had wandered away, I shook him awake and said the name. "Tell me about *her.*"

He stared at me for what felt like ten minutes before saying, "Okay." Yes, he was seeing her. It was a relief, he said, to admit it.

When I asked if he loved her, he responded, "What's love?"

What's love? For the first time, I knew I was in oh-my-God trouble. Nothing, I felt, could be worse...until I asked how long this had been going on. When Kevin said, "Two years, on and off," my gasp was a thunderclap. It wasn't possible. Not from the man whose integrity was among my life's building blocks. He couldn't have deceived and misled me, wrapped his generous heart around someone else for *two years*.

The man in my bed had done that. So I asked him, "Who *are* you?"

He stared at me. I stared back, *two years* looping around my brain. The room tilted.

Seated by a stranger in that hushed, still space, I waited: For the room to right itself. To be consumed by enough deafening *what the fuck* rage to hurl books, overturn lamps, scream like someone being ripped into a thousand splintering pieces. Yet my shock was so paralyzing, I couldn't have toppled a matchstick.

Somehow I rose. Making my way to the bathroom, I slid inside and shut the door. Lowering myself into the dry white tub, I squeezed my hand over my mouth so Kevin wouldn't hear my hot, wet disbelief. Silently I sobbed until "two years" was replaced by a certainty:

My marriage is over.

Crouched in the tub with my dead marriage, I asked myself the customary questions: *Had I been blind? Is this what giving your complete trust to a man gets you?*

Was I warned?

I remembered a fierce argument a few years earlier. We'd been tearing into each other over a long-divisive subject: my desire to be courted the way women in books and movies are wooed. Fictional guys find a thousand creative ways to demonstrate true love: Impulsively gathered wildflowers. Boom boxes held aloft in the rain. Banjos and balloons outside Macy's.

Kevin was actually adept at loving gestures. His romantic greeting cards featured messages of soaring poetry; he remembered birthdays and anniversaries with gifts so thoughtful—tiny metal hearts in a bejeweled box, diamond earrings, surprise trips to B & Bs—that I felt enfolded in his love. I just wanted more of that feeling between special occasions.

I knew I'd married a real guy, not a movie character. That it was my rare luck to have a husband who hardly ever asked *me* to be more. But he'd married a woman who couldn't overhear his vaguest complaint about needing sweat socks—or a warm hoodie or a nicer trench coat—without supplying what he hadn't really requested. I bought tickets to hear his favorite jazz musicians, foraged stores for the perfect wineglasses (I barely drank), and offered full-body massages when he was stressed. When Kevin got his first book contract, I surprised him by clearing our junk-strewn basement and buying furniture for a home office. He never asked for these things, sometimes even said, "You don't have to do so much." But I couldn't stop supplying the gifts I longed to receive.

I was, it seemed, addicted to giving—and to getting back. My compulsion wasn't healthy, but where's the 12-step program for over-giving? Kevin seldom refused my gifts. Yet they came at a cost.

Giving as relentlessly as I did without receiving in kind left me empty in places I expected my perfect husband to fill. So I did what ravenous wives often do: Warned my mate of the risk in ignoring my emptiness. What if another man tried to fill it? At times I grew stingy, withholding my smile, my warmth, my affection. Hoping to sharpen his desire, I pushed him away further.

My simmering dissatisfaction became as unbearable to

Kevin as my hollowness was to me. Resentment bled into every part of our relationship. During one of my soliloquies about how much sexier things would be if he acknowledged me more, Kevin exploded. Between me, bills, needy kids, a leaking roof, college tuitions, job obligations, and the pressure he felt to be everything to everyone, he wanted "something— just one thing—to be easy!"

The word resounded like a slap. "Easy" haunted and enticed me, too. I knew what it promised: More fun. Less stress. Time to think, read books, make love…slowly. Like me, Kevin wanted a break. And I recognized: Of all the words I'd heard used to describe me, "easy" wasn't among them. I *understood*.

Then anger—at the fury contorting his face, at how he'd gotten me to feel *his* pain without empathizing with mine— swept it away. "Why should things be easy for *you* when nothing is for me?" I'd yelled, knowing it was futile. What gnawed at me seemed so slippery, so undefined, so *female,* he'd never understand. I remembered a recent revelation about an unlikely scourge:

Lint.

Lint is the blackfolk of household annoyances: People unwisely ignore it until it clogs their machine…or ignites a fire. Every week, millions of women and a few good men rout this gray plague from their dryers' mesh traps. Unlike the action-packed, highly visible tasks that men prefer—snow shoveling, lawn mowing—lint removal aptly symbolizes "women's work." Tackled in basements without cheering witnesses, it just has to be done.

My revelation had been inspired by a clot of Superlint, lodged deep in the downstairs washbasin. Wash load by wash load, this unholy alliance of dirt, loose threads, and sweater pillage had narrowed the path through which spent water flowed until the morning I found the sink stopped up. For five seconds, I regarded the sink-swamp with pure hatred. Then I inhaled—*who else is going to do this?*—and lowered my arm into the icy dankness. Feeling my way to the drain cover, I inserted a finger and extracted a slimy, burr-sized mass. *Gross.* Wiping it on a paper towel, I kept diving, extracting, wiping, as water drained out. Then, maneuvering tweezers into the cover, I withdrew the last loathsome remnants.

Staring at my hideous slime collection, I felt the full futility of millions of women's lives—and my own. Born at a time when we can do anything—drive buses, racecars, and election campaigns; conduct symphonies and national diplomacy; run schools, corporations, and governments; write soaring words and music—we're still life's lint pickers.

It didn't matter how talented or astute I was, how evocative my prose or trenchant my insights. The lioness's share of my household's soul-deadening chores fell to me. Like other women, I did them while juggling family schedules, school-work and meetings, preparing meals, laundering, grocery buying, supervising repairs, mailing birthday-holiday-sympathy cards, and a zillion other tasks about which we ask: *Who else is going to do this?*

We do it—while trying to be available to our kids, sexy for our spouses, efficient at work, and this side of sane for ourselves. Not only does no one notice; griping about such "small" stuff makes *us* seem small. I was as smart and as gifted as my husband. Yet I'd come to see something as inconsequential as lint representing me.

Why not? What I most yearned for from Kevin wasn't tulip bouquets or romantic dinners, but to be *seen*—for the thousand tiny details I daily addressed for him, for my hourly sacrifices of time, talent, and self. For stuff like lint, that nobody gave a shit about.

Now, burrowing deeper into the hotel tub, I contemplated how brutal life was about to become. I envisioned the separation, the accusations—the *divorce*—awaiting me and the man who'd wanted easy. I thought of his lover, who'd never had to bother Kevin with stuff as unsexy as unpaid bills, kids' school problems, or his limited help around the house. She could be above such pettiness. Be easy.

Once upon a time, I'd been *easier*. But two years as the wife of an addict and eight more as the single mom of small kids had drained me of simplicity. Doing it all had been unavoidable; by the time Kevin appeared, my pattern had hardened into cement. Plus, I'd liked showing him how capable I was, how well I pleased my kids, my bosses, and readers. Like many women, I was sending a message: *imagine how well I'll take care of you!*

But who would be taking care of me?

I hadn't asked because for years, I'd done it myself. Besides, Kevin loved me. He'd fill that role.

Now I needed to know what role the stranger on the bed wanted to fill. Emerging from the bathroom, I felt my husband's gaze on me more intently than I had in months. For ten years, we'd zoomed past each other, always there, always right under each other's noses. Yet he'd stopped seeing me.

Now he couldn't look away.

I did what journalists do: asked questions. Now that I knew the "who" of the story, I needed the what, when, where, and especially the why. Some spouses forbid their mates to speak of their lovers. Please. A woman I'd never met had willfully taken what was mine. She'd read my columns, knowing my assumptions about my kids' security and husband's devotion to be false. Finding out more about her would disempower this stranger who'd turned me into something I'd never thought possible: The victimized wife. The misguided wren with no idea her man "just isn't into her."

For decades I'd seen myself as powerful and confident with men. Suddenly I was in a 1950s melodrama in which a stranger had usurped the fun, bombshell role and handed me the part of the clueless matron. I was so retro, I actually wondered: What kind of woman pursues another woman's husband? In the '50s, such interlopers were portrayed as pathetic sluts. On TV and in movies today, some single women pursue married men with a single-mindedness that's almost sport: cool, hip, so *Sex in the City*.

Some things, thank God, don't change. Once the affair was discovered, Kevin made it clear he had no desire to lose me, or his family. "Whatever you decide, I'll abide by it," he said, before adding what I longed to hear: "But I hope you'll forgive me." He would end things with her the moment we got home. I told him to visit her once more, to tell her to her face that he loved *me*. After that, he'd never see her again. If he couldn't tell her that, *mean* that, "just stay there," I said. He agreed.

Eyes still on me, he waited. So far, so good.

I had to know more. For hours and then days, I asked every question I could conjure: *How did you meet, when did it start, how often did you see her, where did you hook up, what did you tell her about me, who else knows, how could you, how could you, HOW COULD YOU?* Kevin, glad to be telling the truth again, answered every one, even those whose responses made him look worse. When I was out of questions, I said we could stay together if he joined me in marriage counseling. Then we would see.

I couldn't tell him the truth. As lacerated as I felt, I loved him—his affability, his intelligence, his warmth, his unwavering commitment to our kids. Nothing, not the hugeness of his mistake, not the incomprehensibility of his lies, not even *two years*, could wipe away what I knew him to be. For fifteen years, he'd seeped inside me. I couldn't just unmingle us. Night after night, I lay next to him, my pain so palpable that it woke him like a shake. Wrapping me in his arms at three a.m., he asked, "You want to talk about it?", listening when I did. I didn't want to lose him.

Our between—the space where we'd overlapped—was too large to abandon.

In the next few weeks, I effortlessly lost ten pounds. Even when Darrell had died, I'd been able to eat; for the first time, food held no beguilement. Kevin repeatedly took my emotional temperature, endlessly asking, "Are you okay?" and saying "I'm sorry" more.

Like countless men and women whose infidelity has been discovered, he seemed like someone shaken out of a dream. The undefined shape of the consequences of his actions had become wincingly clear; it was the difference between seeing a car crash in a movie and actually being in one. He wasn't just sorry. He saw himself through my eyes and the world's, and it shocked him.

As my own shock receded, I knew that I'd sustained psychic scars that might never fade. As a grown woman, I thought I understood the realities grown-ups accept because living requires it. And although some childhood dreams can't pass the tests adulthood administers, my girlish romanticism—my secret belief in dragon-slaying knights—had never faltered. It had withstood blackness (Negro girls aren't supposed to believe in fairy tales), breakups, and even divorce before being rewarded with a prince. This dream's collapse felt like a death.

As long as I lived, it would rankle, knowing my husband and this stranger shared private jokes, tender moments, a carnal connection whose depth and tenor I would never know. This interloper was still *out there,* possessing, perhaps cherishing, an intimate knowledge I'd thought was mine alone.

Yet what infuriated me most was all that my husband had accepted from *me* during his dalliance. I cursed every pan I'd baked of his favorite lasagna, every shirt washed, each I'm-tired-but-let's-go-for-it intimacy. I wanted them all back, every ounce of exertion squandered on a man who could have saved me the time and effort by telling me the truth.

Why hadn't he told me? Fear of losing his family? Of losing me? Or was a hidden affair "a male rite of passage," as my friend Connie put it? "So many guys do it," she explained, each one creating an agony whose toxic residue reminds her of the torture suffered by a friend of hers who years ago killed a stranger while driving drunk. "Who hasn't had too much to drink and driven home?" Connie asked. "I know I have. But until I saw what she goes through, I had no idea of the pain it could cause.

"An affair is like that," she said. "You think it's a game, but you're hurting your life. And you can never take it back."

Never. I reared back when Connie uttered it, the only thought as brutal as *two years.* What if I never recovered, never understood, never got the room to untilt? "Never" was why I was glad to settle with Kevin onto the comfortable couch of a highly recommended marriage therapist. Maybe I'd find freedom from the rage, the questions, the inescapable him-with-her images.

Maybe I'd come to accept that even princes can have dragons within that need slaying. Maybe, if I sat with my hands folded decorously in my lap on that somber-hued couch, I could express my outrage without screaming.

Maybe we'd find some way to survive this.

Visible

Kevin and Donna, 2011.

A few years after I started writing my column from home, I heard wonderful news: My friend and Post *colleague DeNeen Brown had won the ASNE feature-writing award. One of the most prestigious in print journalism, it's an honor I'd been thrilled to win myself. Excited that a friend—and another black woman—had also won it, I drove downtown to cheer her. In his congratulatory speech before gathered employees, executive editor Len Downie told the assemblage that DeNeen had joined a select circle of previous* Post *winners. He named several—all of them white men. Though I'd made a special trip to be there and stood just a few feet from him, Downie didn't mention me. Working at home, miles from my coworkers, had made me invisible.*

Later, pondering whether I should have said something to my boss, I had to laugh as I wondered: Would a man who hadn't seen me standing right in front of him have heard me?

Even when things are god-awful in a relationship, some memories are too sweet for banishment. Like those of the night I met Kevin. After losing and finding each other on the riverboat, we'd spent an hour talking on the waterfront before moving our conversation to a half-dozen nooks in the convention hotel. Hours later, still grooving to the romantic-comedy vibe that inspired me to tell Kevin, *"Find me,"* I cocked my head and said, "Tell me a secret."

Pausing long enough for me to wonder if I'd struck a wrong note, Kevin began. Days ago he'd attended a relative's funeral. As he wandered into his beloved kinsman's bedroom after the service, his eyes had landed on a hairbrush that had belonged to the departed. Taking the brush in his hands, hefting it, Kevin found himself studying it. Suddenly, he *saw* it—how clearly it evoked the man who had for years touched it, used it, become part of it. And after days of holding himself together, he'd finally let go of his grief.

I was undone. This undeniably cool brother could have told me anything, yet had shared something so unguarded, I felt he'd seen *me,* someone who'd appreciate the instant's import. At that moment, I knew Kevin would be a vital part of my life.

In our therapist's office, I thought back to that first secret, and to the scores of secrets we'd shared, and failed to share, since. Just as I'd hoped, it *was* satisfying, sitting on the safety of that couch and sharing my confusion and rage and pain—until the man whose actions brought us to it started describing how angry and inadequate my resentment and expectations had made *him* feel.

I froze. Being betrayed by the man for whom I'd done everything wasn't enough. Now I was supposed to listen to how *I'd* fucked up? Gripping the sofa, thinking, Screw this, I felt my legs tense to lift me, my mouth prepare to say I'd had it with this bullshit. Who would blame me?

Remembering all that was at stake, I kept my seat.

Everyone wants to be seen. Who knew that better than me, the invisible lint picker? Yet I'd had no idea of my own blindness, of how often Kevin had felt transparent, as unappreciated by me as I was by him. The longer I listened to him, the more I saw myself through his eyes: as someone who envisioned herself as a perfect martyr, not as a flawed human being whose bitterness had made her incapable of seeing him and all he'd offered me.

I saw how maddening it had been, hearing about his supposed ingratitude when he had for years given me compliments, cards, presents, praise for my beauty, and loving criticism of my work. Yet "none of it matters," he said. "I don't get any credit for it." He'd given me weekend trips, surprise gifts, dinners out, countless hugs and kisses, and it wasn't enough. My resentment had been so palpable that he, the most confident of men, began to feel he could never make me happy. Resentment—along with the demands of a ready-made family, a new baby, mounting debt, and a challenging career—had ripened him for a no-strings offer of sex from a woman who claimed only to want a good time. Maybe, he'd told himself, I was screwing around, too. *Hadn't she said she could be tempted?* Increasingly, Kevin continued, he felt "smothered," with no free time to see friends, have an after-hours drink, or just breathe. It seemed that he had to ask permission to do anything on his own, and that I greeted every request with a groan.

I squirmed when Kevin raised a tendency that my friend Jeff years ago dubbed my "rather-be-right-than-have-a-million-dollars" mind-set. My much-criticized husband insisted that I hated admitting I was wrong—about anything. Too often when I could have admitted a mistake or apologized, I explained the reasoning behind my actions, a sensible response that inevitably muted my regret. Sometimes, he said, people just need to hear "I'm sorry."

What a frustrating pain it had been for him: a live-and-let-live guy wheedled and harangued by a trying-to-be-perfect-and-so-should-you girl who seemed blind to her own imperfections.

Let me be clear: Nothing Kevin said on that couch excused his infidelity. Nothing blotted out my rage and disappointment at his deception. Yet hearing what had pushed him toward it was as enlightening as it was disconcerting. Most unexpected—and frankly astonishing—was how tormenting the dalliance had been for *him*. Yes, he'd had fun, enjoyed feeling desired and admired. But for two years, Kevin had betrayed his view of himself as one of the good, straight-up brothers who do the right thing. His unequivocal shame over his disloyalty to me and to himself couldn't be faked. I found myself believing something I never could have suspected: Throughout the affair, he'd been tormented by all he was forsaking—hence its on-and-off quality. I'd assumed it was a nonstop frolic.

Hearing what my husband felt was almost as illuminating as uncovering unexpected truths about myself. I considered how being the child of a needy, abandoned mother and a silent, withdrawn father had sharpened my craving for acknowledgment, how being my brothers' sister, Greg's wife, and a single mother had exacerbated my inborn giving impulse. Exploring the affair forced me to explore my feelings toward *everyone* who hadn't given—or hadn't known how to give—as much as I easily offered.

The problem was more than the imbalance. Part of my despair, I think now, was rooted in my brother. Once again, I had unwittingly allowed distance to creep between me and a man I loved. Again, I was being punished with the death of something irreplaceable.

I had so many frustrations to share on that couch: My certainty that Kevin was dismissive of the difficulty of working at home while managing a household and family. My suspicion that like most accomplished men, he was on some level uneasy with a woman who was his match. My disbelief that anyone as honorable as Kevin would have an affair at all. And that there was no magic wand anyone could wave to make it disappear.

I wanted my old life back. I wanted to be able to go to a party, restaurant, or grocery store without wondering if *she* might be there. I wanted to hear him say he was going for drinks after work or to shoot hoops with friends and not think: *Really?* I wanted to feel I wasn't living some enabling lie that made our lives together look normal—look easy—when the reality was so painful.

I couldn't shake a feeling: As apologetic and candid as Kevin was being, some part of him couldn't accept how deeply he'd hurt me. He'd apologized profusely, joined me in therapy's torture, done everything I asked. Why, he seemed to wonder, wasn't I getting over it?

It had taken months to absorb that the unimaginable hadn't just happened, but had happened over two years. Once I believed it, the real anguish—my deepest rage and most piercing recriminations—began. Get *over* it? I'd just started feeling this fresh agony, this new infusion of ungovernable emotions that ricocheted from acrimony to affection to indignation. Now that I no longer feared losing my husband, I could wonder, "Why am I holding onto him?"

A primal reaction to an internal struggle, an affair unleashes equally primal urges in its victims. When a spouse crosses that line, it can be natural for the betrayed to be consumed by thoughts of revenge. I know I was. What better way to make Kevin understand my agony than by having my own affair? Let *him* imagine someone else's roaming hands and mouth on his spouse. I feared no repercussions; the infidelity had given me a get-out-of-jail-free card. Mentally I auditioned a dozen candidates—ex-beaus, *his* friends, strangers who flirted on the street.

Fate lent me a hand. Two old boyfriends whom I hadn't heard from in years got in touch. Out of the blue. Like it was meant to be.

Joe, a former Stanford tennis player whom I'd dated when he spent a semester at Hampton, was a strikingly handsome attorney who called out of nowhere to "reconnect." When he mentioned he was still single and searching for love, I thought, *Hmmm.* When he said he'd spent several years teaching yoga—

which I'd begun teaching at a local gym—I smiled. When he said he was living in Philadelphia—the city where Mani was studying after having transferred to Temple University—I laughed out loud. I was already planning to visit Mani; Joe and I scheduled dinner.

Joe was the only man I'd dated more devoted to inspirational chats, books, and lectures than I. Unencumbered by a wife or kids, Joe spent most of his free time and income on spiritual workshops, retreats, and studying with various masters; his insight and openheartedness reflected it. In phone calls before our dinner, we discussed the affair. Gently, he helped me explore how I felt, what I might do.

Meeting at a hip Philly eatery, we had a fun, wide-ranging exchange about our lives and work. Later on the phone, Joe confessed he expected to find me bedraggled from my situation. "But in fact, you were quite sexy," he said. Asked if I'd like to get together closer to my home, I said yes, though I was unsure exactly for what. Just before our meeting, Joe—who's spiritual but still a man—clarified things by asking, "So are you feeling...naughty?" I thought about it. Confused, hurt, vengeful? Yes. Naughty? Not so much. Meeting didn't seem the best idea.

Hoping to get my head on straight, I scheduled a trip to my favorite retreat: Rancho La Puerta, a magical Baja California fitness spa near San Diego. Days before my departure, Tony—another ex-beau, this one from grad school—called from out of nowhere. He, too, was headed to San Diego, he said. Could we meet at the spa?

What, I wondered, was God up to?

One of the funniest people I've met, Tony was also a lifelong truth seeker; our discussions about race, gender, and culture had always been electrifying. Smarting from having recently left his own contentious marriage, he, too, was a great sounding board.

Because we'd dated much longer than Joe and I had, Tony seemed more of a threat. *But to what?* I asked myself. A marriage my husband hardly considered while screwing his girlfriend?

Over a scrumptious vegetarian meal, Tony and I reminisced, guffawed, commiserated. Back at my room, I lit a blaze for us in the stone fireplace. Motown ballads floated from the CD player.

On a sofa warmed by the flames, we talked about our marriages, our disillusionment, our pain. Tony stretched out, opening his arms; I sank into them. We said soft, comforting words to each other. We fell asleep. A week later, Tony called and said, "Nothing happened, but that was the most romantic night I've had in years." For me, that solace-filled evening held a lesson: As attractive as Tony and Joe were, I didn't want an affair. I wanted my husband. I wanted my marriage back, untainted.

Impossible. But the only path that would get me anywhere close was forgiveness.

A fact: Some people believe adultery should never be forgiven. They wonder why, when I rose from that tub, I didn't collect my bags, get on the first thing smoking, and immediately start divorce proceedings. In their screw-him-if-he-screws-her world, a betrayed wife who works to save her marriage is a fool. Infidelity can't be tolerated, and forgiveness is tolerance in spiritual packaging.

I marvel at these folks' conviction, but I'd never thought of infidelity as a deal killer. My vanity and idealism prevented me from envisioning any man betraying *me*, but I'd noted countless times how sexual desire inspires people — especially people with penises — to do self-defeating things. If humans could remove the overwhelming need for sex from their repertoire, divorces—as well as "What was (s)he thinking?" scandals— would plummet. More than half of married men (some estimates say 70 percent) stray. I was twelve when I saw the film version of William Inge's *Picnic* on TV. One line hit me like a punch: "You don't love someone because he's perfect."

Decades later, I'd be living proof. As someone who loved her husband and had always judged adultery on a case-by-case basis, I decided in my case to try to learn from it. I wasn't ready to unload a man who'd done so much right for one spectacular wrong—no matter who felt it was the smart move.

Besides, I knew myself to be generous, compassionate, and spiritual. My spouse was repentant, my marriage worth saving.

How hard could forgiving my husband be?

Americans, I soon realized, aren't crazy about forgiveness.

In our public and private lives, those who forgive are dismissed as naive; the forgiven are thought to have gotten away with something. We excoriate officials who utter the racist or sexist beliefs millions of us harbor, and demand resignations from unfortunates caught in sexual situations in which millions more participate. Wives of famous cheats are denounced when their husband's cheating doesn't immediately spur them to kick him to the curb.

That's a lot of unforgiveness for a nation in which 75 percent of citizens say they're Christians, and whose savior forgave those who shouted for his killing. The truth: We all slip, and badly. Forgiveness is a clear-eyed nod to our shared, inevitable brokenness. What offers more opportunity for it than an institution in which two flawed, unknowable people swear to persevere "for better or for worse"? Do we truly expect to encounter only the better?

Damn right we do.

Forgiving when you've been hurt to your marrow is the most arduous of spiritual directives. Considering all that it *won't* do, forgiveness hardly seems worth it.

Pardoning a partner doesn't mean you'll never again suspect him. It doesn't mean you won't catch yourself staring into space as your memory runs high-def replays of his every lie. It won't save you from wondering if you're foolish *for* forgiving, nor make his lover (so familiar to your spouse, so mysterious to you) disappear or share the agony she helped create. Forgiveness doesn't mean that molten *where's-my-fucking-gun?* rage never has you in its grip.

Forgiveness wouldn't obliterate Kevin's knowledge of what *he'd* lost, but couldn't acknowledge, by leaving his lover: the sex, the sweetness of the forbidden, the delicious illusion of one complexity-free relationship. On some level, he'd known it was a fantasy. But fantasies are fun. Marriage—with its ongoing *who-left-on-the-lights, what's-wrong-with-the-baby, where's-the-flashlight, why'd-you-look-at-me-like-that, did-you-move-my-gloves, wait-you-said-WHAT?, who-scolded-disrespected-insulted-raised-a-disbelieving-eyebrow-first* din—seems anything but.

Marriage is back- and heart-breaking work. Yet some days, the sacredness of what Kevin and I hoped to save inspired a gratitude so boundless that I wished *her* well, hoped she'd found happiness after threatening mine. Other days, I felt so weary from pulling myself out of my seething cauldron of misery, I envisioned her dead—or at least trapped in some sunless, faraway galaxy.

Forgiveness. Lost in prayer, I longed to welcome it, to absorb it like the only salve offering release. Then my brain would shout, "No!" Forgiveness was the smirking enemy who'd whisper to Kevin, "She's *over* it, man. You won." And I wanted no part of it.

I knew I wasn't one of those practical women who tolerates a man she despises for the sake of her kids or her budget. Kevin was my *husband;* I wanted to trust him again, absolutely.

But I'd already given him so much—starting with his life, according to the friend who kept half jokingly reminding me, "You could have shot him." I'd let him remain in his home with his family. I'd listened as he expressed his frustrations, even when it meant choking on mine. I'd handled this horror with as much grace as I could muster. Would forgiving finally be giving too much?

Or would I finally be offering the only thing that mattered?

The situation seemed simple. I wanted to forgive my husband. To keep my family and my sanity intact, I *needed* to forgive him. Yet the part of Kevin that had trouble accepting my bottomless grief inflamed the part of me that couldn't absolve him. We were stuck. To get unstuck, we would have to go deeper. For the tenth, the twentieth, the hundredth hellish time, our therapist had us repeat—with feeling and without judgment—each other's views about our relationship, however harsh or tender. Weeks of repeating each other's words, *owning* each other's feelings, began to paralyze our defenses. As hard as it had been for me, the "blameless" wife, to acknowledge the unseen wounds I'd inflicted upon my husband, what Kevin had to do was more daunting: own something as cruel and ill-considered as an affair, and the fact that our marriage might never recover from it.

Sometimes, stepping outside one's basic moral code requires mentally pulling oneself apart. I remember at age six being at a supermarket with Mom, mesmerized by the shiny wrapping of a piece of candy she'd forbidden me. When she turned away, my fingers, seemingly unbidden, floated toward it. Only Mom's slap on my wrist snapped me out of it. I thought, Was that *my* hand?

Months before, I'd asked the adulterous stranger in my bed, "Who are you?" because the man I loved, trusted, *knew*, couldn't have maintained such a deception. Kevin knew it, too—that at his essence, he wasn't someone who'd turn his back on his wife, family, and so much he believed in to behave deceitfully. Accepting that he had done those things, and done them for so long, was torturous. It was like taking responsibility for the sins of a stranger.

Accepting the selfish, unthinking part of ourselves *as* ourselves is tough; few rush to embrace their darkness. But the more he accepted his actions as unforgivable, the more seriously I could consider forgiving them. I had no desire to be free of the man I still knew to be real: The father who'd unhesitatingly raised *all* my sons as his. The companion whose affability balanced my intensity. The writer whose pride in my talent was unmistakable. The husband whose eyes still followed me hungrily and whose words convinced me he found me ever more beautiful.

If I lost my marriage, I'd lose him. He was worth holding on to. And though I sensed myself inching closer to it, I still couldn't forgive my husband.

At my wit's end, I found guidance from two unexpected sources: Mom and the dictionary.

Observing the pain I was in, my mother made an astounding confession: at an especially bleak point in her marriage to Daddy, she'd had an affair. I sat speechless as she described falling in love with a coworker as open and affectionate as Daddy was not. For four years, she shared hidden interludes with him. Not once did she consider leaving my father or us.

She was only admitting this now, she said, to help me see "things happen that people don't plan." In hopes that I'd forgive Kevin for doing what she had done.

My heart melted at the courage and love that prompted her admission. And though Mom's words gave context to Kev's transgression, forgiveness still terrified me. Why was this worthy concept so forbidding? Looking up "forgive" in the *American Heritage Dictionary,* I found the challenging definition that taunted me: "1. To excuse for a fault or an offense; pardon. 2. To renounce anger or resentment against." None of which I could do.

More promising was the word's root: the Latin word *perdonare,* which means "to give completely, without reservation." When *perdonare* was adopted into the Germanic language that gave birth to English, "per" was supplanted by "for," a prefix in this case meaning "thoroughly," and *donare* was replaced by *giefan,* "to give." The resulting word—*forgiefan*—in Old English meant "to give up, allow" and (this seemed ironic) "to give in marriage."

According to the *Oxford English Dictionary,* the word "forgive" meant "to give" as late as AD 900. It was centuries before the meaning evolved into pardoning an offense and renouncing resentment. Amazing. In its earliest form, the word "forgive" not only meant to give, but to give thoroughly and unreservedly.

My specialty.

What if that was the meaning intended by mystics who'd exhorted followers to forgive? If, rather than instructing us to get over our disappointment, they were suggesting we offer our transgressors our best, despite their culpability? That was interesting—a forgiveness fueled less by my bitterness than by my behavior. I remembered trying to manipulate Kevin into being more loving by withholding affection—and making him colder. Being generous with my warmth had inspired similar warmth.

Now the warmth I needed to inspire was my own. I couldn't change or pardon my husband's actions. But I could govern my own. Forgiving in the form of giving I could try. Hell, I was already giving to Kevin again; his amazed gratitude touched me. Giving-as-forgiving meant I could stop second-guessing the generosity I couldn't quite stanch. Such absolution, I was learning, didn't just serve Kevin. Seeing him through a lens of suspicion and blame was depleting me.

So in the interest of *forgiving* my husband, I got more comfortable with *giving* to him, and by extension, to myself: His continued place in the center of our home. Apologies for the many ways I'd hurt him. My slowly unclenching heart. Sometimes I gave, no, hurled at, him stabbing words sharpened by the certainty that they couldn't hurt him as badly as his disloyalty had hurt me. And at other times, I offered him the grudging admission that every honest soul must acknowledge: even wonderful people do really messed-up things.

For five months, I joined him on that couch. Sometimes we sat shoulder to shoulder, fingers intertwined; other times we sat as stiff as planks on opposite ends. Until the unexpected morning after an unsatisfying session when we stood outside the therapist's office, inhaled the fresh, spring day, and realized: dredging up old stuff was making our time on that couch the least effective, the least loving, of our week.

Wrapping our arms around each other, we shared a lingering kiss. Kevin drove to work. I headed home. We kept going.

Without drumrolls or fanfare, we had our marriage back. Not the shiny new match we'd first forged, nor one of those cool-eyed take-it-for-the-team arrangements some couples negotiate. We had a *marriage,* as passionate and connected as the one we'd lost, and in some ways better. Knowing your partner's real selves is instructive. So is proving all that you can still be together if you do love's heavy lifting. We lifted.

Smashed in the tub on that ghastly night, I'd envisioned everything but this: that a year and a half later, Kevin's fingers would still reach for mine when a throng enclosed us, that his lips would find mine before he nestled into the next pillow. I couldn't have imagined still finding him the sexiest man at any party, or my ironclad certainty that he's still one of the good guys. That I could see him, and he could see me, and we could love each other more for the seeing.

Maybe we aren't that unusual. "Some of the best marriages I know of came out of affairs," author and family therapist Linda Carroll later told me. "An affair is like a death; a couple has to build their marriage from the ground up. So it's a new structure.... It's like the landscape after a forest fire; everything's destroyed and desolate. But give it time, and all these surprising things, flowers you've never seen before, can grow there."

When Kevin asked, "What's love?" in that moonlit hotel room, I was devastated. Yet I had no idea how little *I* knew of love's reach and elasticity.

Love, forgiveness taught me, isn't all lilt and rosebuds. It's as raw as meat, and as piercing as a knife wound. But if it lifts and heals you more than it plummets and destroys you, it's worth it. Worth it even when my mind wanders into the groove *two years* carved into it, even when I ask God why there wasn't a less onerous way to learn this:

Two flawed human beings who make a wedding's impossible promises—and who fight for their marriage after seeing the awful truth about each other—can win.

And at times, almost make it look easy.

Other People's Kids

Jason, 2004.

Sitting in the small, neat living room, I try not to flinch as recriminations—in Spanish and English—blow like confetti around my ears. The rage isn't directed at me. But so much bad blood is boiling, so many ancient angers stomping around the room, that I can't calm anything, even my wildly beating heart. I'd come to Jason's father's house to broker a peace: between the fed-up Dominican father who'd turned him out and the embittered, American-born son who was happy to leave. Each man, it's clear, feels abandoned. Each craves an invitation, a forgiveness, that isn't forthcoming. Jason's stepmother has her issues, too. Her tears are like oil, tossing the flames higher.

Classic black-family stuff, I thought. In Spanglish.

Jason was seventeen the first time I resolved to save him. Six years later, never learning my lesson where a black man is concerned, I tried again.

It hurts less when I remember I was only listening to God.

It was 1998, and our family had just returned from one of the out-of-town Hoop It Up basketball tournaments to which Kevin loved taking our boys. Jason was part of Mani's three-man crew. I'd first noticed him five years earlier, when Jason's unashamed tears at a grade-school graduation program had amazed me. Saying good-bye to a beloved teacher, Jason—the coolest kid in Mani's class—stood wet-faced and smiling. Only a *really* cool twelve-year-old could publicly embrace his tenderness in an era in which only the chilliest brothers were admired.

On this post–Hoop It Up night, I found the handsome teenager on our basement couch, exhausted from competing. Asked how he was, he whispered, "Not great." Pressed, Jason said he was considering leaving tenth grade. It was too hard, he explained, stocking shelves at his part-time job at CVS while trying to study in the cramped apartment he shared with his cousin, sixteen, her husband, and their two babies. He'd flunked four of his six classes. Neither of his divorced parents wanted him around. Working full-time made sense.

Sometimes, Jason admitted, death seemed better than his life.

I was stunned. Except for his occasional hotheadedness while playing hoops, Jason—the curly-haired son of a Dominican father and a Puerto Rican mother—had always presented an image of self-satisfied affability. In fourth grade, Mani had just gotten into a rare fistfight with his friend Loren when, out of nowhere, Jason had appeared. This small, confident kid Mani barely knew inserted himself between his and Loren's flailing arms. Putting each boy into a teasing headlock, he said, "C'mon," his tone suggesting, "You don't really want to fight." He pulled the battlers closer; kids hoping to witness a throwdown moved in, too. In the midst of this boy cluster, Mani and Loren discovered they *didn't* want to fight.

Soon afterward Jason attended a birthday party for Mani. Strolling up our tree-lined walk, this striking kid paused in front of our unremarkable three-bedroom home and announced, "Hamani, you live in a mansion!" I instantly liked him.

When Kevin and I moved with the kids to an even larger "mansion" (four bedrooms!) nearby, Jason joined Mani's hoops crew: hulking, Shaq-like Duke; intense Simon; thickset Carey; and tall, talented Robert. Kevin, a former high school basketball star, still lived for the game. Every summer, he and three friends played with fearsome intensity in street tournaments across the Northeast. Mani and Darrell each recruited pals in their age divisions; we transported the boys to Philly, New Jersey, and Delaware to play.

Brothers (& Me)

That night in the basement, I stared at a boy I'd known for years and traveled with to five cities. And I'd had no idea what his life was like. Later, I told Kevin, who was equally shocked. Not quite believing I was doing it, I asked Kev how he'd feel about asking Jason to live with us.

I fell even more in love with my husband when he replied, "I think we should." Because a more practical, less wonderful man would have responded, "As if."

As if we weren't already gasping for breath, keeping afloat two careers, a house, bills, parents, siblings, and sons ages fifteen, twelve, and two. As if we could easily afford feeding, housing, and clothing a fourth kid. As if it wasn't risky, inviting a seventeen-year-old whose peripatetic life had included drinking, drugs, sex, and license-free driving into our family. As if I, who worked at home, wasn't already smack in the tornado's eye. But I kept bumping into another "as if."

As if God—the ultimate Man to whom I wanted to give—wouldn't want us to try. At times I wondered if my need to give was my soul's response to God's biblical directive that we inspire and sustain our fellow man. Whatever the source of my *help him, reach out to her, give him a break, tell her something lovely about herself* impulse, I knew I would need Divine help on this one.

In some ways, opening our home to Jason made perfect sense. If ever an at-risk youth seemed perfect for rescuing, it was him. His past was complicated, but his present instincts couldn't have been more positive: he was bright, sensitive, quick to see and address the needs of others. Add good looks and a sweet disposition, and you had a youth whose potential was unlimited.

I first met with Jason's thirty-something mother, a pretty,

petite woman consumed with raising her adorable brood by her second husband. Her courtesy couldn't disguise her puzzlement: Why would we take in a child who had given her fits? Thanking me, she agreed Jason should live with us. At the start of the new school year, he moved in.

Kevin's and my first concern—that our streetwise charge would adversely influence our very suburban boys—proved unfounded. Jason honored our rules despite finding them "excessive." He stayed home on school nights, went to bed at prescribed hours, and informed us of his whereabouts on weekends. He joined our boys in homework sessions, happily babysat for Skye, and did more housework than either Mani or Darrell. Part of him had yearned for someone to keep tabs on him, to encourage him, to lovingly call him on his mistakes. Every day, Kev and I felt more like we had another son to advise and buy school supplies for, and with whom to discuss the future. Our kids chafed a bit at receiving less attention, but the nuts-and-bolts part of the arrangement was comparatively easy.

School was harder. It didn't take long to understand why Jason had considered dropping out. He had long ago decided academics were relevant only to natural brainiacs or the privileged; he'd shrugged off school and taken outside jobs. Now he was a full-time student. The first six months he lived with us, I spent more time meeting with his teachers than with Mani's and Darrell's combined. In one such meeting three months after Jason moved in, I expressed disappointment over the D+ he had earned in English. "But for Jason, a D-plus is a major *improvement*," the teacher explained. "When I told another teacher who'd taught him he'd made that, she couldn't believe it. It means he's working. And I'm sure he will do better." The instant fix I'd secretly hoped for wasn't forthcoming. But we were committed to giving him what he needed.

In fact, every family member benefited from Jason's presence. Jimmy, Mom's post-Daddy love, found Jason to be a helpmeet who, unlike my sons, knew his way around a toolbox. Jason had lived in homes where broken appliances were dismantled so they could be fixed. At the Britt-Merida abode, we called a repairman. A retired steel mill machinist, Jimmy (who at age eighteen was among the first black workers to integrate U.S. Steel's apprentice program) enjoyed repairing furniture and household appliances at our home. Jason loved assisting him, often anticipating which screwdriver or hammer Jimmy needed.

Mom was wary at first of this interloper, and of the incomprehensible gift we were offering a near stranger. She kept an observant eye on him for weeks before pronouncing him one of the least mean-spirited people she'd ever met. Jason called her "Grandma" ("I *became* his grandma," she said), and he wrapped her in hugs even warmer than her grandkids'. Understanding her abandonment issues better than any of us because he had grappled with his own, he listened attentively to her every way-back-when tale.

Not surprisingly, Hamani, Darrell, and Skye got the biggest kick out of their new "brother." When Kev and I went out, Skye was entertained and fed by a babysitting veteran who'd helped raise five younger siblings. As Skye grew older, he admired the video gaming skills demonstrated by his "other big brother," who taught him valuable shortcuts and tricks.

Darrell would have enjoyed having a Spanish-speaking big brother who'd lived in exotic Puerto Rico even if Jason hadn't been so much like him. Both were tempestuous, wary of trusting too quickly, and unsure as to how much they were loved. Jason worried that his mother was more enamored of his younger siblings; Darrell found living in Mani's perfect-kid shadow stifling. In some ways, Jason was more relatable than his own brothers.

Darrell understood Jason. Both were into hip-hop music; Jason had actually experienced some of the rawness celebrated in the videos I hated but that Darrell admired. Jason's Latino friends Alex, Baloney, and Danny and his seemingly hundreds of cousins were tough guys whose swagger brought a whiff of danger into Darrell's placid life. Darrell knew that if he ever stumbled into "shit" on the streets, Jason's boys would help him handle it. Jason was convulsed by Darrell's humor, by how he cleverly employed what he'd learned in school ("I'm so hungry, my liver just ate my pancreas!") or plucked out of his imagination. As sad as we were to hear that Tupac Shakur had lost a testicle in a shooting, we had to laugh when Darrell asked, "You think they're gonna call him One-pac?" Mani and Jason scandalized Darrell with jokes about masturbation, an activity that Mani and Jason called "Plan B."

Conversely, it was Jason's and Mani's differences that drew them closer. They were near-perfect counterpoints. On the surface, both were happy, popular teens. But Mani's smile was born of genuine equanimity, of his appreciation for his affection-filled life. Jason's grin provided cover for agitation and deep distrust. His caution suggested to Mani that it might be wise to sometimes temper his guilelessness. At the same time, Mani showed Jason the benefits of openheartedness—the courage it took to be vulnerable, the trust it could foster. The more-experienced Jason became Hamani's personal girl-coach, a sexual consigliere who showed him that girls often like guys who keep them guessing, whose confidence (even if it's feigned) helps them "own the room." Jason lacked faith in his ambitions and goals; he watched how Mani, a wannabe film director, studied movies as if they were holy writ. Some school nights, the two slipped downstairs as Kev and I slept, playing Mario Kart when they weren't jawing about life and girls.

Teenagers are humankind's most passionate specimens,

and our boys had three unwavering obsessions: the NBA, Michael Jordan, and the sneakers hawked by both. This was the late 1980s. Jordan was a sports, cultural, and media god so inescapable, he seemed poised for world domination. In addition to Jordan, naturally muscular Mani also idolized buff Seattle SuperSonics power forward Shawn Kemp. Darrell, who had a scar over the same eye as Orlando Magic sensation Anfernee "Penny" Hardaway, bought Hardaway-endorsed shoes and tucked pennies into them. Jason acknowledged other players' "sweet" moves, but his heart and sneaker money belonged to Jordan. Fierce family arguments often erupted over Jordan's place in history when Kev dared ask if he was truly better than Magic Johnson and other legends. By high school, the boys' fascination extended to action movies; they thrilled to Arnold's, Bruce's, Chuck's, and Wesley's bone-crunching adventures. Like their smart-mouthed heroes, the boys relentlessly jonesed on each other's high-top haircuts, walks, annoying habits, and body odor: *Man, your breath is kicking like [martial arts star Jean-Claude] Van Damme!*

Jason reminded us of how blessed Kevin, the boys, and I had been, growing up in stable, loving homes. He was effusively grateful for stuff our crew barely noticed: an attentive ear for every problem; money set out for his school lunch; the reliable appearance of the new socks or schoolbook he'd requested. He made me realize that for kids, consistency is as vital as love; maybe it *is* love.

This Latino kid, one part hustler and more than a smidgen saint, shared lessons he'd learned from his less-affluent, less-stable, less-educated existence, which my privileged sons would never have known. *He* was the gift. The "other" who became ours.

*   *   *

Just because someone belongs to you doesn't mean he'll stay. Almost a year after moving in, Jason said he wanted to "temporarily" move in with his mom. We weren't surprised.

Our beloved new son had lived as an adult for so long that becoming a kid again felt stifling. He missed his freedom. As the parent who helped him with homework, listened to his problems, and stayed on top of his dozen daily crises in addition to handling my own kids and my "real" job, I craved a respite. A few weeks later, Jason called to say that his mom needed him permanently. She was "guilt-tripping" him, he said, "asking why I'm not helping her." He wouldn't be coming back. When we protested, he said he had learned enough from us to keep studying and improving his grades.

Six months later, he dropped out of school. Taking a full-time job, he promised to get his GED. Angry, hurt, and confused about the time and money we'd apparently wasted, I ruminated for weeks. Finally, I invited him over and asked what had gone wrong.

Sitting with me in our den, Jason admitted that after moving in, he felt as if he'd wandered into the Brady Bunch. He'd always believed that Mani's family had everything a kid should have: two parents who got along, had open minds, and provided a safe place where kids could talk about sex, drugs, or whatever came up. "Kevin wasn't like dads who were always trying to prove something," Jason said. "He showed strength without using violence or profanity or putting other men down." Before Jason joined us, he'd had offers to sell drugs. He'd always said no, but living with us gave him a hint of the many options that were out there to pursue. He told himself, I can have a life like this someday.

Suddenly he was in the "perfect family." He was living in a big house; he had brothers his age and loving parents with nice cars who let him drive them. To honor this "dream come true," he came directly home from school, did his homework, and got decent grades. Not everything was perfect, he said, "but things got solved. And not through violence, like I'd seen."

I felt better listening to him. Yet he'd left us. I had to know: "Did we fail you?"

Jason's response was so grown-up: "*I* have to prove I'm not going to end up a failure," he said. Once a person leaves school, he said, people assume his chances for success evaporate. "But I've just begun," he insisted, adding that he had every intention of getting a diploma. He said he knew Kevin and I didn't agree with his decisions to leave our home and quit school. "But they're my decisions."

That was that. We didn't fail him, I decided. But we didn't make much concrete difference, either. And he was gone.

I was spent. Taking a three-month sabbatical from work, I hung out with Mani as much as possible before we transported him to the College of Santa Fe to study filmmaking. Returning to work refreshed and in control of my time, I felt liberated, juggling only two kids after raising four.

Yet Jason was still very much in my thoughts. Leaving as he had with so much undone disheartened me. If anyone deserved a quiet interlude, it was me.

Do you think I got one?

The one thing I wasn't good at giving: myself a break. God knows I tried. For weeks after Jason left, I ignored my friend Bob's weekly request for help with a Costa Rican exchange student from the American Field Service, the nation's oldest exchange program. The poor girl had been kicked out of her adopted U.S. home when her host family's daughter balked at sharing her mother. Now she had no home. Could we take her in? Finally, I couldn't say no.

Maybe it'll be fun, I told myself. Before Jason's first stay with us, my fourteen-year-old niece Raquel, Melech's bright, lovely daughter, had spent a year with us. Her mother, Malcah, had felt her accomplished daughter could be a huge help with newborn Skye and that I'd be a good role model. It was wonderful. Raquel got great grades, was terrific at cooking and chores, stood her ground with her male cousins. Yet what I relished most was her *girl*ness, our talks about shoes, clothes, friendships—everything except the sports that dominated chats with my boys. Maybe this exchange student would be as feminine and engaging.

Our Costa Rican "daughter," Martha Torres Solano, turned out to be an affectionate sprite whose charmingly accented voice ended every sentence with an exclamation point. ("My homework isn't done!" "I am reading this magazine!") Her stay with us was indeed a blast—until the day Martha was arrested for shoplifting at Bloomingdale's after a blond classmate coaxed, "C'mon, all American kids do it!" After her arrest, Martha cried a *río*, spent $500 on legal fees, and fulfilled her twenty-four-hour community-service sentence. Her record was expunged. Today, my memories of Martha aren't of her deeply regretted mistake, but of her squeals over Telemundo soaps, her iffy empanadas, and how much I enjoyed her.

Still, when a chastened Martha returned to Costa Rica, my friend Mireille gave me a hard look and asked, "Have you finally had enough of opening your home to kids who aren't yours?" My heartfelt response: "Are you kidding me?" I couldn't have been happier to be out of the "other people's kids" business.

I had no intention—none—of getting into it again.

*   *   *

Four years later—six after he left us—we learned that Jason was jobless and adrift.

I wish I could say I was surprised. He'd never resumed his schooling and was living the rudderless life we'd feared. I was sincere in my resolve about not getting involved again. Yet I couldn't look away; months of laughing, crying, fighting, confessing, arguing, and forgiving as a family couldn't be undone. Kevin and I couldn't stop wanting to help Jason fulfill his enormous potential. Mani was away at college; we had the physical and psychic space. When we asked our "other son" how he'd feel about moving in again—provided he got a job and earned his GED degree—Jason said, "It would be a dream come true."

Once again, we were bringing this complicated spirit, now a grown man, into our family. We knew the move could have unimagined repercussions. So what? He was ours.

Jason looked into when local GED classes started. With Mani away, Darrell was thrilled at his prodigal brother's return. Exploring music, movies, and videos together, Jason and he picked up their insult-fest where they'd left off. Darrell cracked on Jason's oil-glistening Afro; his play-brother made fun of his cornrows. Night after night, would-be music producer Jason drove my Explorer to studios across metropolitan Washington, recording with other fledgling impresarios. Nothing thrilled him like creating music. After weeks of checking want ads, he found administrative work with an apartment rental company. Daily, he woke up at an ungodly seven a.m. so Kev could drop him on his way to the *Post*.

Things were looking up, and they soared even higher when Jason met Vickie. A vivacious Teri Hatcher look-alike, Vickie had a petite body verging on tiny—until you got to the bodacious booty that delighted the men who watched her demonstrate Latin dance moves at clubs with her best pal, a salsa teacher who was one of Jason's closest friends. We saw how warily Vickie and Jason inched toward each other; both clearly were scared of where they might be headed. But there was no denying it: Jason was in love. Vickie, whose middle-class upbringing contrasted with Jason's, seemed equally smitten.

So when Vickie announced that she was visiting family in Puerto Rico for four months, Jason was floored. Four *months*? He knew her family was nervous about their relationship; what did this trip mean? A month after she left, Jason's abandonment issues in full force, he bumped into his first love at a party. After several drinks, he fell into bed with her. Genuinely remorseful, he confessed to me what had happened. Should he tell Vickie? I told him yes. "She'll be hurt and angry, but I think she'll understand if you explain," I said. "Promise her it'll never happen again. She'll value the courage it took to tell her when you didn't have to."

Calling Vickie, Jason confessed, apologized, and explained why he'd strayed. She dropped him flat. "I could tell the hurt in her voice," he said, sounding truly wounded. "She said I broke her trust. That what I did was unacceptable."

Damn. I had advised him to take a risk that honored the man he was becoming, a risk he'd considered not taking because he didn't want to lose Vickie. Sleeping with an ex is a major screwup, but Jason had taken responsibility, done the brave thing. And he'd lost his new love. "Honey, I'm so sorry," I told him. "But maybe a girl who can't forgive a mistake you've admitted and asked forgiveness for isn't for you. You deserve someone who'll love you even when you mess up." He nodded but was deeply hurt.

Then one of Jason's superiors at work, a man whom he suspected was gay, began saying how well Jason's clothes fit him, occasionally massaging his shoulders, touching his hair. When Jason pulled away, the man told him he wasn't working hard enough. Like many Latino youths, Jason was intensely macho; the man's actions made him uncomfortable, then angry. Since his first impulse—to knock the crap out of the guy—was out of the question, we explored other options with him. "Tell him firmly how inappropriate this is," Kevin and I advised. Then: "Put it in writing, and tell him you'll report him. What he's doing is illegal." Jason said he'd consider it. A week later, without discussing it with us, he quit, saying, "I couldn't take it anymore."

Inhaling, we suggested he try working around something he loved: cars. He got a sales job at a car dealership. Though he hated wearing a suit and tie, Jason loved the response the look elicited. Women's eyes lingered on him. One morning at 7-Eleven, "a woman opened a door for me!" he reported. "No one's ever done that in my life!" But the job paid by commission. Jason stood all day in the August sun, talked persuasively to a dozen potential buyers and—after having paid for food and transportation—came home poorer than when he'd left. He knew about cars from helping relatives fix them. But *selling* autos is a different skill: "I work ten-hour shifts, but if I don't sell anything, I don't make anything."

Again, he quit. Kevin and I took another deep breath. In the next few months, we tried reuniting Jason with his estranged father; their initial warmth soon morphed into recriminations. Next, I told Jason about Election Protection, a nonpartisan group I'd written about that was working to ensure voters' rights in the 2004 election. Jason was sent to Florida, where he was moved by his coworkers' commitment and felt useful helping Spanish-speaking voters negotiate the polls. But coming home was a letdown. He seemed even more directionless.

One night a few weeks after his return, Jason stormed into the house, livid about having been "disrespected" by a friend. Depressed, he'd gone to this man's home and ended up discussing his problems with the guy's pregnant wife. Unthinkingly, he sat beside her on the bed. Walking in to find Jason on his bed, the man abruptly told him to move. Stunned, Jason questioned his friend's anger. Back and forth it went until Jason left fuming. Now he was furious.

"I'm getting my gun!" he said suddenly. "*That'll* force him to admit he's wrong." Flabbergasted, I blurted, "You have a *gun?*" Even in his outrage, Jason looked stung. "You know I'd never disrespect you guys by bringing a gun here," he said. "But I know where to get one!" It took an hour to convince him that any husband might feel uncomfortable about seeing another man occupy such a private space with his wife. "Don't you see how this could escalate if you start waving a gun?" I asked. "How you could endanger *us,* since you live here?" When he calmed down, I wondered: *What the hell am I dealing with?*

I was dealing with Jason, of course, the tenderhearted, volatile young man we'd always known, who was becoming increasingly complicated. Then came the awful news that two of Jason's young cousins had been in a horrific motorcycle accident. One died at the scene; the second survived for only a week. Even as I comforted him, I felt defeated. So did he. A helpless desperation had overtaken him, the old "nothing ever goes right for me" weightiness that had pressed his thin body into our sofa a decade ago. It wasn't just that he couldn't find work. There was no career he wanted to pursue, except for music, which pays the bills only for a lucky few. So we tried to help him with that, setting him up with local producers, offering introductions to people with industry contacts. Convinced that he'd never be taken seriously, Jason seldom followed up. He knew we wanted to support him. And he was just as certain that there was little we could do.

After a year and a half of life with the adult Jason—eighteen months of family crises and relationship dramas, jobs lost and found, promises made and broken—Kev and I had to act. Jason was still helpful, painting the den bathroom and the patio's concrete floor. He was still funny, kind, and had a listening ear for anyone in need. But he was in his midtwenties, jobless, and had given up even the pretense of getting his GED. Jason was getting free room and board, driving my car, coming in at all hours, and requiring counsel for an array of problems. We gave him a deadline by which to get a job or leave. He missed it. We gave him another.

This time, we made it stick.

Once again, our "other son" left us. Grateful for the respite, we lived without Jason for months before realizing that a year had passed with no sign of him. Most of our frustration with his myriad complexities had drained away, leaving just our love. Another year passed. Was something wrong? He'd missed so much: Silverado, the dog with whom he'd enjoyed countless long walks, had gotten sick and been put to sleep. Kevin's book *Supreme Discomfort: The Divided Soul of Clarence Thomas* had debuted to great acclaim. Darrell had nabbed a role as a drug enforcer on the acclaimed HBO series *The Wire*. Mani's screenplay about a sweet, directionless Latino kid was generating serious interest in Hollywood. And we had no way to tell Jason.

I started searching for him everywhere: Among the throngs at movie theaters and outdoor concerts, in the face of every honey-colored, five-foot, six-inch guy in line at Starbucks. Any wiry, curly-headed brother with his head thrown back in laughter could be him, but wasn't. Was he with family in Puerto Rico? Had he returned to Florida? His mom had moved; I'd lost his father's address. Friends of Jason's whom we ran into reported he was "okay, living with his mom, I think." Calls to other buddies got the same response: "I don't see him much. But I'll say you asked about him."

Did he now count us as among those who had abandoned him? Had my disappointment been so palpable he was afraid to face me?

My failures with Jason (I should say "our" failures, but no one had invested as much in him as I had) forced me to examine my need to give. I didn't regret having him in our lives; even as things dragged out, he'd more often been a source of joy than frustration. I was proud of my family for having reached out to him, enfolded him. Yet this prolonged, unexplained absence hurt. I had been the one who'd invited him in, who'd been most free with my time, imagination, money, and experience. Jason knew our family's most intimate workings. And he'd dropped out of sight as completely as if we'd never met. Didn't he miss us at all? Didn't our connection mean anything to him?

It had to, I told myself. But he was still gone.

The God who'd years ago insisted Jason move in wasn't done with us. Here's how it happened:

Driving to pick up Skye from school one April afternoon, I swerved away from a speeding motorist. Scraping the curb, I heard a loud *pop*. A flat. *Dammit*. Pulling into the parking lot of a nearby tire store, I saw a new Mercedes pull up beside me. A tall, handsome young man got out and exclaimed, "Donna! It's me, Loren!" Gaping at his hugeness, I hugged him, saying, "I've been thinking about you! Remember the fight you and Mani got into in fourth grade that Jason broke up?" He laughed. I asked, "Do you have Jason's number?" Said Loren, "It's in the car."

Two days later, I was headed to see my prodigal son. It had been three years since he'd left us, since I'd started searching for his chin-to-the-sky canter on every street. It was the sea-son's first balmy spring day. Moms were out enjoying the sun with their kids, strolling, riding bikes. A weightlessness filled me, lifted the corners of my mouth.

Heart pounding, I'd phoned him immediately after seeing Loren. Jason's voice answered, "Donna?!" in a tone so happy, it seemed that we'd spoken just weeks ago. Catching him up on big events in our lives, I was reluctant to ask why he'd disappeared. His voice in my ear was too precious to risk. It wasn't until I pulled up before his mother's home eight miles from ours and *saw* him, on a porch twenty minutes from ours, that I could relax. Finally I could ask, "What happened to you?" without worrying that he would disappear.

After leaving us, Jason began, he felt totally demoralized by his cousins' deaths. The friends of his that we'd seen had told the truth. He was "okay." But he was withdrawn. Sadder. More aware of time's passage and his own mortality. Then his grandmother died, causing him to retreat even deeper as he worked construction jobs. The day I'd phoned, his family was facing a new tragedy: the drive-by murder of the husband of the cousin with whom he'd been living when he'd first moved in with us.

Listening, I felt the old puzzlement stir. Why did such epic heaviness attach itself to this charismatic young man, follow him like a lovesick puppy? How many other men and women were similarly enmeshed? Jason's formative years had been steeped in drama—the clamor of too few opportunities clashing with too many dreams. Drama is what he knew. It knew him too, finding him when he wasn't looking for it. What could free him from its grip?

Yet he'd stuck with his deepest passion: music. Working with one of his innumerable cousins, Jason had set up a small recording studio in his bedroom. Once he'd haunted other artist's studios; now he was the one "making the beat, recording it," he said. "I have control." His company, Calesent Music Academy, helps artists write verses, record tracks, produce CDs. Living with us did set an example, he said—just not the one I'd envisioned. We'd seen him as "a kid in a bad situation who needed a couple of pushes," he said. "But everything I did—apartment managing, selling cars—I kind of hated. I only loved the music and I didn't know how seriously I could take it." My intense focus on writing and Mani's on movies used to fascinate him. "Sometimes when you'd write, we'd be talking loud, you'd be in the zone, tell us to shush....Now when somebody talks to me when I'm trying to put some music together, I'm like that," he said. "You have to *feel* it."

Later, watching Darrell, Kevin, Mom, Jimmy, and Skye each wrap Jason in a crushing hug, I reflected on love's doggedness. For three years, Jason had made it impossible for us to share our lives with him. Not once had he bothered to see how any of us (particularly Mom and Jimmy, who were getting along in years) were faring. A voice inside me raised tough questions:

Why didn't you forget him like he forgot you? Doesn't his inattention suggest a lack of gratitude, of love? What if his sense of rejection means he'll always abandon the people he cares for?

The questions made sense, but I didn't care. None of us did. Jason belonged to us. He'd long ago seeped inside us in ways that time, distance, and frustration were powerless to affect. He'd made me aware of young men everywhere whose lives seemed foreign, unknowable. Searching for him in their faces, I saw their humanity because I'd seen his. These strangers resembled Jason not only in their youth and beauty, but in their hidden, inestimable preciousness. They weren't other people's kids. They were mine.

Yet the voice wasn't convinced:

C'mon! Hasn't a decade of letdowns cured you of wanting to support and be connected to this complex, perplexing young man?

And I heard my answer:

As if.

The Death Look

Donna getting exasperated, 1975.

All my life, I've been the lone girl among boys. Even my mother was so potent a force that her arrival home from work inspired Bruce to whisper, "Death rides in polka-dot hot pants!" The most feminine resident in our testosterone-steeped home, I immersed myself in the study of four very different males, especially my brothers. Men in training whose protective shells haven't hardened, boys show their sisters the vulnerability they'll one day take pains to hide. Melech, Darrell, and Bruce taught me to question men's bluster, to sense the hurt that can burrow beneath a man's bleakest scowl. Loving them taught me to trust guys I shouldn't have, to open wide my heart and other areas I should have slammed shut. My brothers taught me something else I relearned, over and over:

That a girl—yes, me—might be stronger than any man.

At long last, I was ensconced with my friend in a booth at the cheerful suburban eatery where we'd been trying for weeks to meet. Ilena and I grinned like madwomen over having pulled off this brunch despite everything—her job as a media personality, my book writing, our kids' schedules—that had conspired to keep us apart.

A girlish redhead, Ilena enthused about a recent mother-son rafting trip she'd taken with her eight-year-old. When she asked about my writing, my face fell. I kept getting distracted by obligations, I confessed, invoking a Michelle Obama speech I'd recently stumbled upon in which the then candidate's wife admitted to waking up wondering how she would pull off the "next minor miracle" to get through the day.

As the primary caretakers in most homes, Mrs. Obama said at a 2007 campaign event, women manage an endless swirl of duties: "Scheduling babysitters, planning play dates...supervising homework, handling discipline. Usually we are the ones in charge of keeping the household together. [You men] try to do your part, but the reality is that we're doing it, right?"

The soon-to-be First Lady had joked that her famous husband "had her back." Audience members cracked up at that, at the thought of a man running for president, or any man, pitching in equally.

I was smiling myself until I noticed a deep sadness inexplicably suffusing Ilena's face. "That speech made me want to cry," she explained. "I know I'm far from perfect. But sometimes my life as a wife and mother and career woman is so unbalanced, I think it's making me crazy, or just making me forget who I am."

Grabbing a napkin, she dabbed her eyes. "There's a real irony here," she continued. "Women who grew up after the women's movement wanted careers, to be strong individuals before partnering up. And we *are* that independent woman, outside the home. But in our family relationships, that power is lost."

This woman who minutes before had exulted in racing her son up a mountain looked beaten. "We hate admitting that," she said. "We hate how we just give in and do whatever's asked of us. Until the day we ask, 'What have I done?'"

Ilena shook her head. Sitting across from her, I watched as her face changed, hardened. Within moments, it wore the grim expression—my friends and I call it the Death Look— I'd seen innumerable times in the mirror. Ilena spoke: "I am tired of acquiescing."

Who isn't? I wanted to shout at her. What woman doesn't wrestle with her acquiescence, with giving, and giving up, too much? I told her about the innumerable times I'd carried more than my share in my home, how often I'd halted my writing to soothe, instruct, scold, lecture, or advise the resident males who'd do anything for me but leave me alone.

Surprised by my sudden bitterness, I asked, "Why do we keep doing so much with so little help?" Ilena snorted. "Because no one else will do it." she said. "Because we can't live in a house that looks like a cyclone went through it," I added. "Or wash our clothes and leave theirs dirty," she countered.

Because we're the wife, we agreed. The mom. The girl.

Millions of Death Look–wearing women ask, "What can I do?" yet few embrace the obvious answer: *Stop!* Stop with the cleaning, the arranging, the cheerleading, the shopping, the whole relentless shebang. Some who do stop see their homes' disarray devolve into a chaos that's unbearable — for them, not for their families.

Driving home after brunch, I considered for the first time how much more rewarded I felt for the work I did for the *Post* than for my offerings at home. A woman can be a waitress or a CEO, but her contributions at work have a better shot at being acknowledged than anything she does at home. A paycheck alone is an acknowledgment. Whatever its size, it's proof that its recipient's efforts merit payment. I knew I was lucky: I got paid for work I loved, regular raises, praise from readers and my bosses.

Few of my time- and spirit-consuming duties at home got noticed, let alone earned praise or thanks.

It's natural for disparity to exist between reactions to the work we do for our families and the jobs we perform for our employers. Yet the gap between the two felt so huge to me, I began to wonder: Was my time somehow less valuable than that of my husband? Than of my kids, who seemed to avoid, forget, or grouse about every chore?

Like most women, I enjoyed doing everything I could to enrich my loved one's lives. Like countless moms, I spent my days in a blur: Moving fast, swallowing hard, managing a challenging job while pressing family members into contributing *something* while I did everything else. "Doing it all"—all the while sensing an unnamed, mounting resentment.

Then the inevitable happened. Jason left for good, Mani settled in Los Angeles to write screenplays, and Darrell started his freshman year at Hampton. Left at home with Kevin and just one child, I slowed down. Caught my breath. And saw—really *saw*—what should have been obvious: My life was completely out of balance. And like Ilena, I was no longer sure who I was. When I measured the time, thought, and energy I spent ensuring my guys had all I could give them against what I received in return, I was incensed.

Even in my fury, I still felt blessed to be a wife and mother. Yet I was so much more: Still the voracious meaning-seeker who'd asked five questions in class for other kids' one. Still an award-winning writer and columnist. Still a sought-after public speaker. Still me.

So why was *I* the person doing an inordinate amount of our family's scut work? The one whose writing Darrell, twenty-one, felt he could interrupt for the third time one afternoon to quiz me about a shirt stain? "You already think I'm your nurse, your maid, and your shrink," I snapped. "Now I'm a laundress?"

Like a hospital orderly calming a mental patient, Darrell patted my shoulder, saying, "You're a *mom*. You're all of those things."

Surprised, I laughed rather than asking, "So what are you?"

Whatever he was, he felt no compunction to tackle duties he could easily have performed, that my own parents had no problem making my brothers and me do. Why had I allowed that?

But I had allowed so much, mostly without realizing it.

Working at home had changed a lot more than I'd bargained for. Abandoning the office had seemed so simple: I'd save money on work clothes, lunches, gas, parking. "Commuting" from my bed to my desk rather than driving downtown would give me more time to write and to mother Skye, then an infant. Sure, I'd be vulnerable to distractions, interruptions, the misperception that I was always available. But I'd also be freed from so much: Pointless meetings. Making myself presentable before rushing with my boys out of the house. Envying unfettered coworkers who never missed a deadline to dash home to a feverish kid.

Not once did I acknowledge a major factor in my work-at-home decision: my wariness of the world that had killed my brother. As Mani and Darrell moved into their teens, I wanted to keep them close. Mom had left home to go to work...*see how that turned out?* So what if Darrell had been an independent adult when he died? My subconscious had no use for such distinctions. Working at home, I could keep tabs on my sons, give them counsel, protection, discipline—stuff I was as good at providing as I was inept at demanding help. Once I began, my sons were glad to have me around and never got into real trouble. I didn't regret it.

Yet my world shrank. Abandoning the office meant jettisoning stimulating adult conversation, collegial lunches, after-work socializing. Months later, I noticed: my home and the people in it had gone from being important to being my entire focus.

No wonder my family's untidiness ate at me: their messes sullied my *workplace,* the symbol of an identity I still cherished, even as it became less evident to everyone but me.

In 1996, my twice-weekly column was syndicated, eventually appearing in more than sixty newspapers; articles in *Editor and Publisher* and *U.S. News and World Report* cited me as an influential new voice. Suddenly I was receiving fan letters from Seattle, Grand Rapids, overseas, even Gary. I loved syndication—until a family emergency sent me into a tailspin in which I struggled to produce even one of the week's two columns. After Skye's birth, I cut back to one column per week, effectively nixing syndication. Kevin supported the decision, though it meant less money for our family. Feeling I had to choose between my kids and syndication, I chose my kids—and my sense of balance and well-being. Many of my colleagues didn't understand.

There was plenty *I* didn't understand: My absurd assumption that married life would be easier. My unease that Kevin's success at the *Post* had made my former stomping grounds his province. My confusion about whether I could be a "real" journalist as well as a stay-at-home mom. The executive editor's failure to mention me as a former ASNE award winner at my friend DeNeen's celebration despite my standing right in front of him confirmed what I already sensed:

A valued part of me was disappearing. And I wasn't happy about it.

Nothing disheartened me more than those moments when the kids whose lives my presence was meant to enrich bore the brunt of my frustration. Hour by hour, I alternated between displaying Buddha-like forbearance and the shortest of fuses.

Darrell was in seventh grade the day his Spanish teacher phoned about a letter that I had allegedly signed alerting me that he was failing her class. Having never laid eyes on such a document, I told the teacher to inform my little forger that the jig was up. "That day dragged on longer than any day in the history of the world," Darrell recalls. Walking home, he prayed either to be hit by a car or to learn *I'd* been in an accident—anything to avoid my ire. Entering the house, he found a note: "We'll talk later." When I finally walked in, Darrell, steeled for mayhem, was heartened to encounter only silence. Thrilled, he thought, Maybe I beat the rap! When Kevin got home, we sat Darrell down. His life for the next month, I explained, would consist of "doing nothing": No TV. No pals' visits. No video games. No movies. No phone calls. Nothing. "It was a classic example of you taking no shit," he said.

That time, I was the picture of motherly restraint. A year earlier, I'd been anything but. After sharply telling the boys for the third time to stop arguing, I was stalking upstairs when I felt a tennis ball slam hard against my butt. Turning, I flew down the stairs with so much rage blazing in my eyes that Darrell, the hurler, screamed, "MANI DID IT!" Mani, still grappling with the fact that his insane brother had *thrown something* at this she-devil, froze. Mistaking his silence for a confession, I smacked him. Mani wailed his innocence; Darrell shouted him down. "I don't know why you believed me," Darrell says now. "But I loved that the people I was mad at—you and Mani—were mad at each other."

Such out-of-control episodes were rare. Yet they made me feel like an imposter. I had told myself that I'd given up syndication for the sake of my kids. Yet here I was making them suffer. My phony selflessness couldn't obscure the pissed-off bitch I really was. My daily meditations, religious readings, and regular church attendance felt like a sham.

Yet sometimes, I felt I wasn't the problem at all. At such moments, my mind was like a heat-seeking missile, latching onto anything or anyone else to blame for my vexation.

Like the morning I pulled myself out of a juicy writing stream to make some fresh coffee. Filling the coffeemaker, I noticed that the dishrag was filthy. Tossing it down the laundry chute, I thought, Better wash a load. Passing the den on my way to the laundry, I spied dishes covered with half-eaten food. *Damn.* Scraping them, I heard the phone ring: Kevin with a question. By the time I turned on the washer, forty minutes had passed—and I'd internally listed the sins of every male— Kev, the boys, the dog, God—responsible for the bedlam. *Woe is fucking me.*

In the midst of my Oscar-worthy soliloquy, I remembered: *I could have just gotten the coffee.* Nobody made me do the other stuff, except the part of me that craved some small semblance of order. As tragedies go, schlepping after guys who adored me wasn't so terrible when millions face war, poverty, and disease.

Any honest exploration of women's outrage at our unbalanced contributions must acknowledge how we feed the problem. The secret pleasure we take in being so essential. The ego boost we get, knowing that if our contributions halted, the whole house of cards would collapse. The power we wield, having final say over how well chores are done, and over our kids' hobbies, diet, playmates, even our mates' attitudes. Hate half-folded clothes and barely scrubbed dishes? Do them yourself. Detest hubby's frown when, for the third time, you ask him to walk Prince? *Do it yourself.*

Sometimes, I had trouble being firm with my own family. Afraid of being a nag, the girl who'd seldom backed down from her brothers worried she was too *nice.* Like innumerable unsuspecting mothers, I'd become a victim of Mom-empathy, the unerring wavelength detector women develop after giving birth. Great for discerning kids' feelings when they're inarticulate tots, Mom-empathy is counterproductive when toddlers become housework-avoiding preteens. Hating every second of it, I'd remind one of my sons of a chore. Rolling his eyes, he'd do it, but his reluctance gave me a tiny jolt of anger. Reminding another son elicited an exasperated head shake, and another Mom jolt. After the hundredth sigh, shrug, or protestation of a headache, some overjolted women give up, or wonder, Why can't these guys *see* what needs to be done when it's right under their noses? One day, while picking up the seven hundredth wadded-up tissue, the answer came to me:

Hardwiring. Prehistoric men were *hunters*. Stalkers of prey needed laserlike attention to track their quarry; every unnecessary detail faded. Centuries later, guys in my house were similarly riveted by the newspaper and PlayStation 3. Kevin wrote a whole book in an office ten feet from the laundry room—and never washed a load. I *allowed* this. His first book was too important to be disrupted by a mere basketful of darks.

Want to guess how many loads I washed while writing this book?

But I'm a woman, hardwired to be a multitasker—or multi-*seer*. The hunter's mate needed eyes that could sweep vast landscapes, assess her child's, mate's, and elderly relatives' well-being while locating hidden fruits, medicinal herbs, and poisonous plants. Scientists say men and women viewing the same landscape see different things. Women see more colors and textures, hear and smell details men rarely note. Is it any wonder that men don't see our needs or respond to them as we do theirs?

During a recent party at a friend's house, I sat in the kitchen chatting with Larry, the out-of-work host. Something, I didn't know what, felt wrong. Then I realized: the whole time we were talking, Larry was *working*, wiping counters, loading the dishwasher, rinsing plates. I'd had countless chats with multitasking *women* during parties, but never with a man. After weeks of doing chores while he looked for work, Larry viewed a party chat as I might: a chance to get stuff done. I recalled dinners where I'd watched male hosts clear tables and wondered, What's off here?

What was off, of course, was me. The forces that rocked the nation's social and economic firmament barely tweaked men's and women's basic natures. Though I was grateful for the opportunities provided by the women's movement, I felt frustrated by the flip side: doing nearly as much at home as my 1950s counterpart, with as little appreciation. I wasn't just invisible at the office I'd left; I was transparent to the family I'd left it for.

Where was the victory in that?

It's time I addressed the feeling that transformed Ilena's face. The one that inspired me to wrongfully smack Hamani, and that routinely engulfed me as I made my Invisible Woman rounds in my home.

I'm talking about anger.

I hate to go there. Unlike women who "celebrate" their rage, I find unchecked anger repellent. Sometimes the intensity of my fury scares me.

None of which keeps me from being consumed by it.

I'm talking about the rage familiar to nearly every woman who has a significant man in her life, the acrimony she feels when he displays the stubbornness, contempt, or willful blindness toward women—toward *us*—that can infect the most enlightened of men.

Women's anger often appears out of thin air. I can't count the times my husband has blurted, "Why are you so hostile?" during seemingly innocuous arguments in which my face and voice morphed into a slasher-flick villain's. There's nothing pretty about this kind of rage. So many of us bury it, until it explodes when we least expect it, making us react in foolish or self-wounding ways because, as Ilena says, "We're not making it count where it should."

Some measure of the outrage we spew at loved ones is actually directed at ourselves. We suspect the ways we're culpable, the hand we have in our own diminishment. Unable to stop ourselves, we wonder why it's possible for us to notice the slightest moan, grimace, or sigh from our family members while they remain blind to our flailing. Which only increases our anger.

Sometimes we don't need words to express it. Most people would describe me as warm, even kind. Yet sometimes when a guy irks me, a glance my way suggests that likable woman has evaporated.

In her place is an identically dressed stranger wearing the Death Look.

Unlike women's typical expressions, the Death Look wishes instant annihilation upon the man who summons it. Recently it appeared on the face of my friend Anne after her husband announced he'd made a major decision for them both without discussing it with her. "Was that okay with you?" he asked.

After the Death Look froze him, her intrepid spouse dared to ask, "Why did you look at me like you wanted to kill me?" despite the obvious answer:

She wanted to kill him.

Oh, all right, Anne didn't want her husband dead—any more than I've wanted to disappear Kev, my sons, my brothers, or the male friends at whom I've shot the Death Look. What we long to obliterate is the impulse that makes them ignore, dismiss, snap at, or go back on their word to us.

Other weapons in women's anger arsenal include sarcasm, slammed doors, withheld affection and sex, brooding silences, and, rarely, physical violence. Because the intensity of these responses is often out of proportion to the actions that inspire them, I'm convinced women's fury can be traced to the centuries of oppression they've endured.

From the beginning of time, women have terrified men—through our sexual power over them, our ability to bear life, our connectedness to, well, everything. Fear inspired them to deny our brilliance, burn us at the stake, bar us from pulpits, prohibit us from voting, and otherwise disempower half of humankind.

Yet the vast majority of women have still wanted men in their lives. My brothers softened me up toward guys long before I could develop defenses. That's what families do: drop incomprehensible people in our lives, show us their worst, and make us love them anyway.

But if a woman really wants to be truly buffeted by adoration and apoplexy, she has to have children.

Recently, I was lost in my work when Mani, visiting from Los Angeles, asked if I'd seen his keys. Torn from my writing for what felt like the twentieth time, I snapped *"No!"* and threw him the Death Look. His baffled expression stung me. How could he know that rather than hearing him ask if I'd seen the keys, I'd heard him insinuating I should know their location, or worse, stop working to find them? I hated the absurd sense of protectiveness that made me want to shield him from something as minor as misplaced keys.

A mother's compulsion to safeguard her children can be wholly irrational. So can our giving. There's no one on whom we're more driven to lavish our time and attention. Bonds that primal are hard to govern, so sometimes we lash out at our kids.

I can't speak to the seismic undercurrents affecting mothers' reactions to their daughters. But having sons has meant that the gender-based fury I sometimes feel toward men gets directed at them—at times deservedly. Like racism, sexism is in the air, ripe for absorption through everyone's tender skin, even our boys'. You think Darrell would have thrown that ball at Kevin?

As a black woman, I see women's out-of-nowhere acrimony as symptomatic of the wrenching pain felt by members of any long-oppressed group. Too often, women *are* assumed to be less important and capable than men. We're paid less by some, shushed for speaking disconcerting truths by others, and treated like walking breasts and butts by far too many. These nicks and bruises accumulate like ash, gas bubbles, and dirt in a dormant volcano.

Our explosions aren't just inevitable; often, they're justified. Once upon a time, I reveled in the cleansing *"Hell, YEAH!"* I felt after releasing my wrath. But at some point, I noticed how depleted I felt afterward. The tense silence that invariably followed such explosions felt nothing like the peace I craved.

Women's rage often doubles back on us. Draining us, it alienates those whose empathy, not fear and resentment, we hope to engender.

At some point between fuming about my workload and wondering which role I was more invisible performing, I knew: my problem wasn't just with men, but with women. One woman:
Me.

The hardest place to look when you're assigning blame is the mirror. But I couldn't help noticing: some women didn't have my problem. Yes, some had mates and kids who gladly contributed around the house. But there also were women whose shrewdness, self-discipline, or training helped them get more of what they needed from their families. Other women decided they could live with modern life's messes. Still others

Donna Britt

gladly took on nearly every family-related task. It was as instinctive to them as writing was to me. I admired these women, wished I was one of them.

But I wasn't. I needed order. And I wasn't just annoyed by what my men didn't see and fix. I was fed up with the part of me that couldn't stop seeing and fixing stuff for them. Rejecting that giving impulse felt impossible. Surrendering to it felt like defeat.

I knew I was as smart and as capable as any of the men I'd given to—and that for all my anger, I loved having a life where I could use my gifts in both my home and my career. Feminism had made that versatility possible, provided the blueprints for striking down the barriers that would have prevented it. I couldn't have been more grateful.

But where was the blueprint for changing...me?

Escape

Darrell playing a gangster for acting class, 2006.

*A*fter months of alarmed speculation, midnight arrived uneventfully on December 31, 1999: Y2K, the moment when the twentieth century finally spilled into the twenty-first. My delight that a new century had begun without computer systems crashing and misdirected planes falling from the sky lasted until three a.m., when I heard Mani's key in the door. Listening as stumbling feet ascended the stairs, I realized our seventeen-year-old son's voice was too shrill, and his friend Mike's shushes too urgent, for there to be any other explanation: our "perfect son" was roaringly drunk. The guys had taken the subway to the Capitol, where they'd sipped bottles of Coke and cranberry juice spiked with Smirnoff while awaiting the new millennium. Appalled, I lit into Mani about the dangers of drunkenness. Years later he'd confess that he'd started drinking and smoking cigarettes in high school to feel sophisticated. "I just didn't want to be a kid. Adulthood meant being my own man." That's why he started working at a local video store at age fifteen and chose a college 1,700 miles from home. I'd thought he was being brave and industrious. In fact, he was plotting his escape.

One other thing about the night I scolded Mani for his inebriation: Watching his humiliation from the upper bunk, his little brother Darrell couldn't have looked happier.

I don't recall the subject of my meditation that morning in 2007, or the errand I had agreed to run for my son Darrell. Deep in contemplation on the couch, I felt my mind drift from God to the more pressing matter of my to-do list. How could I squeeze in Darrell's request? I breathed.

And just like that, I saw — no, felt — a fleeting thought that

I must have had hundreds of times without noticing: *I have to do this or he could die.*

My eyes flew open. *"What?"* I blurted, though no one was there to hear me. Had I actually thought something as irrational as, "If I don't run an errand for my son, he could *die?*"

I had. Then, just like that, I understood: Three decades after the fact, I still felt responsible for my brother's death. When Darrell died, putting one foot in front of the other had felt impossible. In such a state, I couldn't begin to process how culpable I felt, but I'd been acting on that culpability ever since. For twenty years, my brother Darrell had been my heart. When we grew apart, I told myself the gap would disappear as we settled into adulthood.

But Darrell had *died*—an event so huge, so inexplicable, that someone besides the policemen who'd pulled the triggers had to be to blame. Of course I chose me. I hadn't done anything wrong, so I turned to what I hadn't been doing: paying attention. I hadn't been watching Darrell, checking in with him, keeping him beyond the reach of pistol-wielding cops. I'd dropped the ball and there was no retrieving it. Back when I'd known Darrell's every move, he'd been safe. Stepping away had made him vulnerable.

I had let my brother die.

Of course I'd never thought this consciously. It took three decades for me to even capture the quicksilver thought born at my brother's death, to grasp it solidly enough not just to respond to it but to *hear* it:

If I'd been there with him, tending to him, supporting him, he wouldn't have died.

No sane person knowingly embraces such a lacerating belief. Yet unconsciously, I was convinced of my guilt. So I resolved that no one else I loved—certainly no man—would die because I wasn't there for him.

*   *   *

It's ironic that an errand for my middle son sparked my realization about his predecessor. Two decades of kinship with the brother I'd named him for had had the sweetest sense of ease.

A single day with my son Darrell could feel like a thousand years of hard labor.

The biggest challenge any over-giving woman is likely to face is her kids. Especially if she has a kid like Darrell. Daily, my middle son tested me. The boy whom I'd prayed wouldn't be born on Melech's birthday was every bit as exasperating as his uncle.

It wasn't fair. Motherhood was an adventure I'd felt born to undertake, and everything about my firstborn, Hamani, suggested I was stupendous at it. Why else was Mani so popular, honest, and affable? Yes, he sometimes got impatient or agitated, but he never lingered there. Like at twelve, when he confessed to me a crush on a classmate. Days later, he phoned from school, an alarming tightness in his voice as he asked, "Mom, can you pick me up?" The girl, he said, had rejected him for another boy. Mani was an A student who never avoided school; I couldn't say no. The next day, he was quieter than usual. Then, emerging from his funk, he said, "If she likes him, she should be with him. She should be happy."

Happy? I was still fighting the urge to storm the school, find the ungrateful twit, and shake some sense into her.

Mani's little brother's purpose seemed to be shaking *me*, out of my smug sense of competency as a mother. By age seven, Darrell was greeting my "good morning" with a scowl, dodging school- and housework, and ensuring that the slightest skirmish escalated into World War III. Everyone was against him, especially me. As if to ward off attack, the kid even slept with his eyes half-open.

This tiny boy's smoldering sense of aggrievement puzzled me. I couldn't have loved him more. Why didn't he believe it? As the mom who slipped praising notes into his lunchbox— *You're the best!*—I couldn't have guessed one source of his pain: the examples set by his successful parents and paragon of a brother. "I felt early on I couldn't live up to the family name or my older brother," Darrell later confessed. "So I thought, Screw it. If I couldn't be great, why not be really, really bad?"

His overachieving brother made him feel irrelevant. Being the rebel, the bad guy, gave him an identity.

"It became good versus evil," he said. "I started to enjoy it."

My most difficult son was a teenager on the morning I sat stunned on the couch after realizing I felt responsible for my brother's death. Though pinned to the sofa, I felt an unbidden sense of liberation envelop me. The life-limiting belief I'd harbored—*if I don't give to them, protect them, do for them, they'll die*—made my over-giving make sense. If sacrificing would stave off some horror, these offerings weren't just about guilt or subjugation. They were acts of love.

My revelation, I suddenly knew, wasn't just about me. I recalled the day that my public relations executive friend Gwen had startled me by describing a program for at-risk youths as "perfect" for me to write about because I had "that *thing* for young black men." Gwen had seen something that I'd hoped my feminist trappings had hidden: I'm a guy's girl, particularly a black guy's girl. Like most black women.

Don't expect us to admit it. Like independent white women with a soft spot for men, sisters talk a good "I'm my own woman" game, warbling with everyone from Gloria Gaynor to Beyoncé about our self-sufficiency. For years, when a man bullshitted a black woman on TV, her "Say *what?*" response was a cliché: Her head swiveled. One eyebrow arched. Her don't-even-think-about-it finger snap said, "Honey, I am *not* having it."

Please.

Let a black man, any black man, be publicly compromised. Let one be fired, arrested, swept up in a melee he had no hand in or caught in a crime he masterminded. Let a *prominent* black man be accused of anything, from asking a female employee about pubic hairs on a Coke can to raping a virginal teen beauty queen, from sleeping with boys at his fairy-tale ranch to stabbing to death his blond ex-wife and her friend.

Guess who'll be his staunchest, if not only, defenders. Of dozens of possible explanations, one is irrefutable: No group of women has a more agonizing history of seeing their fathers, sons, and husbands snatched away from them, of shrieking helplessly as their men were dragged into the night. The cruelties visited on black men have scarred them in myriad ways, and cut black women just as deeply.

Finger snaps and platitudes can't dismiss the sense of lurking tragedy many black women feel, or their unthinking response to it.

Before that moment on the sofa, I'd never connected the dots. Darrell's undeserved killing had inspired me to heedlessly dedicate myself to supporting and protecting black men as penance for my failure to protect him—and as insurance against tragedies to come.

How many other black women were doing the same thing?

How many sisters were putting their dreams and well-being on hold on behalf of the men in their lives, men often unaware of their efforts? How many were taking a backseat to brothers, in private or in the public consciousness? Far more has been written about "endangered" black men than about their equally threatened sisters—with barely a peep of protest from the ignored. The disproportionate attention focused on black men results from brothers inspiring more fear than black women. If *I'd* been in that ditch behaving as the cops described, I might have been spared.

And the person who's most likely to die is the one who's "endangered," correct?

Survivors of such killings know better. Darrell was gone, but Mom and I, as well as my father and brothers, had to live on and endure it. The carnage that has decimated the nation's population of black men barely acknowledges their shell-shocked kin, the thousands of wives, lovers, mothers, daughters, and, yes, sisters left behind, many of them emotionally and financially devastated.

No one can tell me they aren't endangered.

By the time my son Darrell was nine, my own hidden array of fears had spurred me to enroll him in tae kwon do. His roiling dissatisfaction in a world hostile to angry black boys frightened me. Perhaps the Korean form of karate would boost his confidence. Besides, the kid was skinny with an attitude. It seemed prudent that he learn to protect himself, if only from me.

Inspired by movie martial artists like Jackie Chan and Ernie Reyes Jr., Darrell happily attended classes and learned quickly. Though frustrated that his early training focused on *hyeong,* a precise series of intricate movements, rather than on the high kicks he'd admired on-screen, he appreciated the system's rigors. When his instructor suggested Darrell was proficient enough to enter a kids' tournament, I signed him up.

Arriving at the competition, Darrell, Mani, Kev, and I were immediately surrounded by dozens of grunting, kicking kids in uniforms tied with various colored belts. As loudspeakers boomed the results of separate contests, I watched Darrell warily absorb the noise and activity. Feeling his caution slide into terror, I offered every assurance I could think of: "Isn't this cool? You're going to do great! Look, there's the medal you could win!"

Finally, it was his turn to compete. As five other beginners lined up, Darrell stood aside, studying them. He'd never seemed so tiny or vulnerable.

Suddenly he spoke: "I'm not doing it." Sounding as resolute as he had at the airport when he stated he was *not* going to St. Louis, Darrell added, "Nope, not doing it," and headed for the door.

Desperate, I ran after him. "C'mon, you're really good at this!" I called out to him. "If you leave, I'll be really disappointed in you... So what if you don't win. Just try!"

Jumping between Darrell and the door, I placed both hands on his shoulders. Bending over, I looked in his eyes. "Honey, please don't do this," I pleaded. "Don't quit."

Eyes locked with mine, Darrell inhaled. Turning, he joined the other contestants. I couldn't breathe. Mouth set, he awaited his signal, then moved through his paces with perfect precision. I didn't care what the judges thought. He'd done it!

So when the loudspeaker announced that he'd won first place, I was astounded to hear screams—mine—and feel a perplexing wetness engulfing my face. I'd burst into tears. How could this pint-sized person have such power over me? It didn't matter because I knew:

Darrell wasn't alone in having won that day. Everything was going to be okay.

Any black woman can tell you: Our kids aren't the only ones who surreptitiously burrow inside us. So do our men.

Yet so much has been written about the tensions that divide

black men and women, it's easy to overlook what unites us. Ours is a dance of mutual affection and hostility, dependence and distrust, fascination and resentment. This push-pull dynamic has forged a gap between African-American women and their men that yawns, shrinks, and yawns again. The breach contributes to 70 percent of black children being born to unmarried mothers— and the vast majority of those babies having black fathers. Statistically, sisters are the least likely of *all* U.S. citizens to marry outside their race, though we're far less likely than other women to be permanently linked to our children's fathers.

As dismaying as such statistics are, and no matter how many beauty shop rants black women begin with the words "All brothers are dogs!" we won't give up on black men. We won't let them be dragged into the night.

My revelation about the man I'd lost made me reflect more on the guys whose well-being now consumed me, especially my sons. Who would I even be without Mani, Darrell, and Skye? Their births taught me that the stretching required to push something as substantial as a baby through a tiny opening is too profound to be merely physical. Becoming a mother opened me like nothing else, and no one else could fill the space they'd created.

Surely I would have felt the same if I'd borne daughters. But I'd had three black *boys*. Years after their births, I still asked myself what every mother of black sons must: Did I have what it took to equip them to become strong, loving men in a harsh, unloving world?

By high school, the sweet certainty I'd felt after Darrell's martial arts triumph was a distant memory. Sometimes, wading through the tumult of clothes and sports gear in his room, I'd run across his gold medal and gaze at it in wonder.

Its recipient had long since abandoned tae kwon do—along with playing sports with any seriousness, pretending to care about school, and listening to me.

I still offered Darrell praise, encouragement, and surprises; nothing pleased him for long. His resentment was so palpable, and our fights so fierce, I wondered if he hated me. Sometimes I wondered if I hated *him*. I'll never forget the day he hurled a taunt at me so piercing that I lunged at him, wrapping my hands around his neck. Immediately, I pulled away, flabbergasted by my fury. Darrell's expression was more shocking. Though enraged, he looked as if he felt he deserved it. Feeling desperate and defeated by his hostility, back talk, and lies, I studied brochures from military academies. But I couldn't send him away.

If not for Mani and Skye, I would have felt certain I was an atrocious mother. But these sons, like my brothers Bruce and Darrell, not only welcomed my efforts, but reciprocated them. Like the time Skye, who as a preteen despised shopping, wheedled his way out of a trip to buy school clothes, leaving me to guess at his sizes. Returning home, I found a sorry-about-that fruit salad he'd fixed me on the counter. Modest and self-sacrificing to a fault, Skye was the most likely of my sons to say, "No, Mom, you take the last brownie/comfortable chair/extra taco for yourself." No wonder he won his middle school's "Quiet Giver" award, voted by fellow pupils and teachers as the student most "helpful and generous in ways that might go unnoticed due to his quiet nature."

Mani, too, took my example to heart. "Trying to please everyone is a gift and a curse I inherited from you," he told me. "When I was little, I saw how tirelessly you worked to please people. What better way to earn people's love and respect than to be the one who never lets them down? I wanted friends, people I worked with, my girlfriends, to think, Mani always comes through."

My eldest was also like me in a less noble way: enamored from day one of the opposite sex. The toddler who'd pinched the legs of the prettiest girls in my journalism workshops became a man who adored women, to the point that he often warned potential lovers he couldn't swear to be faithful (though his innate honesty wouldn't allow him to be *un*faithful). Darrell's vaunted opinion of him notwithstanding, Mani wasn't perfect. A casual observer of the two brothers would have assumed Darrell, the hip-hop scowler, was the liquor-and-drug experimenter. In fact, Darrell never drank or got stoned, once saying, "People get high to *be* me." Mani, on the other hand, not only drank wine, beer, or liquor at every high school party; he eventually experimented with weed, coke, and even ecstasy. He got away with such behavior because he was like me in another way: a born discloser. How do you stay mad at someone who instantly confesses, and apologizes for, his sins?

But Darrell was like me, too. His sudden rages and refusals to back down resembled mine more than I liked to admit. But his riotous humor was delightfully—and disturbingly—reminiscent of someone else's: my late brother's. My other hilarious Darrell had been volatile, too. Knowing what it may have cost him was frightening—and impossible to discuss with his namesake.

By the time Darrell left for Hampton (we figured my small alma mater would be more nurturing to a complex youth than a huge state school), I'd surrendered my perplexing middle son to God. I certainly wasn't having any impact. I hadn't stopped loving him or trying to reach him. Yet when I told him, "I think I'd have to die for you to appreciate me," I meant it. Darrell just looked at me.

Although I missed him when he left for college, I reveled in our home's relative peacefulness without him. It didn't last. Like me, Darrell found Hampton's intimate campus restrictive. Unlike me, he had the presence of mind to transfer, to the theater program at the University of Maryland, Baltimore, a half hour from our home. Darrell and his drama were back.

During a talk with Kevin and me about our frustration over how he kept his life and feelings hidden from us, Darrell, who had seemed unusually nervous, made an astounding confession. At Hampton, freed from parental prying, he'd unleashed his inner outlaw. Lacking funds to buy the stylish sneakers he craved, Darrell started stealing them. Channeling Melech, he described entering a store, slipping on a pair of desirable shoes, and studying them in the mirror. When the salesclerk got distracted, he'd slip his old pair into the empty box and boldly stroll out in the new ones.

As if that wasn't enough, Darrell (who still didn't get high) briefly sold marijuana, though only to people he trusted. Unbeknownst to me, my son had been risking his freedom, his future, and his family's reputation. And he didn't care. "It was all about me, what I wanted," he admitted. "I was smart about it so I knew I wouldn't get caught. And if I did, so what?"

So what? I'd spent years working to instill character in my sons, certain to assure their actions would reflect and prove their worth — *black people's* worth. Yet Darrell had blithely validated the worst stereotypes, flirted with the possibility of jail, and behaved in ways that suggested my integrity, too, might be a lie. I'd lost my brother because others had only thought he was stealing. The son I'd named in his honor was actually doing it, throwing himself to the very wolves I'd tried to shield him from. How could *my* son — nephew of my slain brother, a teen we'd taught about the criminal justice system's harshness with black youths — be so reckless?

"What were you thinking?" we asked him. "I wasn't thinking," he said. Asked "What were you *feeling*?" Darrell was silent. Then:

"A lot of it had to do with just not wanting to be around," he said slowly. "I almost think I wanted to die. It seemed like an escape. I had no direction, I felt useless and didn't care what happened to me. So I said, 'Fuck it.' Since I was a burden to everyone, if I got locked up, no one would have to worry about me."

Escape. Utterly at a loss, I remembered the times I'd been confounded by reports of black and brown youngsters whose prison-or-death mind-set suggested a desire to bolt from life. Yet these kids were impoverished; their most compelling role models were in prison or their graves. Darrell had spent his life surrounded by encouragement and success. Why would a kid from a stable home commit minor criminal acts? What had *he* hoped to escape?

Searching for answers, I reminded myself that many wild-oats-sowing white youths also behave badly. Then I wondered if Darrell's lifelong antipathy was at all linked to his having been just five months old when I left Greg. Hamani had been four—old enough, perhaps, to know his father, to feel assured of his love. Darrell had always grieved more for the man whose connection grew increasingly tenuous after I married Kevin. Millions of black boys lack *any* father-son connection. That has a huge effect, no matter how loving or giving their mothers.

And there was this: for every child like Mani, whose sense of self is solid from birth, there's one like Darrell, whose inborn fear of being unloved and unworthy haunts him. Such kids come in every shade, yet those who are black or brown hear whispers that support every nasty thing they fear—*you're not good enough, you'll never succeed, we'll never accept you.* Hearing such messages as a girl, I decided to be so perfect that "they" would be forced to accept me. Darrell decided differently. Unwilling to try to live up to an impossibly high standard, he set his own: a low one.

The fact that a multitude of kids were like him didn't make

his behavior, or the cavalier attitude behind it, tolerable. Too crushed for words, I left the room.

The next day, Darrell found me in my office. Sitting at my computer, I'd been staring at the screen, trying in vain to write. All I could think about was my son's confession, and its suggestion that I'd been an even bigger failure as a mother than I'd suspected. Turning in my chair, I stared mutely at my son, contemplating his charisma, humor, insight, and preciousness, none of which he believed in, and all of which reminded me of another irreplaceable Darrell's.

Tears filling my eyes, I found words. Darrell remembers them clearly. "You started telling me about your brother," he recalls. "How he had all this promise that got thrown away. You said you'd secretly feared that the same thing could happen to me. You'd given me his *name*. Now you were worried about what it meant for me."

My macho middle son remembers that he started to cry. "That was a defining moment," Darrell says. "It was the day I promised to not let the same thing happen to me."

After years of failing to make my son understand how loved he was, he believed me. After two decades of wondering if I was the wrong mother for my son, I felt I was the right one. All because I'd told him what I'd hardly admitted to myself: how vulnerable losing my other Darrell had made me. For years, I'd feared that admitting my terror to my sons would somehow put them more at risk. Yet it had the opposite effect: Darrell, sensing how much this confession had cost me, finally understood that he was as essential as the brother I'd lost. As he put it:

"Seeing how much *we* meant to you changed everything."

*   *   *

Countless black women spend a lifetime terrified by the vulnerability kindled by their inseverable link to their embattled brothers. Sometimes, as with my cherished middle son, that connection pays off. Sometimes not. And sometimes, after a brother's crisis has passed and he has moved on without noting or acknowledging our support, we ask, "Who supports *me*?"

More often than we'd like, we must do that for ourselves. At times I've wondered: Is that such a bad thing?

Self-sufficiency was one of the chief traits I'd hoped to engender in my sons; by 2005, they were twenty-three, twenty, and ten, old enough for me to begin to gauge my success. I knew my brother's death had made me feel unduly responsible for their welfare. To shake free, I had to feel my boys were on the right track.

Skye, our youngest, most easygoing son, was already his own (young) man. Telling him to do something that made no sense to him was like bitch-slapping the wind: pointless. No argument, threat, or intemperate display disturbed his monk-like peacefulness as he swatted away directives from teachers, peers, and us. Skye's sense of honor was stronger even than Mani's; he never abandoned anyone or anything, including homework if he didn't complete it by bedtime. He kept plugging away, finishing every assignment no matter how late it got or how forcefully we ordered him to stop. A violin student from age five, Skye performed at recitals with ease, and acted in school plays with as much ferocity as Darrell, who said, "Skye's the only person I know who's fearless."

Mani, no surprise, was his usual, accomplished self. After junior-year internships at PBS and at Tom Hanks's Los Angeles film company, Playtone, he'd spent a semester in Rome. At the term's end, I joined him in Italy's Eternal City for three days; afterward we visited Paris and London. Of course my "perfect son" was admired by teachers and peers, and knew as many hip nightclubs as he did Italian phrases.

There was one problem: Mani, now a man, had passionate opinions. About *everything*. We clashed about when to rise, where to eat, which ruins to visit, how to fit luggage in Porta-John-sized hotel rooms. When I asked where my congenial-at-all-costs son had gone, Mani insisted his disappearance was—get this—my fault.

"The value you placed on the truth has made me into a frank, sometimes inappropriately honest man," Mani explained. "You always stressed that lying was worse than whatever I was covering up. Now I'm so honest, it gets me into trouble with people, but they usually come around when they realize it's a sign of respect.

"Thanks to you," he said, "I can't lie."

Not even on one trip? I wanted to shout. At least our feuding made me feel better about his plan to move to Los Angeles after he graduated magna cum laude, an honor which Darrell, unimpressed, dismissed as "magnum cum latte, a coffee drink, right?"

At twenty, Darrell was still Mani's opposite, pushing my buttons with his apathy rather than his passion. Performing in a summer drama production, he astounded us with his virtuosity. "I'm going to be an actor," he stated afterward, describing the Porsches, Oscars, and Halle Berrys his genius would earn. Yet for months, he took only the courses required for his filmmaking major. No extra acting classes. No auditions. No inquiries into Mani's Hollywood contacts.

"You have to *work* for stuff in this world!" Kevin and I insisted. "You think an acting career is going to fall into your lap?"

"I'm going to be an actor," Darrell repeated. "In my own way."

In 2006, he asked our friend, Emmy-winning *Post* writer-turned-screenwriter David Mills, to introduce him to the casting agent for *The Wire*, the HBO series about life on Baltimore's drug-decimated streets. "If you can't act," David warned him, "they won't hire you." Darrell auditioned, winning a one-line role as a drug dealer in the series, which filmed near his college. Darrell's tiny part grew into a two-year featured role, Mani heard later, because he "gave his throwaway character a voice." A promising acting career had all but fallen into his lap.

In the months after I confessed my fears about him ending up like my brother, I watched Darrell warily. Would his toxic *woe-is-me*-ness return? When remnants of it did appear, they evaporated quickly. Eventually, the kid who craved a work-free career launched facebookwastaken.com, an effort-intensive online video series of quirky minute-long comedy sketches. We expect miracles to be announced by lightning bolts and cymbal clashes. Yet Darrell's slow slide into self-awareness was as miraculous as any burning bush.

So was his gratitude that I'd never given up on him.

"I still can't believe you stuck by me," Darrell told me years later. "I really was an asshole. But even when I hated you, I felt you were the only woman who could have been my mother.

"God gave you to me because it was the only way I would survive in the world."

Talk about a miracle: my refusal to stop offering love and support to Darrell had saved him from the allure of the ultimate escape. But now, relatively assured of my sons' independence and well-being, I felt every instinct telling *me* to flee, from them and everyone else I loved. Something in me clamored to escape from the people I couldn't stop doing for, and to examine the doing.

Who can become whole in a place where everyone has a piece of her?

*   *   *

Escaping can be tough for oversubscribed women—and not just because of the problem of who'll fill in for us. Anne Morrow Lindbergh wrote about it in *Gift from the Sea*.

A mother of five and firm believer in retreats, Lindbergh admitted that for a woman, even briefly leaving her family feels like "a limb is being torn off," until the richness of her aloneness makes her feel more whole than before. If this homemaker could ditch her family for her sanity a decade before anyone even heard of women's lib, surely I could swing it in 2007. Who said change was easy?

But after finally escaping from my home and my sense of obligation to everyone in it, I had a different thought: maybe change *is* easy.

It certainly looked that way as I gazed at a postcard-worthy stretch of blue-sky mountains outside my window. Underlying the spare loveliness outside my Baja California room was something more exquisite and exotic:

Silence.

Not just the room's silence, which filled me like hot water plumping a tea bag. The silence in my mind. An unaccustomed clamorlessness had overtaken me. *Look at me,* I thought, words spreading slowly as just-spilled honey across my mind. *Not parsing my problems, cursing my duties, planning my next move.*

I was ten again. Peering outside, replete with...nothing much.

Kevin had first visited Rancho La Puerta while we were dating; he'd read a *GQ* article describing North America's first destination fitness spa as a paradise where he could eat organic meals, hike a sacred mountain, and exercise four times a day. Arriving home six pounds lighter, he'd taken pity on my broke, single-mom self and awarded me a $1,200 "scholarship" to join him the following year. A few years later, I started going alone.

Each time I visited, I relearned something Mom always knew: Every aching woman, especially every bruised *black* woman, needs a place where she can find the peace and clarity to keep going. When I was small, Mom baffled me by escaping—alone—to a motel. "I need to get away," she said, refusing to apologize for addressing a need few women admitted in the 1960s.

I don't apologize, either. I can't count the times I've retreated; if not to the spa, which I couldn't always afford, then to an empty office at work, a vacationing friend's home, or just an unoccupied bathroom. I couldn't afford *not* to hole up in a quiet space with a door that closed. Where the only person I was beholden to was me.

I'd escaped to Rancho La Puerta this time because I couldn't explain how at odds I felt with how I was seen by my husband, my kids, and my employer. Now I asked who, really, was to blame? I'd abandoned my office for home, assigned myself the impossible roles of "perfect" wife and mother, and immersed myself in duties I hated. Brilliant.

Alone in my room, I let myself wonder: What, really, was wrong with my life?

I still found Kevin sexy and supportive; somehow, the affair and its aftermath had resulted in us cherishing each other more, being more devoted. Years afterward, I half joked that as much as anything, fear of losing the boys, especially Skye, had kept him with us. Surprised, Kevin replied, "That would have been awful, but people make that work. I didn't want to lose *you*." I knew exactly what he meant.

Our sons, though far from flawless, were terrific. I hated that the world wasn't as welcoming as they deserved, that I daily put my boys, my *heart*, in God's hands. But wasn't that where they'd always existed?

Most problematic was work. A popular columnist for fifteen years, I wanted to do more. Like every newspaper, the *Post* was facing an alarming drop in readers. I spent weeks conjuring ways to help bring them back: moving the column to another section, "bouncing" it between sections to tackle different issues. All were rejected. Once, my bosses couldn't see me. Now they couldn't see me differently. *Why rock the boat?* I felt them asking. *You're doing fine.*

Staring from my window, I had to agree. Things *are* fine. Why am I so unsatisfied?

And just like that, I knew. This time, the revelation didn't appear in a flash. Dawning as slowly as the sun over the Mexican horizon, the truth, like the sun, had always been there. My love-hate relationship with giving was a symptom of something deeper. The problem wasn't between me and my job, my kids, or my mate.

It was between my brother and me.

Thirty years of pushing him away, of trying to escape his memory and meaning, had failed. Writing for the *Post* didn't satisfy me because what I needed to write about was Darrell. Freeing myself from family obligations was impossible because I was terrified of leaving loved ones vulnerable, like I'd left him. Resenting what I gave to men did nothing to stanch my generosity because in fact nothing I did for anyone was enough. Because nothing could erase my sense that I'd failed Darrell.

There was no escape. Getting a handle on my giving and moving forward with my life required facing the man whose life and death had shaped so much that I'd become.

I had to make peace with Darrell.

Finding Darrell

Darrell and Bruce "riding" Taffy and Scooter, 1975.

*W*hen Bruce dreams about Darrell, his departed brother
usually shows up at a family gathering at the old house,
the one Daddy and his friends built with their own hands. Darrell saunters right in, looking just as he did at twenty-six—his
smile knowing, his solid body broad, his eyes alight with the same
mischievous glint. Each time Bruce dreams it, "Everybody tiptoes
around Darrell because they're afraid to ask him where he's been.
The understanding is that he just had to go away for a while to
get his head straight. And we're so glad to see him, we don't ask
any questions.

"But there's this palpable tension about where's he been."

I didn't kid myself. Freeing myself from my entrenched give-or-
someone-will-die demons wouldn't be easy, especially if it meant
confronting the brother who had so profoundly affected me.

Decades after his death, I realized that as the years had
passed, I'd thought less and less about him, and thereby was
hurt less by his goneness. Now when I spoke of Darrell, it was
with dry eyes and a near-steady voice. My attitude was remark-
ably similar to the one I had in grad school before he was
killed: *Darrell and I aren't close now, but someday we will be
again. And it will be great, like before.* Much as it did in 1977,
it worked for me.

Until it didn't. The revelation that I'd locked myself in a
must-give, must-help, must-prop-up prison led to my sense
that exploring my life's defining moment—Darrell's death—
might explain those tendencies. Yet the decision to reexamine
my brother's life and death brought the most surprising realization of all:

I had lost Darrell. I mean, really *lost* him. I had plastered what he represented onto male friends, lovers, coworkers, husbands, and sons whom I'd cheered, pushed, and sought to protect. Each had provided an outlet for my ongoing need to give to my brother. But now I wanted Darrell, not stand-ins. And he was lost to me.

Lost.

When my father died in 1999, I was struck by the cards I received expressing sorrow for my "loss." At least a dozen kindhearted people said, "Sorry you lost your father." The words lent his death a hint of impermanence, as if Daddy was a cell phone I'd misplaced and might yet recover. My father had *died.* But nobody wanted to say it. "Dead" is too redolent of decay and final resting places. So we speak of our "loss" and of our loved ones "passing." Both terms imply movement and action, leaving room for the possibility of realms beyond the one in which we're enmeshed. Room for "it ain't over."

But can't people die without being lost to us? Can't we continue to savor their way of regarding us, the spread of their smiles, their voices' timbre? I'd retrieved my brother twelve years after his death for the article I'd written for the *Post* about what his death taught me about the value of black life. But the excavation required to write the piece was agonizing. After its publication, I let Darrell slip quietly away.

To some extent, my brother's fade from my memory was natural and protective. But when I wanted him back—when I felt sturdy enough to entertain him again in consciousness—I couldn't find him. I invited his return to my dreams; he remained a no-show. I meditated, hoping he'd rise in my awareness. I found solace and quietude, but no Darrell. Closing my eyes, I mentally returned to our Gary home. Peering in long unvisited rooms, I saw myself staring in the bathroom mirror, Steve peacock-walking through the den, Bruce's head thrown back in a preteen guffaw. But Darrell was largely missing. Wherever I'd buried his memory had become matted and overgrown.

Once again, I became aware of a fact that had shaken me decades before: I didn't know Darrell anymore. Back then, at least, I had memories, some so vivid, it ached to evoke them. Now, only a few well-worn moments were easily recalled. *Darrell*, the essence of the man who'd been my joy, was gone.

I had abandoned him again.

In 2007 when I decided to write this memoir, I knew I'd have to hack through the thick, protective walls I had erected to find my brother. Yet I was paralyzed.

One afternoon while lamenting my quandary, I was riffling through a little-used drawer for a turtleneck when I happened upon an unfamiliar clear plastic bag. Curious about the yellowing papers inside, I unzipped it—and gasped. Years earlier, Mom had thrust into my hands a plastic duvet bag filled with Darrell stuff—notes, doodles, and letters taken from his apartment after he died. Terrified of it, barely looking at it, I had pressed it deep inside this drawer. Forgotten it.

Heart thumping, I briefly leafed through the bag's contents—and then pushed the treasure trove back in its hiding place. For weeks, I couldn't reopen the drawer, confront Darrell even in this indirect way. I wanted him back but couldn't face him. Few people knowingly rush headlong toward pain. But the depth of my reluctance at a time when it was imperative that I face Darrell bewildered me.

Why was I afraid to find my brother?

It was during this period of searching for Darrell while keeping him at bay that I remembered my friend Kathy's experience with hypnotherapy. Studying to become a family counselor, Kathy had been skeptical of this aspect of therapy until a professor hypnotized her and she recalled details of her child-hood she'd had no idea she had retained. Could hypnotherapy bring Darrell back, with a minimum of pain?

Settling into a chair in the office of Betty Silon, a psychia-trist recommended by a colleague of Kathy's, I waited for this kind-looking woman's instruction. Would she ask me to gaze at a swinging watch? Count backward aloud? Alarmingly, she launched into questions, about Darrell, me, our family. "I want you to *feel* your emotions. Emotions will take you where you want to go," she said, placing a box of tissues beside me. Staring at the box as if it were a grenade, I thought, It took decades to learn *not* to feel Darrell's death. I'm not filling any more tissues with my tears.

But I was in her office, with no backup plan. Inhaling, I answered her questions. They did take me deeper into my feel-ings, which felt...good. On my third visit, she asked why finding Darrell frightened me. My answer was so obvious, it shouldn't have surprised me:

"I want to protect him."

I'd treasured my childhood memory of Darrell the hero for so long, I was terrified of learning anything that might destroy it. What if he wasn't as perfect, as pure, as I recalled? What if the golden light in which I'd bathed him was undeserved?

For thirty years, my view of what had happened in that Indiana ditch had been ironclad: My sensitive, warm, and car-ing brother—an innocent black man—had been unjustifiably killed by a pair of rogue white cops. If he'd been white, he would still be alive. Simple as that.

But was it that simple? Darrell and I had drifted apart. Who was the man in the ditch? The born-again minister-to-be? The slow-to-boil powerhouse whose eruptions stunned me? The confused soul whom the truck owner saw as a thief he was "holding," a description that probably got my brother killed?

A man whose fascination with mysticism and drugs had backfired in a baffling, tragic way?

Learning that Darrell was complex could make him culpable. Make him like all those other black men whose all-too-human behavior resulted in their deaths—and meant nobody had to give a shit about them.

I couldn't risk handing a weapon to those who believed every problem a black person has is his own fault while simultaneously giving every benefit of the doubt to whites. I hadn't forgotten the 2008 presidential campaign, in which some of the very people who bleated about Michelle Obama's being "really proud" of her country and her husband's angry pastor blithely overlooked John McCain's thirteen cars and multiple residences as well as Sarah Palin's pregnant and unwed teenage daughter. Such issues surely would have sunk Obama.

Black people had to be perfect. After decades of trying to achieve perfection—or just be good enough—I'd decided to forgo the approval of hypocrites. But the prospect of learning that my childhood hero wasn't so heroic terrified me. What if Darrell *was* like those imperfect, all-too-human brothers whose behavior contributed to their deaths? Whose shootings even I had dismissed? What if he was...human?

No, *black* human. Someone whose death—and by extension, life—hardly mattered.

Thousands of black men have been murdered in this nation—millions if you count those who died with women and children on the Middle Passage. How many of their deaths were mourned? When I unconsciously resolved that no other man would suffer through my inattention, I joined countless black women who've harbored similar guilt and remorse. So what if their men were lost through racial violence or through other black men's brutality in a tragic criminal loop? They, too, heard an ancient blood memory whisper that the "reasons" for their men's slayings weren't reasons at all.

One murdered brother whispered too much about freedom. Another "didn't work his share." That one made a pass, real or imagined, at a white woman. Yet another one refused to bow down to white men. One man's prosperity made him dangerously uppity; another's destitution made him a burden on society. Still another's land—or wife or goods—were coveted by his white neighbor, and the fool wouldn't part with them. And don't forget the ones whose drug deals went sour or who dissed the wrong thug. And what about the one who wanted to be a comic, then a drug counselor, then a preacher—who stood in a ravine with a pot on his head, acting so crazy they shot him like a rabid dog?

Whatever the rationale for these men's "punishment," black women knew them as guiltless, or at least worthy of the benefit of the doubt. They were ours. If we didn't fight to preserve their innocence, who would?

Feeling all of this, I grabbed for a tissue. And whispered to Dr. Silon, "I don't want people to think he deserved it."

Regarding me with gentle eyes, she said, "The man you've described to me *was* sensitive and kind. He protected his little brother from his older brother's attempt to make him use drugs. He counseled addicts. He appreciated you, helped you love yourself. Every day, I listen to women speak of brothers who are very different, whose behavior wasn't loving or kind. Nothing you learn about Darrell will change who he was to you.

"It's okay to let him have his complexity."

Wiping my welling eyes, I knew she was right.

I started where I always had: with questions. At first, they were addressed to those whose remembrances were unlikely to wound me: Bruce, with whom I often spoke but seldom about our brother; Melech, whom I barely talked with at all; and Mom, whom I had for years discouraged from bringing up Darrell. Finally, I contacted Darrell's friends, boys-turned-men with whom I'd hadn't spoken in thirty years.

"Tell me what you remember about him," I said, steeling myself.

"Remember the blue Mustang?" Bruce asked. And just like that, I did. *Royal* blue, a 1970 model with an eight-track tape player from which Hendrix, Parliament/Funkadelic, and Santana blasted. Darrell drove left-handed, Bruce reminded me, and shifted with his right, a move so cool that Bruce mimicked it when he bought a car. Bruce reminded me of the pair of huge speakers, the rock-concert type as tall as I was, in Darrell's bedroom. And he related the time Darrell approached him, his music protégé, saying, "I got some free tickets to a concert. Never heard of the group, but you wanna go?" Bruce said, "Sure. What's their name?" When Darrell said, "Kiss," Bruce shrugged. *Whatever.* "It was one of the best nights of my life," he recalled. "The lighting, the candelabras, the makeup, the group in all-black leather with their funk moves dancing across the stage. It was Kiss's first national tour, in a little movie theater in Hammond, Indiana."

Melech had never told anyone what he was doing the moment he heard Darrell had died: smoking pot with some street types when a drug dealer who also happened to be a cop arrived. "He comes in and says, 'I think your brother has had an incident. You need to go down to the police station,'" Melech recalled. "That's how I found out. I went [to the morgue] and viewed the body." Long pause.

"It was just shocking to see someone who's alive...who's not alive."

His closest brother's death "tempered and bent all of our

lives," Melech continued. "You put a rock on a plant, and the plant will bend to grow around that obstacle. The rock has a steering effect that cannot be ignored." And though he, too, wondered if drugs Darrell had taken much earlier had triggered an altered state, Melech said, "I chose the biblical perspective. My understanding of the Creator comforts me, tells me that it was Darrell's time. I believe he made it, that he will be in the Kingdom."

Mom welcomed the chance to talk about her departed son. When he was killed, she said, the surreality of the circumstances made her replay everything she knew about her son through a new lens. She'd thought back to Darrell's high school graduation, how after the ceremony he had bopped joyfully down the aisle inviting girls on either side to kiss him. "Give me some lips!" he had called to them. Had he been high, she wondered, or just excited? He'd told her he left college because he couldn't decide on a major. But someone whispered to her that he'd fallen for a married woman. Back home from Bloomington, Darrell had stayed in his room for a week, she said, emerging only to eat. Had his heart been broken?

Darrell's friends were harder for me to reach out to. These men knew my brother in ways I hadn't. What might they reveal? How would they feel about opening a long-closed wound? It took me a week to unearth their phone numbers. Yet when I considered actually dialing them, my heart's terrified dance stopped me.

Another week passed. Finally, I couldn't put it off any longer.

I called Vernon first. Vernon Williams had met Darrell in kindergarten. I can still see him back in the day, wearing thick Clark Kent glasses and oozing confidence. Now an Indianapolis public relations exec, Vernon seemed thrilled to talk about his first best friend, whom he alternately called Darrell and

Chip, as in "chip off the old block." "Block" had been Melech's college nickname; Darrell's had been an homage.

"We were 'boy boys,' getting dirty in foxholes, Indian wrestling," Vernon began. "We played a game called burnout: take a hardball and stand forty feet from each other and throw to each other. First at a moderate speed, then harder, until we were almost breaking each other's hands. Invariably Darrell and I would be the last two."

From the time they were small, Darrell "was a little better at every sport than the rest of us," Vernon said. As teens, they'd attended a frigid doubleheader at Comiskey Park, the Sox versus the Angels, for which their thin jackets were inadequate. Yet "neither of us considered leaving," Vernon said. "It was a *doubleheader*. We stayed till both games were over and nobody was left in the stands."

Our former neighbor Lanel Chambers surprised me, saying he believed Darrell should have pursued a baseball career. "He was a very good hitter, *very* good," said Lanel, a sportswriter for the *Gary Crusader*. "If I could have laid out his life, he would have made a living in baseball, as a player or coach. I wish he had gone to college near a minor league team where he could have tried out."

Lanel had become buddies with our family when we moved to the new house Daddy and his friends had built. He can still envision my brother on the rec diamond, where they played. "Darrell batted left-handed, and he could hit a fast pitch. If you ever see film of Ken Griffey or Barry Bonds, they're very similar to him. When he came to the plate, people started backing up. One time in a big sandlot game, I was trying to pitch to him in a way he wouldn't get a home run. He said, 'That's right, you got to be careful, pitching to this dangerous hitter!'"

Each of Darrell's friends recalled what I'd remembered

most clearly about him. "Everybody was funny sometimes, but Darrell was one of the *funny* people who could make people burst out laughing given the slightest opportunity," Vernon said. Because he was "a very keen observer of the world, politics and society," said Lanel, "you couldn't predict what he might joke about."

Attending Indiana University expanded Darrell's worldliness, Lanel said. "We talked even more about current events, history." His humor, too, seemed to expand.

"Chip was the funniest human being I ever met," said Yochanan Israel, whose name was John McCorkle when he and Darrell met as Alpha Phi Alpha pledges. Yet "he could turn his humor on and off like a faucet. Serious and funny, serious and funny. If you got on his bad side, he could cut you up with words, slice you to bits. He didn't even have to cuss."

Cornell Collins, who also pledged Alpha with Darrell, remembers those days as "a golden era."

"Vietnam was winding down, but there were still protests, almost every day a different demonstration," Collins recalled. "Most of the students from Gary hadn't been around whites. In Bloomington there were white kids our age from all over the state and the country. Blacks could mingle with them, be friends, exchange ideas. The environment was so stimulating."

Dave Shelton had also joined Alpha's eighteen-man "Sons of Satan" pledge line, living with his brothers in the organization's very hip frat house blocks from the center of campus. Shelton remembers Darrell had a corner room; its door was always open to a wide variety of friends, male and female.

And though Darrell had dated several women, his friends told me, none of the relationships was serious.

"He was a constant dreamer," Israel recalled. "Very few women could understand him, and he could care less. They weren't the kind of females who could peel the layers off to get to who Chip really was. So they just passed through. At that age, I was of a similar mind-set. We weren't really trying to settle down."

Most of my brother's running buddies paused before introducing the subject that most worried me: Darrell's drug experimentation. "I suppose college is where Darrell discovered getting high" is how Lanel brought it up.

Though Lanel saw drugs as "too scary" to explore, Darrell had no such fears. "He had this basic fascination with life, he was sampling it," Lanel said. "But he had good sense about it. He would tell people, 'Don't do that drug' or 'Stay away from that quantity.' He warned people against risky combinations. Darrell was a reader; he would research and make his decisions based on that. He essentially knew what he was doing,"

Collins suggested that I put my brother's drug dabbling "in perspective," reminding me that he was doing it at a time in which millions of young people were getting high. "We all were doing our experimentation, and Darrell was Chipper the Tripper," he said. "It was no secret he was into this acid thing."

Said Israel: "We're talking 1977. *Everybody* was doing drugs on some level. Chip loved LSD, and he would get the best. He loved the fact that it could take him somewhere else, to a higher state of consciousness. When he went in his room, closed the door, put Hendrix on the box, you knew."

By 1974, Darrell and Vernon had returned to Gary, where they helped found a nonprofit group chartered in the state of Indiana called People's Action Coalition and Trust, PACT, "probably the city's foremost group of young people," Vernon said. Somehow, I had forgotten about it.

"The mayor, councilmen, all the movers and shakers, participated," Vernon continued. "We wanted to give something back; we'd always talked about issues confronting black people. We had Save the Children Week, focusing on children's health issues, a Mr. and Mrs. Senior Citizen pageant, a recreational program for kids."

About that time, Lanel and Darrell, both twenty-three, were lounging in our basement, sipping wine, and watching *The Midnight Special* on TV when Lanel suddenly said, "The Indians sure were stupid." He'd been considering how America's indigenous peoples had embraced the newcomers who would decimate them. "And Darrell stopped me and said, 'No, man, that's not true at all,'" Lanel recalled. "The Indians knew how to live off the land. They were into nature, really smart.' That moment will stick with me forever."

When Darrell was killed, Vernon, then a reporter for the *Gary Post-Tribune,* poked around, heard vague suggestions that Darrell may have attended a party the previous night, though his autopsy showed no evidence of alcohol or drugs. To Vernon, only one thing seemed clear:

"If it had been a white young man, more effort would have been made to talk him through it, even if he was belligerent."

What happened in the ravine "illustrated what Chip and I had talked about all the time," Vernon continued. "When a black person tears a Stop sign down, it's vandalism. When it's a white kid, it's a prank. If there's physical contact from a black person, it's assault. White kids are just 'roughhousing.' Two sets of standards. Even if there was some behavior that wasn't ideal, cops should always think about how they can defuse the situation. I don't think there was a clear threat to the safety of the officers. I believed then and I believe now, it was a matter of them panicking when confronted with the threat of a black man they couldn't explain or control."

Vernon paused. "I will say that occasionally Darrell had a temper. And it wasn't incredible, it wasn't like he needed anger management. If the police were approaching him like a criminal, I can envision him challenging their position, their overaggressiveness, their presumption that he's doing something he's not doing. And I could see them overreacting. That's the best I can do to explain that bizarre set of circumstances."

Israel's explanation is simpler. Darrell's best college buddy and the man who lived with him for months in Miller believes the police account is an out-and-out falsehood. "I knew this guy. He wasn't out there with no pot on his head in the woods," Israel said. "I don't care how high Darrell got, he was never stupid....I lived with him, I *knew* him." The police account, he felt certain, "was a lie. Darrell could tell you which drugs not to mess with, which was primo. He knew what he was doing. He was absolutely discriminating. It was a straight setup. It had to have been. There was no reason for the scenario the newspaper described. It didn't make any sense."

He'll never forget living with Darrell in Miller—their long, profound conversations, how Melech would stay up all night "painting these big wall murals" in their apartment. One December night, Israel and Darrell decided to walk to the beach at Lake Michigan a block away.

"The sand was like concrete, it was so cold," Israel recalled. "There was a full moon over the lake." Looking out over the water, Israel couldn't believe his eyes. Were those *people* marching on the water? He asked Darrell, " 'You see that, man?' " Darrell said, " 'Wow, look at that!' "

"The waves had actually frozen in midwave," he said, his voice still marveling. "And we stood looking at it. The frozen waves looked like people. I remember him saying, 'That makes you think about what the possibilities are. If water can freeze like that...' "

Israel inhaled. "Darrell had a window to other stuff that other people didn't have," he said. "He saw through a window other people couldn't see through. I miss him."

Lanel still remembers the last time he saw Darrell. About a month before he died, "we played basketball at Kennedy-King

Middle School," he recalled. Darrell "seemed to be his basic self—there were no clues that he was going through any changes." Only one thing struck Lanel as odd: watching Darrell get into his Mustang to drive to his Miller apartment as he prepared to go the opposite way.

"We had spent so many years getting in the same car. Going the same direction."

Listening to these men, I felt my brother again. Saw his quick-stepping walk, heard his palpable excitement when he spoke of anything that moved or delighted him. Darrell *had* been a great athlete, but his gentleness with me made me forget his strength, how formidable an opponent he was, how intensely he played on our backyard court.

His friends' words empowered me enough to face the plastic duvet bag. More than a year after realizing I had to write about Darrell, I'd brought the bag to Rancho La Puerta, where I could be alone with this terrifying treasure. Sitting on my bed, I unzipped it as warily as Pandora opening her box. Nestled inside were dozens of folded, wrinkled, and torn papers, most in a cardboard El Producto cigar box emblazoned with a lyre-strumming senorita. *Did Darrell smoke cigars?* Designed to hold fifty 15-cent cigars, the box was stuffed with the dreams, hopes, and imaginative leaps of a searching-for-itself life.

Handling these crinkled sheets like the most fragile parchment, I lifted them one by one from the box, placing them gently beside me. Once upon a time, Darrell had touched them, spilled himself onto them. Surely some wisp of him remained. Among the gems: a bill for $163.18 from Indiana University on Darrell S. Britt's student loan and a handwritten letter from Darrell thanking the university "for your patience."

He had just started working at Bethlehem Steel, he wrote, and would soon repay them.

The scribbled phone number, on lined paper, of a girl named Charlene. And one for Brittany on a torn-out calendar page (April 21, 1976). And a third number written on the most detailed hand-illustrated map I'd seen. Delicately drawn, the map was clearly the work of a motivated woman, including directional arrows, bends in the road, street signs, stoplights, and squares representing a playground and her building. Everything, in fact, but the illustrator's name.

A receipt from Jack's Loan Office, Licensed Pawnbrokers, for "band ring and 2 speakers." Darrell had gotten $25 for a thirty-day loan on his gigantic speakers.

A parking ticket for being "parked against traffic"—for $2 (!). A notice for a "Summer Madness" party at the Gary Armory ("Come!!! Come!!!"). Bills from three auto repair shops for work on the Mustang totaling $310.74. Designs for a logo to represent the Pipe Fitters, a rock group Darrell planned to form in which Bruce would play guitar.

A poem or song titled "Parachute," written in pencil on stationery from the Hollywood Young Men's Christian Association, where Darrell must have stayed in Los Angeles. Admitting he was once "foolish" to think "higher was better," Darrell appears to have written these words for a friend dependent on drugs:

I'd like to be your parachute, to help and bring you down
For no one can live for long suspended from the ground
I know it will be hard at first to mingle 'mongst earthly
*   crowds,*

When you've lived so long on the stars, and danced across
*   the clouds.*

The poem's conclusion states that Darrell had "flown through the skies alone, and no one broke my fall. The trip was rough and I could have died. But instead I came out strong."

There were dozens of white sheets torn from pads inscribed with the logo of the Indiana State Employment Service, where Mom had worked. One was filled with scribbled song titles; others held reflections labeled "Poetry." The largest number were identified as "Comedy" and held notes for sketches that never made it onstage.

Darrell had written one-liners, opening gambits, and what looked like reminders for longer sketches, stuff like "My hair's so hard, Moses couldn't part it" and "Don't think of yourselves as an audience. Think of yourselves as my psychiatrist." One said simply, "You don't have to make sense to be understood."

Some comedic notes were crude, in the style of performers he admired—Redd Foxx, Richard Pryor—and were tough for a hero-worshipping sister to read: "Been meeting a lot of girls lately who don't like to fuck," Darrell wrote. "They like to get high and Disco. I say you dig on this dicko." And "Why dream about me when you can cream about me?" And "I can tell when someone needs sex—I spend a lot of time in the mirror....I grew up in Gary and it used to be pretty rough. I mean, I wasn't handsome, cool, or smart so I didn't get much....Gary bitches didn't give no pussy to just another muthafucker."

The sheer volume of material in the bag was mind-bending. Darrell had written enough for more than a dozen comedy routines, several essays, a portfolio of songs, and a book of poetry. His mind had been ablaze; it must have taken months to have plucked so many words, so much inspiration and insight, from his life and others'. When he left home, I used to wonder how he filled his time when he was alone. Darrell had been serious about his comedy, his poetry, his writing, in ways I had never suspected.

The most probing of women, I have over the years persuaded countless men to reveal themselves to me. Yet I'd never been offered a thrown-open window to a man's naked soul. In a rough draft of a letter to someone unnamed, Darrell wrote:

"I've got nobody special now and too much time on my hands. I like you so very, very much. We seem to have fun when we get together so I don't see why we can't get together more instead of feeling sorry for ourselves....If you're any kind of judge of character, then you should know I'll be only good for you. And if you don't know what kind of man I am, then I invite you to find out."

Who was she? Did he ever mail the finished letter?

A love poem: "When I remember you I shall re-create in my mind those fathomless eyes that...invite me to bathe in the tropical blue waters of your soul. And I'll remember your hands, small and gentle, eager to fill themselves with love. But would it be my love?"

I read and reread the poem entitled "Learnin' How to Die":

Saw a man bent half-backwards
Throwin' up his life,
Couldn't keep it down inside of him
He was learnin' how to die....
Seems people stopped trying to live
And started learnin' how to die.

And this, another poem without a title:

The point of the story,
If you didn't catch it
From our friends,
And Stepin Fetchit
Is that although things for us

Are better than ever before
We've got to come to the slavemaster
If we want more....

Niggers for sale, Niggers for sale
Big as a mountain, dumb as a door
Fine black beauties, make a hell of a whore....

The chains that were once on our bodies
Are now on our minds.
And the key to unlock them,
No one's trying to find.

Entranced, I read through the cigar box's contents for more than an hour—proud, shocked, convulsed, as I drank in the man from whom I had hidden for three decades. Two-thirds of the way through, I paused to breathe in the enormity of holding these bits and traces of my brother in my hands, hearing his voice in my ear. A knot closed my throat. Without warning, a river of hot, confused tears boiled down my face.

I was reading Darrell's private musings, his art, his scatter-shot, unedited thoughts, secrets he never expected anyone to see. Absorbing them felt as wrong as it was necessary. How often had I refused to let editors see my scribblings before I'd shaped them into something reasoned, fluid? Yet I was reading Darrell's nakedest fancies—and planning to reveal his uncensored reflections to the world in my book.

But how could I keep them hidden? These were Darrell's *words,* written in the carefully slanted script I'd forgotten. Thousands of them, all the more sacred for their incaution and incompleteness. Here was proof that my brother had been alive, that he'd been real. Proof of his humanity. His worth.

And mine. Suddenly I remembered the other obvious yet

shattering thing that the psychologist had suggested as I sat sniffling in her office.

"Darrell could have reached out to *you*," she said. "He was an adult; he was equally responsible for the two of you falling out of touch. Yet you've blamed yourself for that. That's not fair to you."

Thirty years after I began giving to men in his memory, my brother was offering himself to me. The more I read, the more certain I was that Darrell wanted me to have this box, to become reacquainted with him at last. Much that was offered, I didn't understand; half skits and musings as free-flowing and limitless as he had been, as uncaged by logic and judgment. Many of the box's offerings lacked the concreteness to satisfy a sister searching for answers. Fragments couldn't explain every-thing about the man my dearest brother had become. Yet I did know this:

The box clasped in my hands was Darrell's last gift to me.

There were two more: A layaway receipt dated two days before my birthday in April 1976, from The Hanging Tree: Clothing for the Contemporary Ms., for a "woman's cloth-ing" item costing $27 on which Darrell had paid $10. And on a folded white paper bag, a long-forgotten Ann Arbor phone number Darrell had recorded. Beneath it was a name, written in my brother's precious, now-remembered hand:

Donna.

Finding Donna

Donna, 1963.

*L*ife is a process of moving in and out of opposites: from light to dark, from day to night, from growing to shrinking to enlarging again. Inhaling, we expand our lungs; exhaling, we deflate them. Blood stampedes into the heart, barely pausing before tunneling out. The tide flings itself at the shore, only to capriciously abandon it. Yet the perfect place may be the between, the sliver of time and space intersecting the opposites: The beach where sea and land unite. The chord born of an impeccable violin note, overlapped by a perfect, harmonizing strain. The gasp of a moment during sex as foreplay ends and intercourse begins, when a woman feels herself opening to receive.

The between. That's why we feel God in the center of our being — the perfection in the midst of our confounding opposites.

Reconnecting with Darrell felt so right, I could hardly recall why I'd been so terrified to find him. It *was* painful, unearthing once-familiar details I'd entombed. But there was profound comfort in remembering why he'd been so necessary to me — and so unthinkable to lose. For weeks, I did nothing with the information I'd unearthed. I just sat with it, savoring every tidbit, enjoying feeling, seeing, knowing Darrell again.

Two months after getting my brother back, I felt ready to truly examine how his life and death had influenced me, especially in regard to my "giving thing." I'd "disappeared" Darrell's memory for decades, yet I had rarely doubted that he'd affected every day of my life. What I had never been sure of was how. Had his slaying closed me off or opened me up? Left me in some ways better? Had his dying really turned a barely noticed childhood giving impulse into an adult imperative? I had always been sure of the *rightness* of giving, of its necessity, if only to soften the world's harsh edges.

Like the Mexican vacation I decided to treat Kevin and my son Darrell to after Christmas 2009. Kevin was exhausted from his demanding new job. Darrell, just out of college, was fearful about moving to Los Angeles to act full-time. I found a great postholiday deal on a beach condo but couldn't afford four plane tickets to Cancun; Skye and I would have to stay home. That was okay, I decided. Kevin and Darrell needed the break more. Yet for a moment, I hesitated. *Here you go again, giving away something you could use!* Ignoring the voice, I offered the trip. The guys were thrilled.

On the January night they returned, I was pulling into the airport pickup area when I noticed: Kevin and Darrell, not needing coats in summery Mexico, had left them in the car. The night was frigid. They'd freeze! Putting the car in park, I made sure no ticket-writing cops saw me before dashing into the baggage area. Tossing the guys their coats, I yelled, *"You'll need these!"* and sprinted back.

Driving home, I savored Darrell's and Kevin's descriptions of eating just-caught fish and watching the sea shimmer from their condo. We were turning onto our street when it hit me: *neither had thanked me for blowing my wad to send them to Mexico!* They'd sunned on a beach while I froze my ass off at home. I wanted some acknowledgment, like the time I returned from a trip and Skye blurted, "Thank God you're back! We were *pathetic* without you!"

Suddenly *I* felt pathetic. Kevin, seeing my face, asked why. Of course he and Darrell thanked me profusely when I told them. But my annoyance had already shifted, from them to me. What was my problem? So what if their excitement about returning home prevented them from paying homage to me? Why did I need props for what I'd gladly given? Or—this felt truly treasonous—should I have heeded the inner voice that questioned the offer?

Later, Darrell, who increasingly seemed as attuned to my feelings as the man I'd named him after, joined me in my office and asked for my New Year's resolution. "To not care when I do stuff for people and they're not as grateful as I'd like," I told him. "To truly let giving be its own reward."

Darrell sighed. "Listen, Mom, I've been thinking about this," he began. "*Nobody* brings coats inside the airport for people who don't ask them to."

I just looked at him.

"They *don't*," he said. "If I'm picking somebody up after a trip, they just better be glad my black ass showed up. But you—you get coats out of the car, run them across two streets, and hand them to people who didn't even ask you to.

"Giving is your *gift*," he added, pausing to see if I was getting it. "Pretend I'm the world's best snow shoveler. When I do it, the driveway is perfectly clear. But when Mani shovels it, he just does it well enough for cars to get up the hill. What matters most? That your car's where you need it, or that he didn't shovel perfectly?"

I started to answer, but Darrell wasn't finished.

"Or look at how Skye is so humble. He just doesn't have that puffed-up thing about him." He laughed. "If you gave me classes on humility, maybe I'd be *less* of an asshole. But I'd never be like Skye. He's a genius at it."

"People give in their own way," he said. "We're grateful in our own way. We just won't be geniuses at it, like you."

Like many genius-level self-sacrificers, I had a problem with accepting—the harsh fact that few people I loved were built to give or to express gratitude as reliably as I. My difficulty with keeping my need for reciprocity in check often made me a royal pain in the ass. But I was even worse at something else: Feeling purely and undilutedly wonderful about my giving.

How could I? I'd made peace with my brother, but not, as I'd hoped, with this stubborn proclivity. I had no idea why I was still doing more than my share at home and in relationships. Every *here you go again* admonition reminded me: I didn't trust my gotta-give reflex.

Such mistrust can make sense. Take my friend Sarah, who supervises a staff of two hundred at a government agency while caring for her attorney husband and three teenagers. My exhausted pal was griping about the hassle of juggling needy workers, messy kids, and a husband so clueless that he asked if antidepressants—rather than a helping hand—would relieve her, when she admitted something astonishing. Sarah not only cooks dinner after her hour-long nightly commute; she then rouses herself to *wash the dishes.* Her family had cowed her, the busiest person in the house, into taking this on, too.

"I hate begging and browbeating to make them do stuff," Sarah explained, looking mortified. "Besides, I'm a feminist. Aren't we supposed to show women can do anything?"

This was too much. "Doing everything for your family and letting everyone else off the hook is *feminist?*" I blurted.

We both laughed. But Sarah's lopsided interpretation of feminism's demands wasn't funny. Many women have self-defeating perceptions of what their independence requires. My impulse to send my guys on a needed vacation was loving and apt, yet I wondered if I would have been smarter to keep the trip for myself. Sarah felt "doing it all" proved her equality, even if it wore her out and made her a servant in her own home. Another friend's pride that her lucrative job lets her indulge her kids in ways her own homemaker mom couldn't pushes her to go overboard. Among the gifts for her daughter's thirteenth birthday: a spa massage, a facial, brunch for ten, a movie outing for six kids, and videotaped shout-outs from four mentors. When I suggested this was, um, *generous,* my friend half joked, "I thought I'd kept myself in check."

It's hard, keeping our giving in check when it comes to people we love. It's even harder admitting how often we leap over the line drawn in the sand that suggests, "Today's independent woman gives to herself first, then to others who deserve it." Wanting to be tougher and more uncompromising than our self-sacrificing foremothers, we conceal or explain away our inconsistencies, admitting our "weakness" only to friends who harbor similar secrets. As if centuries of women being *expected* to give profusely could be wiped from our collective consciousness.

Confused by our over-the-top generosity toward loved ones (especially to men who hardly seem to "deserve" it), women fear being used yet can't curb their helping impulse. As an executive powerless to cut off her big-spending gadabout brother told me: "If another woman in my situation told me she was doing what I do, I'd be wagging my finger at her, saying, 'Girl, you've got to stop!'"

Is it any wonder women sometimes see their "gift" of giving as an affliction?

"Giving truly is a gift," a female life coach once told me. "But it's also a responsibility. Without discipline, anything you're responsible for gets out of hand."

Say you've gotten a puppy, she explained. Without discipline, the creature that enchants you when it burrows in your lap will turn your life into a chewed-shoe, urine-stained nightmare. Over and over, I'd seen mindful giving enrich me—and giving-gone-wild compromise everything from my budget to my self-esteem.

My generosity felt like an out-of-control puppy. But how could I housebreak a stubbornly entrenched impulse?

I was lucky. I had no doubt that the people who could best help me tame this habit—my family—would want to assist. Yet it would be tricky, cutting off the giving gravy train to which my guys had grown accustomed. Who wants to do more and get less?

And though I didn't need anyone's permission to take control of my giving, I wanted my family's support. I recalled my basement lint revelation, how crucial it felt, but how impossible to explain to a man who'd stopped seeing me. Counseling taught me to effectively express my frustration without judgment. Could better communication help with this problem, too?

I had something in my favor: I'm a woman. Any English teacher can tell you girls' language skills tend to be superior to boys'. Men's brains are usually larger, but the parts dealing with emotion, memory, and language are much bigger in women. Researchers say that's why the charge we get from intimate conversation nearly rivals that of orgasm. Is it any wonder women connect through talking, in the coffee klatches, book clubs, and tête-à-têtes that the busiest of us build into our lives?

Communicating wasn't just fun for me. It was my calling. Why not use these skills to help my guys get my concerns?

For months, I'd been reminding Kevin of the multitude of supportive things I'd done when he was writing *his* books. "Clearly," I'd huffed, "*my* work isn't as important to you!" This observation not only failed to inspire his warmth, but it suggested I knew his feelings, when in truth, I wasn't always certain of my own. When I changed my curt "You'd do more around here if you cared about my book" to the more honest

"This book is vital to me; doing more than my share around the house bothers me as a wife *and* an author," Kevin heard me.

Rocket science it wasn't. Mounting verbal attacks on folks sparks their need to fight back; loving expressions inspire commensurate warmth. When the gentle approach proved effective with my sons, I took the next steps: delegating more, making honey-do lists, stuff wiser women had always done. Admittedly, the patient technique was no swing in a hammock. I bristled at having to ask nicely, sometimes more than once, for what should have been freely given. But *things got done.*

Which was great. And yet...

Changing my family's behavior didn't change *me.* Disciplining my generosity didn't extinguish the still-powerful urge to cave in to it. Happiness wasn't necessarily a warm, in-control puppy.

To be truly content, I needed to figure out why I'd bought the damn dog in the first place.

My frustration notwithstanding, I'd come a long way since that day on the couch when I realized Darrell's death had set me on a path of unexamined giving. New mindfulness had freed me from my most thoughtless offerings; I understood how Mom's childhood traumas, Daddy's coolness, and my sibling-imbued love for men exacerbated the impulse. Resurrecting my brother's memory had brought me peace. But I still had precious little insight into his death's hidden effects. And for all my newfound discipline, I hadn't stopped wanting to offer myself more freely than anyone who wasn't named Mother Teresa.

I was stuck.

One day, Mom brought over a sack of old letters she'd found. Filled with correspondence between friends and me when we were in our late teens, the letters made a disconcerting suggestion: I'd hardly changed in thirty years.

Stuff I was passionate about—movies, culture, race—went unmentioned. The letters focused almost entirely on one thing:

Men. Letter after letter between my friends and me detailed breakups, hookups, luring strategies, outrage at guys who'd stomped on our hearts, and our reconsideration of exes craving another shot. But the more I read, the more I noticed: our fixation was less on particular guys than on the place where most women lived, in the shifting landscape of our relationships. These missives from the 1970s reminded me of exchanges I'd recently overheard between my goddaughter, twelve, and her girlfriends; between me and women in their twenties, thirties, and beyond. It's where we *live*.

But surely I'd evolved more than the letters suggested. I asked my best source—Mom—what I was like as a girl. The World's Bluntest Woman jumped right in: with my perfectionism.

"Everything had to be right," Mom began, citing a favorite tale of hers in which I defied her at age seven by cutting my hair and hiding it behind the fridge. "But your bangs were perfect," she admitted.

"Being the only girl didn't faze you a bit," Mom went on. "You were a girlie girl, into clothes and combing dolls' hair.... You asked lots of questions, wanted to know what things meant. And you were very independent. Darrell and Bruce didn't want me out of their sight, but you, you were fine on your own. And you had this deep sense of right and wrong; I never had trouble disciplining you."

She paused for breath. "If there was a leader in the house, it was you.... You acted like a little mother."

Listening, I tallied: Maternal? Check. Independent? Check. Wants everything—my house, my family, my hair—just right? Check. A justice-obsessed girlie girl who asks endless questions, takes the lead, and keeps herself in line? How many checks is that?

I'd barely changed. But why hadn't Mom mentioned my giving? She thought about it.

"The only child I remember as extremely giving was Bruce," she said. "He'd ask, 'Mom, is there anything I can do for you?'...I don't know when you became that way."

When I whispered, "After Darrell died?" Mom didn't hesitate.

"Of all my kids, you were the most affected," she said. "His death changed all of our lives, but you're the one who was... obliterated. I had no idea of the bond between you two."

For decades, I, too, had underestimated that bond—and I was still doing it. I realized this a few weeks later while sitting on the couch in Hamani's Los Angeles apartment, the one Darrell would soon be leaving our Maryland home to move into. We'd all flown to L.A. to visit Mani and see the place he'd be sharing with his little brother. When everyone left to get breakfast, I stayed behind. Glum and alone, I contemplated the rooms that would soon house my departing middle child. Mute tears slid down my cheeks.

Darrell's key in the door shook me out of my reverie. Turning away, I tried to hide my damp face. No luck. Plopping beside me, Darrell pressed me about what was wrong.

"You're moving so far away, and I can't protect you," I finally admitted, trying to gather myself. "First Mani left, now you. I keep thinking about what happened to my brother when he left home."

Suddenly I was sobbing. "I failed him," I gasped, as shocked by my words as by my tears. "He left, and I couldn't protect him."

The son whom I'd spent the most time consoling, scolding, reassuring, and tearing into patted my shoulder.

"Everything you wanted to put into your brother, you put into me," he began. "Everything you didn't get to tell him before he died, you've said to me, Mani, and Skye. But you can't be responsible for what happens to us. If I walked out of here tonight and got hit by a bus, I would leave this earth knowing that you loved me completely. And you would know I loved you completely.

"That's the best you can do, Mom," Darrell said. "We have to be responsible for ourselves."

Everything, it seemed, was tied up in the brother whose name I went months without uttering, whose face I sometimes struggled to recall. Day after day, his loss still haunted me.

Darrell was right. Loving him, his brothers, and others in my life as fully and demonstrably as possible *was* the best I could do. I couldn't be responsible for him, live his life, shield him in every instance. I had to let him—as well as the man I'd named him for—go. It was *time*.

Yet I still felt restive. Unsatisfied. Certain there was something I'd missed.

A month later, I was yakking over dinner with Mireille at an Indian restaurant when I interrupted our chat to address our hugely pregnant waitress. "When are you due?" I asked the server, smiling. "Next month," she said, disappearing with our plates.

Now, Mireille had seen me engage strangers often enough to joke that no maitre d' or manicurist was safe from my probing. Yet this time she looked puzzled and asked, "Why did you do that?"

Surprised, I shrugged. "Because I didn't want the waitress

to feel like she didn't matter to us," I said. Still looking confused, Mireille asked why I needed to send that message.

"Because I wanted her to know I saw *her*, not just her job or status," I snapped. Now *I* was puzzled. "Why?"

Mireille leaned in, her voice gentle. "These acknowledgments you give people...is it possible they have something to do with your brother?"

Her words felt like a slap. The answer—to her question and the one I'd been futilely asking myself—was embarrassing in its obviousness. Yet for a moment, I couldn't speak.

"The men who shot him didn't *see* him," I finally said, my voice unsteady. "He asked for help, but all they saw was an image based on how he looked....I don't want to be like that with anyone."

I took a deep breath.

"I want people to know that I see *them*," I told her. "What they need."

Something cracked open inside me. The realization that emerged felt concrete and true. Halting my giving, I knew in this fathomless place, would dishonor Darrell. Failing to acknowledge anyone's humanity would make me as blind as the men whose sightlessness had stolen him from me. Why hadn't I seen it?

I'd known on the couch that long-ago day that I felt culpable in Darrell's death, and that the feeling had kindled a protectiveness and generosity toward other black men. But the truth was much deeper. It wasn't just black men, or men period, whom I felt driven to recognize. It was *everyone*—Asian bank tellers, female appliance repair people, tollbooth ticket takers of every stripe. I didn't need to know their stories to know they deserved to be seen, heard, acknowledged, as Darrell had deserved it. Not seeing, not responding, was unthinkable.

Thirty years earlier, two cops had seen the strange-behaving guy in the ditch only clearly enough to kill him. They saw nothing that prompted them to talk him through his crisis, wrestle him to the ground, or just give him what he'd requested: a ride home. As long as I lived, I'd be making up for their mistake. For decades, I had prided myself on my insight, on my ability to cut through tangled emotional thickets to get to the heart of things. And the most transparent directives of my own heart had eluded me.

Feeling responsible for my sons, my husband, for all black men, hadn't been enough. I was shouldering the whole world. How could I live and *not* give when everyone with a need represented my brother? When each offering was actually a gift to him?

And I knew this: Though I would be more careful about whom I offered myself to (everyone wasn't my brother, after all), I would never stop wanting to bolster, reassure, prop up, fix plates of food for, and tend to the woundedness of others. My search for the epiphany that would free me from my need had failed because finding it would have meant losing my brother all over again. Accepting this, I *did* feel free. Or just liberated enough to recall what my questions and suspicions had often made me overlook:

Giving can be pure, fucking *joy.*

I was telling my friend Lynne how great it was, how freeing, finally understanding why I couldn't stop giving, when Lynne blinked.

"Why would you want to stop?" she asked.

Well, what the hell, I thought. Why *had* I wanted to reject a trait that comforted, assisted, and inspired people, and that my best instincts pushed me to employ? Was it because the instinct was linked to my life's worst tragedy? Or was it just fear—of being taken advantage of, of being naive or even sneakily self-serving?

Some people see giving as a scam. They say it's selfishness in altruistic clothing, masking givers' real intent: making themselves look good, or their recipients beholden to them. Of course, I'd sometimes given for selfish reasons, to make this or that person think, Isn't she *great?* Yet after years of parsing my motives, I was sure: Far more often, my most selfish reason for giving was the lift it invariably gave me. Greedily, I pursued the fulfillment it offered. Hungrily, I embraced how it aligned me with God. Whether I was signing a check for earthquake victims, praising a beleaguered salesgirl's smile, or letting a hurried deli patron in front of me in line, the person who felt most rewarded was me.

But, hey, don't believe *me.* Even science now acknowledges giving's uplifting effects. More than its dictionary definition as "the transfer of items or actions from one person to another," giving is the transfer of *energy,* of loving vibes that actually lower stress hormones like adrenaline and cortisol in both the giver and the receiver while raising spirit-lifting endorphins.

So giving is clearly much more than manipulation and penance. Yet too often I've kicked myself for it. Like during rush hour, when I've reduced my speed to let a stranger in the slow lane ease his car in front of mine—and he couldn't be bothered to nod, wave, or otherwise acknowledge the courtesy. Once I've gotten over myself, once I've stopped looking for the automotive version of "Mom, we were pathetic without you!" I've recalled why I'll never stop giving: Because it uplifts more often than it disappoints. Because it's the right thing to do.

Because, honest to God, there's nothing like it.

In 2005, my lissome twenty-three-year-old yoga teacher announced she was leaving town. My disappointment turned to astonishment when she asked, "Would you like to train to take over the class?" I was immensely flattered—until a thought plummeted me to earth: With this ass?

I promptly found numerous other reasons to say "No, thanks": Writing columns was enough of a high-wire act. Between home and work, my plate was too full to learn unfamiliar skills. Why would I voluntarily make a fool of myself— *in Lycra*? In truth, I was petrified. I had a choice: Give in to my fear or turn my off-and-on workout into a nonnegotiable commitment.

I knew I'd chosen rightly each time I taught. Time after time, I was astounded that sharing this ancient discipline empowered me every bit as much as writing. I wasn't "supposed" to teach yoga—which only added to my delight.

Today, women confront countless life and career choices we weren't "supposed" to have. They *should* scare us. Because no matter how much we deserve these opportunities, or whether we labor out of love or just for a paycheck, work challenges us differently from the way it does men, especially if we have kids. Can we admit this, stop pretending men's and women's concerns about work and family are identical? Real life isn't like the Enjoli commercial I loved as a child, the one whose sexy heroine sang about bringing home the bacon, frying it up in the pan, and never letting her guy forget he's a man. In real life, women's dual devotion to both home and work isn't a snap.

My fear of teaching yoga was like the reluctance with which I approached every important piece of writing. Time after time, I wondered how I could bring clarity and wisdom to the work while tending to the myriad needs of a complex family and tumultuous home. How could anyone as tethered as I was create anything as ephemeral, as free, as art?

Feared and constrained, my writing morphed into a separate entity, with a voice that asked, *Where's your support for me? Why are you so tempted to abandon this part of you?* Finally, I would write, but not before realizing my craft was like my giving: loved and yet despised for the opposite directions in which it pulled me.

I longed to immerse myself in the *between*. To dive into the tranquil stream that flowed between rejecting my writing and being subsumed by it, between the demands of my family and the cajoling of my craft. Floating on the silken waters where my warring aspirations met and smoothed out, I'd drift effortlessly in the stillness between my contradictory desires.

Emptying myself for others while feeding the artist within.

Millions of women might appreciate a cool dip in their between. Yet what I wanted was contradictory: To make peace with my fracturedness, to find closure about it—but a closure open-ended enough for me to rethink, feint, change. I wanted permission to honor, without guilt or remorse, the disparate claims made on me by family, job, and creativity while somehow remaining whole unto myself. When my search for the between became unremitting, I described it to other women who confessed similar yearnings, felt similarly ensnared in contradiction. Listening to them, I felt what always stirred beneath the video games, balls, and sports jerseys littering my male-strewn life:

I love *women*.

I always had, despite my early life having shaped me into a lover of men and a girl terrified by females' power, including my own. Now, captivated by women and their countless acts of unheralded devotion, I longed to throw my arms around dozens whom I "knew" without ever having met: panic-stricken new moms at the mall shushing crying babies, fifty-somethings whose eyes avidly followed their oblivious teenage daughters, college-aged cuties whose offhand praise—"Great shoes!"—uplifted me. I wanted to throw a parade for Colleen, the furniture saleswoman who whispered as if she were in confession: "I have two jobs: Bloomingdale's and home. My son is thirteen. Every night, my husband asks him if he has homework; he says, 'No.' I get home and know instantly he has bunches. *I* end up helping him. Women do things right, so we end up doing everything."

In my childhood history texts, the mythical Greek figure holding the world aloft was male. In truth, it was always a woman:

The woman who gives sustenance of every kind to her family and to those she *treats* like family. The woman who sees beauty and brilliance in the child others would reject. The woman whose mate has died, dumped her, disappeared, or gone to war, who waits tables, takes over the company, pays the bills, raises the kids, handles every frigging thing in his absence. The woman whose grit, talent, and ingenuity compel her to make art, music, literature, peace, or, hell, just money, despite—or because of—others' disapproval. The woman who refuses to sacrifice her life, her *self,* to marriage, men, or kids, and who instead enriches us all.

Holding up the world—or one garden-variety family—isn't easy. Women should celebrate their giving, revel in how it smoothes the way for others, while lifting them, the world's most tireless givers, light-years above their human smallness. However misguided our offerings may be, what motivates them is often valid—and offers the answer to my question: "How do I honor myself *and* my need to give?

Love.

Love is the between. It's the glue that binds a soul's warring selves, the meeting place at which our opposites melt into and become part of each other.

I turn to love in situations in which I once instinctually gave too much. Loving both my giving and myself, I decide, "This time, I'm giving to *me*." Love is the voice that whispers to us that the separateness suggested by people's genders, colors, and disparate backgrounds is an illusion. Underpinning women's giving, it explains why the closer we get to others, the more we lose track of where their skin ends and ours begins.

What else but love could make a species as dazzling and exalted as humanity resemble last night's boring spaghetti? Left overnight in the fridge, this humblest of pastas becomes infinitely more memorable and delicious when warmed up the following day. People are like the sauce, vegetables, and noodles that share no likeness until mixed together. Marinate us in each other, and our differences melt and disappear, leaving us infinitely richer than we are in our separateness.

It's love—for spaghetti and the guys who adore it—that brought me back to the kitchen where my journey began. Two years after Skye stopped me in my tracks as I packed his lunch for chess camp, I was warming a pot of pasta as I chatted with a chess-loving friend on the phone about the queen in my son's favorite board game.

And I got stopped in my tracks all over again.

"The lone female in chess, the queen is the game's most dominant piece," my friend was saying. The queen can move anywhere on the board and can capture any opposing piece in her way. Typical strategy says it's unwise for a player to bring out his queen too early because "a cluttered board makes her more vulnerable to entrapment," she said.

Wow. Hanging up, I asked Skye, two years taller and wiser, his take on chess's queen. "She's the most powerful piece, Mom," he said, looking up from his homework. "But not necessarily the most important. Lose the king and you lose the game."

Kevin glanced up from his computer. "The queen is most important because she's the most versatile," he said. "She can go anywhere. She does everything."

To which I couldn't help blurting, *"No shit."*

The only female on the cluttered chessboard of my home, I indeed do everything. My versatility is unmatched; I wield more power than I usually acknowledge or employ. I've used that power in the service and protection of others, especially my "king," whether a husband, a son, a father, or a brother long lost to me.

Yet mine needn't be the rules-driven board game Skye went to camp to play. It took half a century, but I finally understood: My game is my own; I decide which rules or limitations to embrace. I determine when and where I move, how I play, whether to keep mining the past or to leap beyond it.

Choosing different strategies will ensure different outcomes. And I can have fun. After all, it's a *game.* Day by day, I can decide where the shifting balance of my love for myself, and my need to give to others, moves me: forward or sideways or diagonally or backward.

Or *between.*

Acknowledgments

It's hard for me to imagine this book existing without the support and encouragement of the following people:

Mom, for surviving so much and still being the most alive person I've ever met. And Daddy, for having loved us in his own unique way.

Deborah Szekely, who with her husband, Edmond, founded Rancho La Puerta more than seventy years ago. Deborah's spirit permeates the sacred place where I did much of this book's toughest soul-searching and writing. If even a smidgen of the Ranch's beauty is reflected in these pages, I'll be ecstatic.

Mireille Grangenois, the sister I thought I'd never have, for offering me thousands of probing questions, gentle critiques, and uplifting prayers—and her husband, Steve Holmes, for the use of their dear, departed cottage Marisol in which to write.

Mary Jo Schumacher, for her love and support, and for teaching me better than anyone that love knows no color.

Jo-Ann Armao, an amazingly supportive, tough, and

engaged editor whose last-minute analysis and suggestions saved many a column and parts of this book. And Mary Hadar, for being a friend as well as the best line editor I know.

My agent, David Black, for year after year checking in with me, believing in me, seeing me as an author, even when I doubted ever pulling it off. And my editor, Tracy Behar, for making this book infinitely better in spite of me.

Jeff Rivers, for being the first man to challenge me to think more imaginatively. Life Coach Wendi Kovar, for that hike at the Ranch that changed my life. Milton Coleman, for seeing me as something I was afraid to see myself as: a columnist.

Gayle King, Shawn Hutchens, Sharon Brown, Pam Bohler, Deborah Allen, Retha Hill, Mimi Harris, Ketrin Grady, Jeanne Fox-Alston, Mary "Masha" McLaughlin, Kathy Rushing, and every other girl and woman with whom I've talked, rhapsodized, fumed, lamented, cried, sermonized, and giggled about men.

Justin Britt-Gibson, Darrell Britt-Gibson, and Skye Merida, for making me smarter, hipper, more loving, and so much better than I could ever have been without them.

Bruce Britt, for always being able to make me laugh and for never living a single unoriginal day. Ben Melech Yehudah, for staying, and staying himself, when Darrell left. To both of them for still being my brothers.

And Kevin, for teaching me more about love, forgiveness, and giving—and how inevitably the three are tangled—than anyone.

About the Author

Donna Britt is an award-winning former syndicated columnist for the *Washington Post,* writing on issues both topical and personal. She worked as a staff writer for the *Detroit Free Press* and *USA Today,* and she holds an undergraduate degree from Hampton Institute (now Hampton University) and a master's degree from the University of Michigan. She has won awards from the American Society of Newspaper Editors, the National Association of Black Journalists, and other organizations, and she has been featured on *The Oprah Winfrey Show,* C-Span, and NPR. Britt lives in Maryland with her husband and youngest son.